THE
Biomechanics
— OF —
ROWING

THE
Biomechanics
— OF —
ROWING

Dr. Valery Kleshnev

THE CROWOOD PRESS

First published in 2016 by
The Crowood Press Ltd
Ramsbury, Marlborough
Wiltshire SN8 2HR

www.crowood.com

This impression 2019

© Dr Valery Kleshnev 2016

British Library Cataloguing-in-Publication Data
A catalogue record for this book is available from the British Library.

ISBN 978 1 78500 133 8

Typeset by Servis Filmsetting Ltd, Stockport, Cheshire

Printed and bound in India by Replika Press Pvt Ltd

CONTENTS

CHAPTER I

INTRODUCTION

This book is intended for rowers and coaches who want to improve their rowing technique, row faster and maximize their results in regattas, given their physical conditioning. Here I have tried to summarize my knowledge of rowing biomechanics, which was obtained from nearly thirty years of working with thousands of rowers and coaches from all around the world: from Europe to Australia, from China to the USA and Brazil. Many of them ended up being Olympic and World champions and I have learned a lot from them. This knowledge didn't come as a divine revelation but is a product of extensive measurements and analysis, continuous attempts to solve many puzzles and exhaustive studies of the efficiency techniques of winning crews. Though inspiration is still important, I believe the only way to achieve it is through hard work and continuous thought.

I can say that my understanding of rowing biomechanics and technique is completely different now from that in 1986, which is when I finished my fourteen-year rowing career and started pursuing sport science. It was a very steep learning curve. In the beginning I had very limited instrumentation and had to rely on experts and literature, which mainly emphasized the importance of 'smooth boat speed' and so on. If someone had asked me

at the time 'How should the best force curve look?' my answer would have been quite evasive: 'It is possible to win with various force curves.' I just didn't know. Now I realize how many mistakes we made at that time.

The logical question that I always ask myself is 'Are you sure now that all these conclusions are true?' The answer I give is: 'They should be correct, on the basis of all the available evidence and its analysis. However, if new facts contradicting the theory should be found, or someone finds an error in the analysis, I have to revise it and develop a new theory.' Of course, misconceptions are always possible, but at least I try to be open-minded.

For example, a few years ago I thought that a pair of horizontal forces at the handle and the stretcher might create a torque, which could lift the whole rower-boat system out of the water and decrease drag resistance. My colleague and friend Prof. Volker Nolte from Canada had an opposite opinion and counted only a rower's vertical accelerations, but I was still hoping that a true lift force might exist. After a few quite sophisticated experiments (see Chapter 2.5.4), I have found that Volker was right: horizontal forces cannot be converted into vertical forces in the way I thought, but some data still remained unexplained. Suddenly, a solution came not from a sport scientist, but from a master rower and engineer, Tor Anderson from California, who suggested an effect of centripetal force, which we had both overlooked.

Very often, the reason for changing the concept is not a fault or mistake but due to new data being obtained when new instrumentation becomes available. For example, a few years ago the dominating winning race strategy was one that encouraged the fastest start. Now we can see a change in this trend, where more and more winners use a more even distribution of effort during the race.

Most of the information in this book could be found in the *Rowing Biomechanics Newsletter (RBN)*, which I write and publish, and have done so monthly since 2001. My original reason to start this project was to keep my brain active in my speciality. Later it became a great tool not only for sharing ideas but also for their discussion and verification. Many thanks to all the contributors whose comments were very valuable in correcting errors and mistakes, obtaining new ideas and making the advance in rowing biomechanics possible. However, this book is not a simple compilation of newsletters. All the information was revised and structured and many contradictions accumulated over the years were corrected.

Quite a common approach as a way of improving rowing technique is to look at winning crews in an attempt to copy them, without considering why they are fast. However, nothing that's worthwhile is ever easy, especially in rowing. Some crews are not winning just because they are; they win in spite of their technique by means of higher physiological power and stronger, better motivation. A large variety of rowing techniques could be found in winners of Elite regattas, so which one should you copy? Remember, a copy is always going to be worse than the original.

I propose a different approach, which is not as easy; it requires some extra efforts and brain power but will help you produce much more consistent and reliable results. What this book can offer you is an understanding of 'how it works', and why. This is a sort of mosaic, a completed puzzle, where the bits and pieces of rowing technique are placed in an organized manner and bound together through mechanical principles. This is not a simple system, and is sometimes controversial. You may try to improve one efficiency component, but lose more on another one. Therefore, using common sense is the rule of thumb here, and all ideas must always be verified empirically with actual rowing results.

This book is also for sport scientists: for people who want to measure numbers in rowing, relate them to technique and give specific advice to coaches and rowers. In general, sport biomechanics is a very specific science, much more than physiology, psychology or nutrition. Sporting technique is completely different in various sports, for example between rowing and swimming, canoeing and athletics, so there are very different analytical models and criteria of effectiveness, measurement methods and equipment. The biomechanical equipment is usually custom-made, and we can't, as it were, 'go and buy it in a shop', unlike the skills of other sport scientists. It takes many years for a biomechanic scientist to obtain professional expertise in a specific area, and they usually can't work across many sports and switch between them quickly, as other sport scientists can do.

Biomechanical models can be very complicated, with many important unknown variables. Sometimes, if you blindly follow an incorrect model, the outcome could even be counter-productive and decrease performance instead of improving it. Again, common sense and continuous verification of your ideas with practical results are absolutely necessary.

INTRODUCTION

Rowing is a unique sport due to its technical complexity, which is defined by the following factors:

- Rowing utilizes nearly all the muscles of the human body;
- Rowing requires complex coordination of the rower's movements, which is determined by many degrees of freedom: the three-dimensional pivoting oar, the moving seat and an unstable boat;
- Coordination of the rowing movements becomes even more complex in crew boats, which require synchronization of the rowers' motions;
- Rowing is the only sport where the athlete moves backwards, which is not natural human movement and dictates inversion of the muscle sequence.

These factors make rowing a very technical sport and explain why rowing biomechanics is so important for developing an effective technique and achieving good results in this sport. Technique is not the only important component of rowing performance; a high physiological capacity is also compulsory. The top results can be achieved only through a combination of these two main factors together with mental toughness. There was evidence (comparison of erg scores and on-water results) showing that an effective technique could make the boat 3–5 per cent faster (10–15 seconds over a 2km race) at the same physiological power production, which is the difference in speed between gold medallists and sixth-placed B-finalists at Elite regattas.

In addition, rowing is a very productive sport in terms of measurements and science; rowing equipment allows many places where the sensors can be mounted to measure forces, angles, velocities and accelerations of the boat, oars and rower. Therefore, rowing biomechanics has quite a long history, originating at the end of the nineteenth century[5,13,15], when sensors were mounted on the oarlock and the rowing force was measured. Since that time, the measurement equipment has been continuously developing. Data acquisition technology is booming these days, since the beginning of the information age in the twenty-first century. However, numbers and curves would be useless without proper understanding of their meaning, how they are related to effective rowing technique and what sort of numbers are required for the best performance.

This book contains eight chapters:

1. This introduction;
2. Measurements – explains technology and meaning of biomechanical methods;
3. Analysis – the core theories behind rowing biomechanics;
4. Technique – practical applications of biomechanical information and knowledge;
5. Ergometer rowing – giving the specifics of using machines;
6. Rowing equipment and rigging;
7. Performance analysis – discusses races and boat speed analysis;
8. Various cross-disciplinary topics – a brief overview of areas on the borderline of rowing biomechanics with other disciplines.

The purpose of this book is to help rowers and coaches to understand better the main biomechanical principles of effective rowing technique, to relate them to what they can see and what they can measure in rowing, and to show them some ways to improve technique and maximize the performance of their crews.

ROADMAP ON ROWING PERFORMANCE

Performance in rowing is a complex matter as it is in any sport. It requires high physiological power production, effective technique, mental toughness and smart management of an athlete's lifestyle and training. The main purpose of biomechanics in rowing is improvement of technique. The main questions are:

- What components of a rower's skills can be *analysed* to develop optimal technique?
- What biomechanical variables need to be *measured* to provide data for the analysis?

Fig. 1.1 schematically shows relationships between components of a rower's skills and biomechanical variables. The real picture is more complicated, since the components of technique are interrelated and usually affected by many other biomechanical variables.

The road map of rowing biomechanics has three levels: *measurement, analysis* and

performance. At the measurement level we collect information from sensors, process it (apply calibration, filters, averaging, and so on), store and feed it into the analysis level.

During analysis, we combine data from various variables, calculate derivative variables (for example power from measured force and oar angle) and values (for example maximum and average force), and produce some meaningful information. There are two separate areas at the analysis level: *theory* and *practice.* In the theory area, we produce and publish some common knowledge, such as average values in athlete groups, correlations, and normative criteria. In the practice area, we compare the acquired data with the normative criteria and produce recommendations for a specific athlete or crew, which are then fed into the performance level.

At the performance level we try to correct rowing technique with instructions obtained at the analysis level. Various methods of feedback can be used at this level: after a session, post-exercise and real-time feedback as well as various drills and rigging adjustments. After a technical correction is made, variations of rowing technique should be measured and

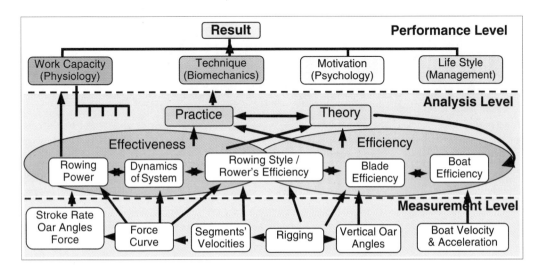

Fig. 1.1 Road map of rowing performance with the main components of biomechanics.

analysed to check their impact and evaluate an athlete's adaptability.

At the measurement level, there are three groups of variables related to very basic mechanical categories: *time* (stroke rate), *space* (drive length – rowing angles) and *force* (applied by a rower). Together these three variables produce the fourth mechanical category: *energy* (rowing power), which is very closely related to the average speed of the rower-boat system and, hence, with *rowing performance*. Below is a brief description of the main measurement areas:

- The force curve defines the total impulse supplied by the rower as well as the dynamics of the system. An optimal force curve must be 'front loaded', full and not have any humps.
- Coordination of the body segments' velocities is related to the force curve and defines rowing style, which is the key component of technique.
- Rigging defines the kinematics of oar and rower and through gearing ratio – the kinetics of the system. Lighter gearing makes the rower's movements faster and, possibly, increases power production but reduces blade efficiency.
- Oar handling skills of a rower could be evaluated using measurements of the vertical oar angle, which is related to the rigging (say, blade pitch and height of the gate) and could impact on blade efficiency.

- Patterns of the boat velocity and acceleration during the stroke cycle result from the dynamics of the system and should be good indicators of quality of rowing technique.

To evaluate the numbers measured in these areas, we usually compare them with target values and curves, or what are called 'Biomechanical Gold Standards', developed based on the combination of two methods, fused together with creativity and common sense:

- The *Statistical* method helps to relate measurements to rowers' performance. Say, if one group of rowers have some common features of technique and always win medals and another group have similar physical qualities but row differently and are always missing finals, then we could conclude that the technique of the first group is more effective.
- The *Modelling* method allows different variables to be related between themselves, and, importantly, with the boat speed and rowing efficiency. For example, based on trends of the best results in world regattas, we could derive a 'prognostic' or 'gold standard' boat speed, which 99.9 per cent guarantee a gold medal in the next Olympics. Then, knowing the drag factors of various boat types, we could derive the rowing power, stroke rate and length and the applied force required to achieve prognostic results.

CHAPTER 2

MEASUREMENTS

2.1 METHODS

2.1.1 Biomechanical Assessment Procedure

An important part of the biomechanics assessment procedure is the testing protocol, which must provide standard conditions and make results comparable between rowers and over the course of time. There are two major factors affecting rowing technique: the stroke frequency and fatigue. Therefore a test protocol was used consisting of two parts:

■ A step-test with increasing stroke rate: for example, 5–6 sections by 250m or 1 minute at 20, 24, 28, 32, 36 str/min with a free recovery of about 3–5 minutes and 30 second maximal effort;
■ Race length of 2,000m with full effort or specified percentage of it (say, at 95 per cent).

This test protocol was quite time-consuming (1–2 hours) and put a significant load on rowers. Therefore, a combined test protocol was designed, which enabled determination of both effects at once. The test consists of one continuous 2000m piece at racing force application, but various rates (see Table 2.1).

This testing protocol received very positive feedback from rowers and coaches. This test was a good training load itself; the first half of it is performed at aerobic training intensity, which allows smooth transition to the second half with anaerobic intensity; only the last 500m is performed with stroke rates close to those used in racing. There can be some variation of this protocol for junior rowers and veterans. For example, sections N5 and N7 could be replaced with light paddling with corresponding reduction of the stroke rate for the next sections. The data samples are taken and averaged at every lap.

2.1.2 Data Processing

The raw data collected during a testing section usually contains many stroke cycles, which have various durations and magnitudes of biomechanical variables (see Fig. 2.1a). If every stroke were analysed, it would create a huge amount of information, which could be ambiguous and difficult to comprehend. To solve this problem and accurately represent the rowing technique, a method was developed which converts raw data into a form representing one typical stroke cycle for the sample, so it is called an 'averaging' process.[33]

Section	Split	Lap	Stroke rate (1/min)	
N	(m)	(m)	Singles	Crew boats
1	0–100	100	Start max	Start max
2	100–500	400	18	20
3	500–1000	500	22	24
4	1000–1250	250	26	28
5	1250–1500	250	30	32
6	1500–1750	250	32–34	34–36
7	1750–1900	150	35–36	38–40
8	1900–2000	100	Max.	Max.

Table 2.1 The standard protocol of biomechanical assessment procedure.

The cycle start time was defined as the moment when the oar (right oar in sculling) of the stroke rower crosses the zero angle (perpendicular to the boat) during the recovery phase. This moment was used as a trigger for the stroke cycle of the whole crew. The average cycle time was calculated over all the strokes in the sample and then each cycle of the sample was normalized to the same average cycle time. The data was then processed (averaged) into 50-point data arrays for each measured variable (oar angle, force, and so on).

Discrete data values (extremes, sub-phases) were then derived using second-order polynomial interpolation based on the four nearest points of the arrays. The normalization algorithm was checked for validity by means of a comparison between the derived values (such as catch and release angles, maximum force, work and power) calculated using normalized data and an average of those values from each cycle in the sample using raw data. The differences ranged from 0.02 per cent to 0.85 per cent, which was considered satisfactory.

Analysis of the typical (averaged) patterns of different samples allows reliable comparison of various samples (various rowers, stroke rates, long-term trends, and so on) and makes the changes in rowing technique very clear. Fig. 2.1b,c illustrates this analysis. The specific feature of the technique (Fig. 2.1b) is a significant change in the timing of the maximal applied force; at lower rates the rower applies more force during the second half of the drive (1), but at higher stroke rates the peak force is shifted to the first half of the drive (2). The comparison of the start and finish sections (3) gives us information about fatigue resistance, which was satisfactory in this case.

Fig. 2.1c shows another example of changes of the force curve at various stroke rates: the force gradient (rate the force increasing) at the beginning of the drive (1) remains the same at all stroke rates, as well as the position of the peak force (2). However, at stroke rates higher than 30 this sculler suffers from the 'hump' in the force curve (3), which is caused by early activation of the trunk at the catch, then a

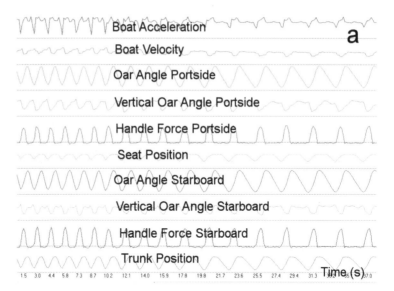

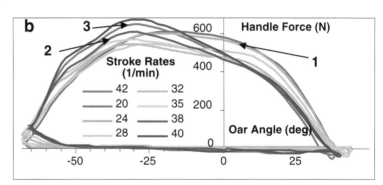

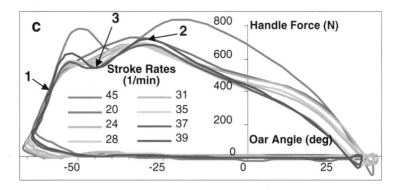

Fig. 2.1 Examples of raw data (a) and averaged force curves at various stroke rates (b, c).

decrease in its velocity when the leg drive is the fastest. The hump occurs at the moment of the second activation of the trunk (see Chapter 4.1.4) and is also related to a weak posture of the sculler (see Chapter 4.5) and very deep burying of the blade (see Chapter 2.3.2). Such 'disconnection' and double emphasis of applied force significantly decreases rowing effectiveness at racing stroke rates and negatively affects performance.

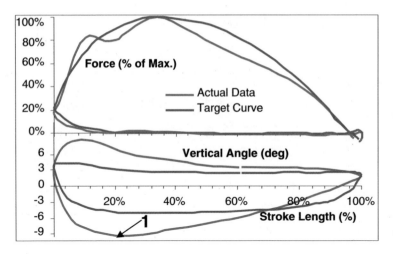

Fig. 2.2 An example of rowing technique evaluation based on comparison with target curves.

It was assumed that the conditions of the second last section of the standard test above (see 2.1.2) are very close to racing conditions in terms of stroke rate and fatigue. Therefore, this data sample was usually taken for analysis and compared with 'targets' to evaluate the technique of each rower. The comparison is made in two ways. Quantitative values are compared with the main criteria and percentage of differences are defined for variables of oar angle (see 2.3.1), force (2.5.2), blade work (2.3.2) and body segments (see Chapter 4.1.4). Qualitative evaluation is made by means of comparison of the real measured curves with target curves (Fig. 2.2), which were constructed based on quantitative values.

This evaluation method allows clear and effective feedback for rowers and coaches and helps to improve technique.

2.2 TIMING

Time is an absolute universal variable, which has only one dimension and direction. Therefore, timing can be related unambiguously to mechanical variables and make the analysis clear and effective. In rowing and also in many other sports, the result itself is measured in the time taken to cover the race distance.

2.2.1 Stroke Rate and Boat Speed

Stroke rate is the most obvious and commonly used timing variable in rowing as in many other cyclic sports. It is always measured by coaches and rowers during training and races and is used to define training and racing intensity. The stroke rate R is defined as a number of strokes N per unit of time T:

$$R = N / T \qquad (1)$$

where T is in minutes – the commonly accepted unit of time in rowing, and R is strokes per minute denoted as 1/min, or min^{-1}. Together with stroke length and force, the stroke rate is one of three components of rowing power, so it is one of the main determinants of performance in rowing. However, it is not possible to increase the stroke rate to infinity to improve rowing results; it is limited by mechanical conditions (inertial losses of energy increase with the stroke rate) and with neuromuscular abilities of rowers (a higher stroke rate would require a faster

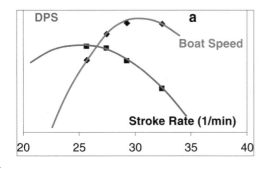

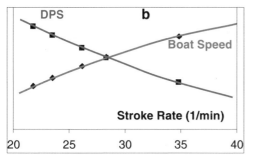

Fig. 2.3 The effect of the stroke rate on the boat speed and distance per stroke (DPS) in two rowing crews.

muscle contraction, which may be inefficient, and quicker coordination of movements). Therefore, it is important to find the optimal stroke rate, which maximizes boat speed. This optimum may be different for different crews and boat types. Fig. 2.3 shows an example for two crews: in Crew A the maximal boat speed was achieved at a stroke rate of 32 min^{-1}, while in Crew B it continues to grows up to and beyond 40 min^{-1}.

To evaluate dependence of the boat speed on stroke rate and find its optimum, we introduced a method[35] based on effective work per stroke (*EWPS*). Previously, distance per stroke *DPS* was used as a measure of the stroke effectiveness. However, *DPS* always decreases at higher stroke rates (even in the best crews), because the duration of the stroke cycle becomes shorter.

So, the question was: 'What do we need to preserve as the stroke rate increases?'

It was decided that the main objective is to sustain the application of force *F*, of stroke length *L*, and of mechanical efficiency *E*. The effective work per stroke, *EWPS*, integrates all these variables and is used as the basis of the method:

$$EWPS \sim F * L * E \qquad (2)$$

The boat speed *V* and rowing power *P* are related as following:

$$P = DF * V^3 \qquad (3)$$

where *DF* is some dimensionless factor depending on the boat type, displacement, weather conditions and blade efficiency. Therefore, *EWPS* can be expressed in terms of power *P*, stroke cycle time *T*, boat speed *V*, stroke rate *R*:

$$EWPS = PT = P (60 / R) = 60 DF (V^3/ R) \qquad (4)$$

For the two sections of rowing with different stroke rates (R_1 and R_2), if the value of *EWPS* was maintained constant and also DF_1 and DF_2 are the same, then ratio of the boat speeds (V_1 and V_2) must be:

$$V_1 /V_2 = (R_1 / R_2)^{1/3} \qquad (5)$$

This means the *boat speed is proportional to the cube root of the stroke rate*: if the stroke rate is doubled at constant *EWPS*, the boat speed increases only by about 26 per cent ($2^{1/3} = 1.26$), and to double the boat speed, the stroke rate must be eight times higher.

Correspondingly, the ratio of *DPS* (distance per stroke) values can be expressed as:

$$DPS_1 / DPS_2 = (R_2 / R_1)^{2/3} \qquad (6)$$

This means the *distance per stroke is inversely proportional to the square of the cube root of the*

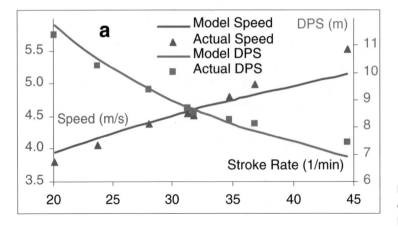

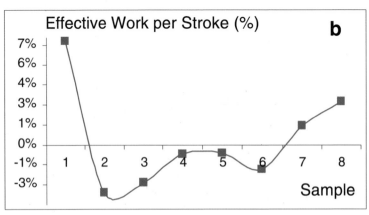

Fig. 2.4 Dependence of the boat speed and DPS on the stroke rate (a), analysis of EWPS (b).

stroke rate: if the stroke rate is doubled, *DPS* shortens by about 37 per cent ($0.5^{2/3} = 0.63$).

To use this method, we do not need to know drag factor *DF*, because it is assumed constant for all samples analysed. However, this is applicable only for the same boat, rowers and weather conditions, which is a limitation of the method. Fig. 2.4a illustrates the equations and represents dependencies of the boat speed and *DPS* on the stroke rate.

The most practically convenient application of the method is the definition of 'prognostic' or 'model' value of the speed *Vm* for every stroke rate:

$$Vm = V_0 (R_i / R_0)^{1/3} \qquad (7)$$

where V_0 is usually average of all samples of the race or step-test. Then, the actual speed in each sample *Vi* can be compared with the 'model' *Vm* and its deviation *D* calculated:

$$D = Vi / Vm - 1 \qquad (8)$$

If *D* is positive, then EWPS in this sample was relatively higher than average over the whole race or test (Fig. 2.4b) and vice versa. This method can be used for race analysis in cyclic water sports (rowing, swimming[20], canoeing), employed for evaluation of the strength- and speed-endurance using a step-test and does not require sophisticated equipment (only a stopwatch or StrokeCoach).

On an ergometer, as the drag factor for

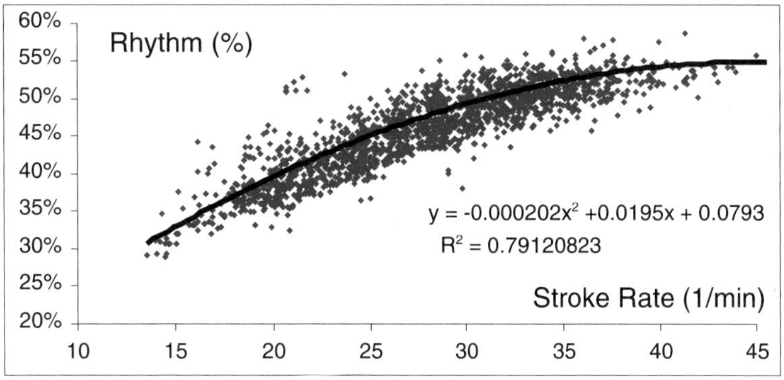

Fig. 2.5 Dependence of the rowing rhythm on the stroke rate.

speed calculation is always constant (in Concept2 erg $DF = 2.8$). This method is applicable without any limitations and can be used for developing normative splits for ergo training. To do this, the target speed V_0 and stroke rate R_0 should be defined firstly, then

$$D = Vi / Vm - I \qquad (9)$$

should be used to calculate normative splits for various stroke rates. For example, your target for a 2km ergo race is 6:00 at the rate of 36 min^{-1}. If you can train at the rate 18 at a split of 1:53, this means your muscles are ready to produce the same amount of work per stroke, as required for your target result and rate.

2.2.2 Rowing Rhythm

The standard definition of rhythm is the ratio of the drive time to the total time of the stroke cycle (50 per cent means a 1/1 ratio of the drive to recovery times). It was found that the rhythm has a strong positive correlation ($r = 0.89$) with the stroke rate (Fig. 2.3) because possibilities to shorten the drive are limited. This happens because rowers increase the stroke rate mainly by means of shortening recovery time, which is much easier to do than decrease the drive time. However, the

stroke rate only explains 79 per cent of the rhythm variation (Fig. 2.5) and 21 per cent depends on other factors.

The standard deviation of residuals from the trend (n = 2881) was $\sigma = 2.5$ per cent, which means that at the same stroke rate the rhythm may vary within ± 7.5 per cent ($\pm 3\sigma$) in various crews. For example at a stroke rate of 32.5 str/min the average rhythm based on the above trend is 50 per cent, but it could be between 42.5 per cent and 57.5 per cent.

2.2.3 Case Study: Factors Affecting the Rhythm

Is it better to have the rowing rhythm higher or lower? Many coaches believe that a lower rhythm is more efficient and ask their crews to shorten the drive time, but does that make sense? Biomechanical variables of two M1x were analysed at the same stroke rate of 32.5 str/min (Fig. 2.6). Sculler 1 (red) had a rhythm of 49.5 per cent or 0.91s drive time compared to Sculler 2's (blue) 52.5 per cent and 0.97s correspondingly; that is, the second one had a 3 per cent higher rhythm and 0.06s longer drive time. The reason for this difference was quite simple: Sculler 1 had a total oar angle of 107.5 degrees while Sculler 2 had 116 degrees; that is he had an 8.5 degree longer stroke length. This fully explains the difference in rhythm and drive time since the average handle velocity during the drive (= drive length / time) had the same value of 1.73 m/s in both scullers. This happened in spite of Sculler 1 applying a 3.9 per cent higher maximal force and 2.6 per cent higher average force than Sculler 2.

What other biomechanical features are related to this difference in rhythm and stroke length? During the recovery, Sculler 2 has to move the handle much faster (Fig. 2.6, point 1) to cover a longer distance in a shorter time, so his average handle speed was 11.7 per cent higher. This was impossible without faster seat/leg movement (2). At the catch, Sculler 2 changes direction of the seat movement much quicker than Sculler 1, slightly before his handles change direction (3). Contrarily, Sculler 1 uses his trunk even before the catch (4). Consequently, the boat acceleration of Sculler 2 has an earlier and deeper negative peak (5), but higher first positive peak (6), so his boat and stretcher move relatively faster (7), creating a better platform for acceleration of Sculler 2's mass ('trampoline effect', see Chapter 3.2.5).

Other technical advantages of Sculler 2 were:

- More effective return of the trunk at the finish (8);
- Better blade work at the catch (9) and finish (10);
- Faster force increase up to 70 per cent of max. (11);
- 1.5 per cent lower variation of the boat speed (0.5s gain over 2km);
- 3.3 per cent higher rowing power because of longer drive.

As a result, the boat speed of Sculler 2 was 5.9 per cent higher (6:34 for 2km) than Sculler 1 (6:57) as well as his performance (world

medallist compared to third finalist for Sculler 1). *Conclusion: The rhythm and drive time cannot be changed voluntarily as they depend on the stroke rate, length and boat speed. The stroke length is the main factor affecting the rhythm. There are other factors, which may affect rhythm (shape of the force curve and depth of the blade), which we may study in the future.*

2.3 ANGLES

2.3.1 Horizontal Oar Angle and Drive Length

The horizontal oar angle is one of the most important variables in rowing biomechanics, which defines the amplitude of the oar movement in a horizontal plane. It is measured from the perpendicular position of the oar relative to the boat axis, which is zero degrees (Fig. 2.7a). The catch angle is defined as the minimal negative angle, the finish angle is the maximal positive angle and the total angle is the difference between finish and catch angles. The horizontal oar angle is used for triggering the stroke cycle, which occurs at the moment of zero oar angle during recovery.

The oar angle can be measured at the oar shaft or at the gate, and these two methods produce slightly different results (Fig. 2.7b). The total angle measured at the gate was found to be 4–5 degrees larger than the total oar angle, mainly because of finish angles. There are two main reasons for this difference (Fig. 2.8):

1. A bend of the oar shaft. When force increases at the first half of the drive, the oar shaft bends and its angular velocity is slightly faster than at the gate. At the second half of the drive the oar extends, and its rotation appears to be slower than the gate rotation. This is the reason for the

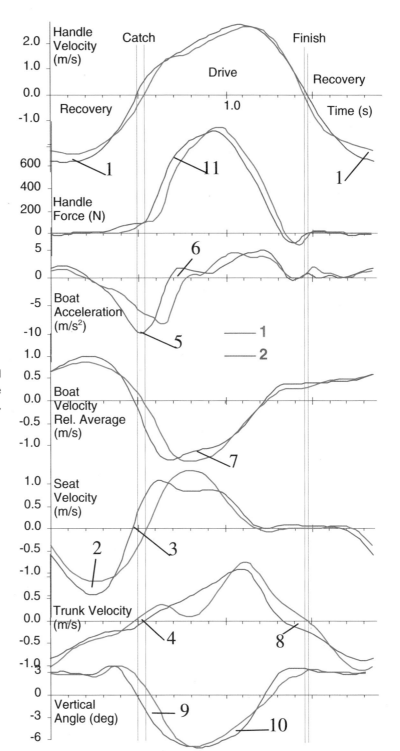

Fig. 2.6 Biomechanical variables affecting the rowing rhythm.

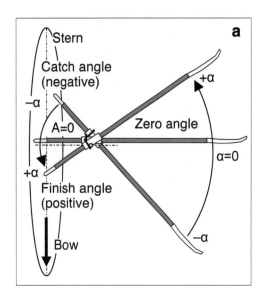

Fig. 2.7 Definitions of the horizontal oar angles (a), comparison of the angle measurements at the oar and at the gate (b).

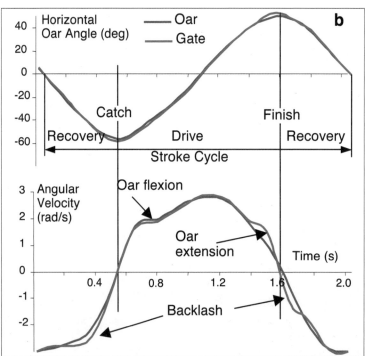

small difference in the catch angle and has no effect on the finish angle, because the force at this point is minor.

2. Backlash of the oar sleeve in the gate is the main contributor to the difference in the finish angle. It depends on the geometry of the gate, sleeve and button, and also on coordination of feathering along with horizontal and vertical movements of the oar. The backlash does not create any

Fig. 2.8 Differences in measurements of the oar angle at the oar shaft and at the gate.

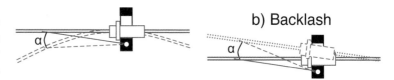

b) Backlash

inefficiency because the blade is already out of the water and no propulsive force is produced at that moment.

The method of measuring the angle (at the oar, or at the gate) usually corresponds to the method of measuring the force and is determined by the following factors:

- If the target is the geometry and kinetics of the rower's movement then the oar angle and force are the best choice. The main advantage of this method is accurate determination of the handle position and power production of the rower.
- If boat kinetics and propulsive forces need to be measured then gate angle and force are quite useful for defining force components at the pin. However, the rower's power cannot be estimated accurately because of unknown actual leverage of the oar.

The drive length is defined as the length of the arc L_{arc} made by the middle of the handle, and related to the amplitude of horizontal angle A and actual inboard $L_{in.a}$ as:

$$L_{arc} = A\, L_{in.a}\, \pi\, /\, 180 \qquad (10)$$

The actual inboard $L_{in.a}$ is the distance from the pin (centre of the oar rotation) to the middle of the handle, and it is related to the normally measured inboard L_{in} (from the collar to the top of the handle) as:

$$L_{in.a} = L_{in} + W_{g/2} - W_{h/2} \qquad (11)$$

where $W_{g/2}$ is half the gate width (2cm for the standard gate) and $W_{h/2}$ is half the handle width, which is set at a standard 6cm in sculling and 15cm in rowing. It is important to maintain this standard, because it makes drive length comparable in sculling and rowing, and is used for calibration of the handle force and provides correct calculations of work per stroke and rowing power.

Fig. 2.9 Stroke length at various stroke rates.

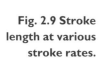
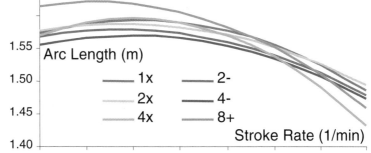

Table 2.2 Target oar angles and stroke length for various categories of rowers.				
Rowers' category	Catch (deg)	Finish (deg)	Total (deg)	Arc Length (m)
Men Sculling open	− 70	44	114	1.67
Men Sculling lightweight	− 66	44	110	1.61
Men Rowing open	− 59	33	92	1.64
Men Rowing lightweight	− 58	32	90	1.60
Women Sculling open	− 66	44	110	1.61
Women Sculling lightweight	− 63	43	106	1.55
Women Rowing open	− 58	32	90	1.60

Usually, the maximal stroke length occurred at a stroke rate of around 24 str/min (Fig. 2.9). The length became 2–3cm shorter at lower rates, and this is probably related to lower inertia forces which help to stretch muscles and ligaments at catch. The reduction of the stroke length is more significant at higher rates, especially in big boats: in 4 × and 8 + it was 10–11cm shorter at a stroke rate of 40 str/min relative to 24 str/min, while in smaller boats it was only 6–7cm shorter.

2.3.2 Vertical Oar Angle

Vertical oar angle is an important variable that could be used for evaluation of the blade work in the water. Fig. 2.10a shows the reference system used for the measurements of the vertical angle (VA). For practical reasons, the zero vertical angle was defined at the centre of the blade at water level. A positive direction means the blade is above water level, and a negative direction means the blade is below water level.

The trajectory of the blade relative to the water level could be plotted using data from the horizontal and vertical oar angles in the above reference system, used for evaluation of the rower's blade work skills (Fig. 2.11).

At the beginning of the stroke cycle (point A), the average vertical angle (VA) was found to be 2.4 ± 0.8 degrees (mean ± SD) and does not differ between sculling and rowing. Before the catch, the blade rises to provide space for squaring, and VA reaches its maximum elevation 4.9 ± 1.2 degrees in sculling and 4.1 ± 1.2 degrees in rowing at point B. The blade starts descending after this point, moving horizontally a further 2–4 degrees towards the bow, and changes direction at point C, which represents the catch angle. The VA at point C is very close to + 3 degrees, which means the bottom edge of the blade is close to the water level.

The catch slip could be defined in two ways:

■ From catch point C to point D, where the centre of the blade crosses the water level. It was found that this is enough to apply propulsive force, which overcomes the drag and starts moving the boat-rower system forward.

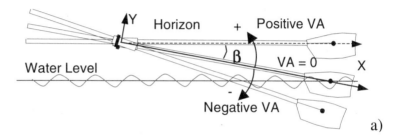

Fig. 2.10 Definitions of the vertical oar angle (a), and sensor for measurement of 2D oar angles in BioRowTel system (b).

Fig. 2.11 The trajectory of the blade relative to the water and definitions of criteria of blade work.

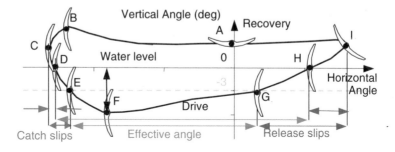

■ From catch point C to point E, where the whole blade is immersed below the water level and full propulsive force is applied. The VA at this point may vary depending on the blade width and outboard length. This criterion was set at −3 degrees, which guarantees blade coverage at all oar dimensions.

At point F the blade achieves its minimal (deepest) VA, which was found to be

−7.2 ± 1.3 degrees in sculling and −5.7 ± 1.2 degrees in rowing. Similarly, release slips could be defined in two ways: either starting (1) from point G at −3 degrees VA, or (2) from point H at 0 degrees VA, both ending at the release angle at point I.

The table below shows catch and release slips and the corresponding effective angles, which are components of the total angle, within which the blade is immersed according to the defined slip criteria:

Boat type	Catch Slip to 0 VA (deg)	Catch Slip to − 3 VA (deg)	Release Slip to 0 VA (deg)	Release Slip to − 3 VA (deg)	Effective Angle at 0 VA (per cent)	Effective Angle at − 3 VA (per cent)
Rowing	4.8	13.1	3.4	14.3	90.1 per cent	68.4 per cent
± SD	2.9	5.1	3.2	7.2	4.6 per cent	8.1 per cent
Sculling	4.1	10.0	6.5	18.5	89.7 per cent	73.1 per cent
± SD	2.0	3.1	3.9	6.5	3.8 per cent	6.7 per cent

Table 2.3 Average values (n = 6600) of the vertical angle criteria in rowing and sculling.

It was found that both effective angles have moderate correlations with blade propulsive efficiency ($r = 0.45$ for the 0 degrees VA criterion and $r = 0.38$ for the −3 degrees VA). Measurements of the vertical oar angle can help to improve the blade propulsive efficiency and increase boat speed.

2.3.3 Rotational Motions of the Boat

There are three main axes in any vessel, defined as longitudinal X, lateral or transverse Y and vertical Z (Fig. 2.12). The rotational movements around them are known as roll, pitch and yaw:

- Roll is the rotation about the longitudinal X (front/back) axis. Positive roll was defined as the port board − up; the starboard − down.
- Pitch is the rotation about the lateral or transverse Y (side-to-side) axis. Positive pitch was defined as the bow of the boat − up; the stern − down.
- Yaw is the rotation about the vertical Z (up–down) axis. Positive yaw was defined as the bow turning to starboard.

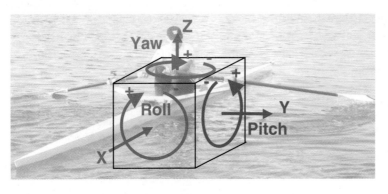

Fig. 2.12 Definitions of the boat rotations.

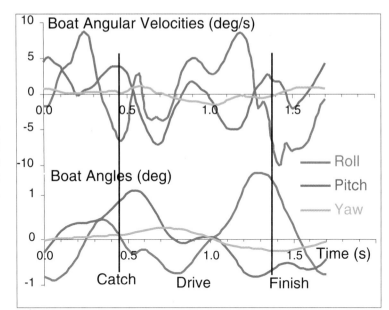

Fig. 2.13 Angular velocities and derived angles of the boat rotations (M1x at 35 str / min).

Modern electronics allow the use of tiny 3D gyroscopes[8] to measure the angular velocities of the boat rotation around all three axes. Corresponding rotation angles could be derived using integration of the measured angular velocities (Fig. 2.13). 3D accelerometers help to define boat position relative to the horizon.

Interpretation of the boat rotation angles is illustrated in Fig. 2.13. Roll is close to zero at the catch, when blades enter the water and the boat is balanced. Then it becomes negative down to − 1 degree (the right gate, port side, goes down), which is the consequence of separation of the oar handles during the drive. At the finish, the boat rolls on the other side by more than + 1 degree (left gate down), because the sculler pulls the handles at even height, but the gate's height is different. During the recovery the boat roll repeats this cycle.

The boat pitch has its highest positive value + 1 degree (stern goes down) soon after the catch, which is related to transfer of the rower's weight from the seat to the stretcher. At the middle of the drive the pitch remains close to zero (the boat is balanced). At the finish the pitch becomes negative, close to − 1 degree (bow goes down), which is explained by an increased seat force and upwards force at the stretcher due to the return of the trunk.

The boat yaw is close to zero at the end of recovery and becomes positive at about + 0.3 degrees after the catch, which is explained by asymmetry of the application force in this sculler; his right arm is pulling more strongly at the middle of the drive. Then, the boat yaws on the other side because the left arm is catching up, and the minimal yaw value about − 0.3 degrees is achieved at the finish. During recovery, the yaw decreases to zero, which could be explained by the stabilizing action of the fin.

The roll amplitude is highest in singles (Table 2.4) and significantly decreases in bigger boats, nearly down to zero in eights, which is the most stable boat. Interestingly, there is no significant difference in roll between sweep and sculling boats.

Surprisingly, the difference in the pitch

Table 2.4 Average amplitudes (differences between maximal and minimal angles) of the roll, pitch and yaw in various boat types.

Boat Type	n	Roll (deg)	± SD	Pitch (deg)	± SD	Yaw (deg)	± SD
1 ×	492	2.70	1.45	1.39	0.27	0.65	0.26
2 −	185	1.42	0.81	1.29	0.16	0.58	0.16
2 ×	317	1.42	1.03	1.24	0.16	0.42	0.21
4 −	137	0.53	0.64	1.01	0.15	0.45	0.15
4 ×	60	0.54	0.60	0.88	0.08	0.11	0.03
8 +	35	0.14	0.08	0.81	0.43	0.05	0.01

amplitude in various boats was relatively small: in the eights the pitch is only 40 per cent less than in singles. The pitch amplitude significantly increases with the stroke rate ($r = 0.86$), which is explained by higher inertia forces.

The yaw amplitude is also inversely proportional to the boat size, decreasing nearly down to zero in eights. In pairs it is slightly higher than in doubles and in fours it is significantly higher than in quads, which is explained by the rigging asymmetry.

All rotational motions of the boat should be minimized: pitch and yaw could increase drag resistance; roll may decrease power production and lead to injuries.

2.3.4 Rotational Motions of the Oar

An oar has three degrees of freedom relative to the boat coordinate system: rotation in the horizontal plane (horizontal angle, see 2.3.1), rotation in the transverse plane (vertical angle, see 2.3.2), and rotation around the oar's longitudinal axis – squaring and feathering. Similar to the boat rotations, the oar rotational motions could be measured with 3D gyro and accelerometers (Fig. 2.14). The frame of reference was set similarly to the boat motions analysis and the axes directions were defined by the design of the sensor.

Interpretation of the data from this sensor

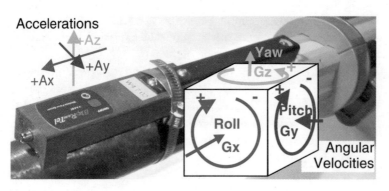

Fig. 2.14 Wireless sensor measuring 3D oar rotations and 3D accelerations as well as handle force.

is quite complicated, because the boat coordinate system is not inertial and the sensor measures not only oar movements but also the boat accelerations and rotations (Fig. 2.15). During the drive, the sensor is positioned horizontally underneath the oar, so Ay and Gy (pitch) are related to the vertical movements of the oar, and Az and Gz (yaw) to the horizontal ones. During recovery, the oar is rolled 90 degrees (feathered), so Ay and Gy became horizontal measures and Az and Gz become vertical ones. Also, the sensor rotates with the oar in the horizontal plane for more than 100 degrees. At the catch, its X axis is positioned at about 30 degrees to the boat axis, so Ax measures the boat acceleration. At the middle of the drive, the X axis of the sensor is close to the perpendicular to the boat, so Ax becomes very close to zero.

The most understandable and informative measured variable appeared to be the roll Gx, which is clearly related to the squaring-feathering of the oar. Fig. 2.15a shows (at point 2) that the squaring takes about 0.35s and completed at the catch, when the oar changes direction, but the blade is still in the air. The feathering in this sculler began when the centre of the blade crossed the water level (point 3) and completed in about 0.25s: that is faster than squaring.

The oar roll for M1x boats was the same at various stroke rates: at a low stroke rate the squaring of the blade before the catch takes about 15 degrees of horizontal movement of the oar. At a high rate, the squaring takes about the same time but twice as long a distance, up to 40 degrees, because of the much faster horizontal movement of the oar. The feathering distance at the finish is independent of the stroke rate.

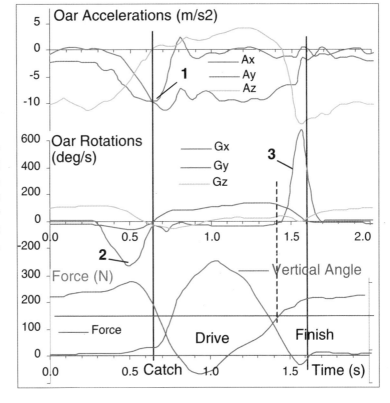

Fig. 2.15 (a) Oar accelerations and angular velocities together with the handle force and oar vertical angle (M1x at 30 str / min).

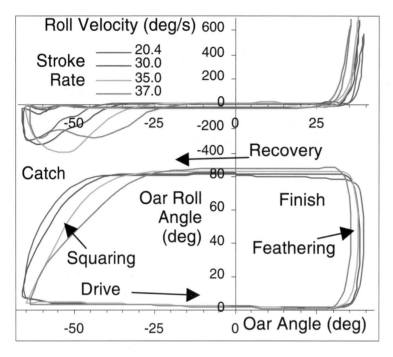

Fig. 2.15 (*Cont.*)
(b) Corresponding oar roll velocities and angles.

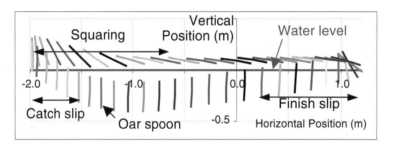

Fig. 2.16
Reconstruction of the oar movements relative to the water level (M1x at 37 str / min).

The oar roll data in conjunction with horizontal and vertical oar angles allows a full reconstruction of the oar movements relative to the water level (Fig. 2.16).

In this sculler, the blade moves nearly half the distance of the recovery in a semi-squared position, which significantly increases losses on the aerodynamic drag resistance. More effort is required to build a mathematical model which will combine the complex data and allow an explanation for other measured variables.

2.4 VELOCITIES AND ACCELERATIONS

2.4.1 Speed and Velocity in Rowing

There are two words that define how fast an object moves: speed and velocity. Speed defines quickness of the movement and has only magnitude, but no direction, so it is a scalar quantity. Velocity is the rate of change of the position of an object over time, so it is a vector and combines both magnitude (speed)

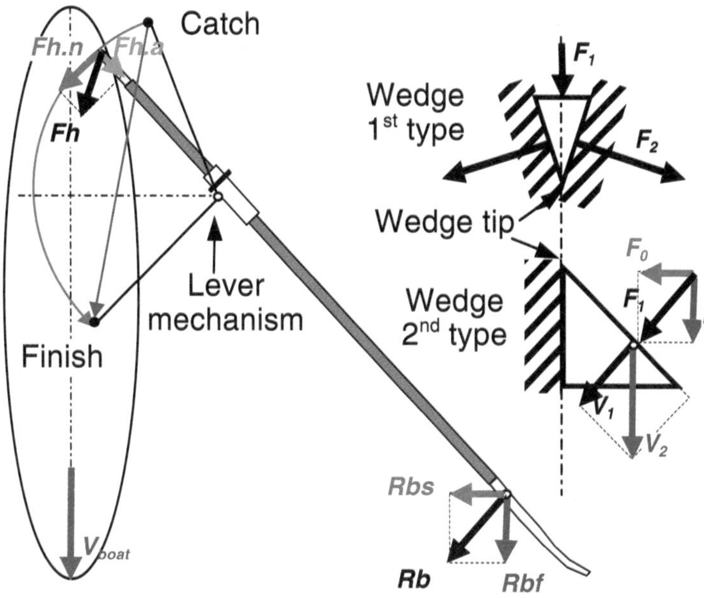

Fig. 2.17 The difference between speed and velocity for the motion of the oar handle.

and direction. With instantaneous velocity, its magnitude at each moment is equal to the speed. Similarly, average velocity during continuous linear motion is equal to the average speed. However, with curvilinear or recurring motion, it is more complicated. Average speed is equal to the average of its instant values, or to the travelled path divided by time. Average velocity is the ratio of displacement of the object to the time. With curvilinear motion the displacement is always shorter than the path, so the average velocity is lower than average speed. With cyclic motion, when an object returns to its starting position, the displacement is zero, and so is its average velocity, though the object may travel a long way and the average speed could be high.

Oar movement provides a good illustration of the difference between speed and velocity (Fig. 2.17). From catch to finish, the handle travels 1.71m (the length of the arc at the middle of the handle at 114 degrees total angle and 0.88m inboard), but the displacement between these two points is only 1.44m, or 16 per cent shorter. Similarly there is a dif-

ference between the average speed during the drive (1.90m/s with a drive time 0.9s) and the average velocity (1.60m/s). If the handle velocity is averaged over the whole stroke cycle, it is zero, because the handle returns to the same position relative to the boat. However, the average handle speed over the stroke cycle is not zero. (It is 2.05m/s in this case at 36str/min.)

Performance in rowing is defined by average velocity of the boat, but not by average speed: the boat must travel from starting point A to finishing point B in the shortest possible time. So we are interested in the fastest displacement between these two points, but the length of the path travelled by the boat is not taken into account. Therefore, effective steering is a part of rowing performance and should provide the straightest path for the boat, which can be a complicated task in head races on curved rivers.

The power applied by a rower is the main factor in determining the boat's speed and velocity. One of the components of the power is the velocity, but not the speed, because the direction of the movement relative to applied force is important. Therefore, power P is a scalar product of two vectors: force vector F and velocity vector v: $P = f\, v\, cos(\alpha)$ where α is the angle between these two vectors. When the force is applied perpendicularly to the velocity, the power is zero, because $cos(90°) = 0$. For example, the axial handle force $Fh.a$ (Fig. 2.17) does not produce power, because it is perpendicular to the instantaneous handle velocity by definition. Only the normal handle force $Fh.n$ produces power.

Speed and velocity can be easily converted with a simple lever mechanism, like an oar. The ratio of the input (handle) velocity, Vin, to the output (blade) velocity, $Vout$, is inversely proportional to the ratio of corresponding forces and defines the gearing ratio G: $Vout\ /\ vin = fin\ /\ fout = g$.

A similar effect can be achieved when a force is applied at an angle to the velocity. This defines another simple mechanism – a wedge, which can also convert velocity and force in two ways (Fig. 2.17): type (1) when the force F_1 is directed towards its tip in the axial plane it magnifies the lateral force F_2 (used in wood splitting) and type (2) when the lateral force F_1 is applied to a wedge slope the output force F_2 is smaller, but the velocity in this direction V_2 is proportionally higher. The component of the blade reaction force Rbs, perpendicular to the boat velocity, used to be considered as energy loss, which was one of the 'myths' of rowing biomechanics for many years: 'force applied at steep catch and finish angles is ineffective'. In fact, the side force produces zero power, because it is perpendicular to the boat velocity $Vboat$, so the energy losses are zero. Sharp catch angles work as a wedge of the second type and make the gearing heavier. This means the propulsive force Rbf is smaller than total blade reaction force Rb, but it is applied at boat velocity $Vboat$, which is proportionally faster than the velocity of the pro-

pelling object – the blade. So, the propulsive power is the same and the only loss is friction, which is small at the blade. Similar examples can be found in nature:

- A skater pushes his skate blade to the side, but moves forward much faster than a runner who pushes the ground straight backwards.
- A sailing yacht moves much faster in a cross wind than in a straight tail wind.
- In archery, a bow pulls the string to the sides, but the arrow flies forward much faster.

The total oar gearing is variable during the drive and equal to the sum of the lever and wedge effects. It must be optimal for each rower. Heavier gearing helps to increase the force quicker at the catch, but may slow down the handle velocity and decrease the stroke rate, and vice versa (*see* Chapter 6.2.1).

2.4.2 Boat Velocity

Certainly, the boat velocity is the most important variable in rowing biomechanics because it defines the race time and rowing performance. However, this is the resultant variable, which depends on many other parameters: rowing power, technique efficiency, weather conditions, and so on. Therefore it would not be very helpful to just advise to 'use a higher boat velocity' but we can use this variable as a criterion, an indicator of various aspects of rowing technique.

There is an old and widely spread idea that the variation of the boat velocity during the stroke cycle is the main factor of energy loss and must be reduced for efficient rowing[32]. Its reasoning is as follows: energy losses due to drag resistance (drag power P_d) are proportional to the cube of boat velocity

v: $P_d = DF\,v^3$ where DF is the drag factor. The minimal P_d could be achieved at constant boat velocity. For example typical values for single sculls of $v = 5$m/s and $DF = 3$, give drag power $P_d = 375$W. However, if the boat speed is 4m/s during half of the stroke cycle, and 6m/s in the other half (the same average speed 5m/s), then the average drag power would be $P_d = (192 + 648)/2 = 420$W, which requires 12 per cent more energy production. If the rowing power remains the same 375W with a similar velocity variation, then the average boat speed will be only 4.82m/s, a 3.7 per cent loss of speed.

Variation of the boat velocity in rowing has only two sources:

1. The periodic nature of the propulsion. Blades produce propulsive force only during the drive phase – about half of the stroke cycle time. Therefore, the rower-boat system accelerates during the drive and slows down during recovery.

2. Significant movements of the rower's mass, which is much heavier (4–6 times) than the boat mass.

Two factors affect the variation of the boat velocity in different proportions which vary with the stroke rate. *At lower stroke rates (below 24/min), the periodic propulsion dominates,* because recovery time is long and a rower moves to the catch slowly and pulls the stretcher easily. The maximal boat velocity is achieved at the finish (Fig. 2.18a, point 1), then it decreases during recovery. *At higher stroke rates (above 24/min), the rower's movement dominates:* the recovery time shortens

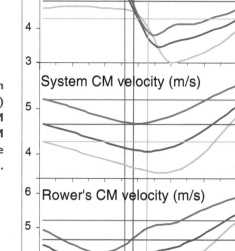

Fig. 2.18 Variation of (a) the boat, (b) the system CM and (c) rower's CM velocities during the stroke cycle.

dramatically, so the rower must move faster and pull the stretcher harder. This force accelerates the boat, which achieves its maximum velocity just before the catch (Fig. 2.18a, point 2), when the seat velocity is maximal and the rower switches from pulling to pushing the stretcher.

The coefficient of variation C_v was defined as the ratio of the standard deviation σ of the mean value of the variable, in this case, the average boat speed Vav: $C_v = \sigma / vav$. It was found that the variation of the boat speed has a nearly functional relationship with energy losses E_l and speed losses V_l ($R^2 = 0.996$): $E_l = 2.5\ C_v^2$ and $V_l = -0.9\ C_v^2$.

A large sample of telemetry measurements (n = 5448) was analysed, and these values were found to be lower than in the above example: C_v ranges 10–18 per cent, E_l 2.7–9.0 per cent, and V_l 0.9–3.0 per cent.

To study the effect of the above two factors, velocities of the rower's centre of mass $Vrow$ and the whole system (rower + boat + oars) $Vsys$ were derived (Kleshnev, 2010), (Fig. 2.18b,c), as well as trends of their dependence on the stroke rate in different boat types (Fig. 2.19). It was found that all the variations were higher in smaller boats, and they depend on the stroke rate: the boat velocity variation increases with the stroke rate, but variations in the rower and system velocities decrease.

At low rates, 60–80 per cent (depending on the boat type) of the boat velocity variation is provided by the system velocity variation, which depends on periodic propulsion only. At high rates, 70–80 per cent of the boat velocity variation depends on the rower's movements: variation of the rower's CM velocity.

For many years, the idea of asynchronous rowing was considered as a way to eliminate both the above factors and achieve more efficient and faster rowing. Phase shift drive should make the propulsion constant; an opposite direction of the rowers' motions

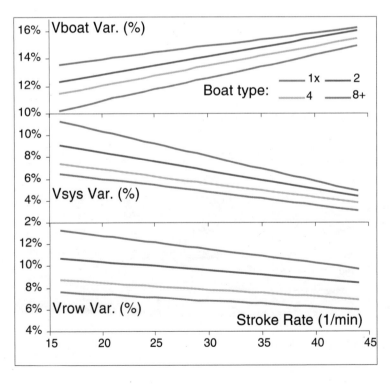

Fig. 2.19 Dependence of variations of the boat, system CM and rower's CM velocities on the stroke rate.

Fig. 2.20 (a) Asynchronous eight at London rowing club, 1929; (b) 1979 world champions W4 + USSR. The boat was designed for asynchronous rowing, but rowed normally, because it was faster.

should cancel their effect. Some efforts were made to implement this idea, but no practical results were achieved[37]. This happened because of dramatically increased inertial energy losses. Instead of moving a light boat in normal rowing, the rowers had to change the direction of the movements of their heavier body mass, and also overcome boat accelerations created by countermovement of their teammates, which made it even less efficient than rowing in a stationary tank/erg rowing (RBN 2010/05). Whilst about 6–8 per cent of energy was saved due to less variation of the boat velocity the rowers had to spend 10–12 per cent extra energy to overcome inertial forces. In other words, V_{boat} variation

was decreased, but V_{row} variation increased, which was especially inefficient at high rates, so asynchronous boats were slower than normal ones.

In rowing technique, an idea of achieving faster rowing by means of a more even boat velocity has created many unproductive outcomes, such as 'do not check the boat at catch', 'pull the handle before you push the stretcher', and so on.

What could really be done through technique to minimize energy losses due to variation of the boat velocity? The two factors above dictate opposite solutions: increasing propulsion time requires a longer drive phase and higher rhythm (ratio of the drive phase to the stroke cycle time). Contrarily, if rowers' movements need to be smoother, then the recovery phase should be longer and the rhythm lower[54]. As we are interested mainly in higher racing stroke rates, where the second factor dominates, it makes sense to follow the second route. This was confirmed through the data: at rates above 30/min, the rhythm *Rh* significantly correlates with rate-normalized variation of the boat speed *Cvr* (r = 0.63, *Cvr = 0.248 Rh + 0.019, Cvr* was derived as a deviation from the rate-based trend line, to eliminate the effect of the stroke rate), so: *the shorter the drive time and longer the recovery, the more efficient the boat velocity.*

Not all methods are productive for shortening drive time: for example, shortening drive length would decrease power and the speed. In general, maintaining the constant boat speed during the recovery should be emphasized, but not during the drive, because the boat speed is much higher on recovery, and creates the highest drag resistance. Here are a few things, which could be used effectively:

- Avoid sharp jerky pulls of the stretcher during recovery. Try to spread stretcher pulling force evenly to produce the most constant boat speed and minimize energy losses (O'Neill[48]).
- Use the optimal gearing ratio according to weather conditions: shorter outboard with a headwind. Avoid too heavy gearing, which makes the drive too slow and requires rushing on recovery to maintain the stroke rate. Shorter recovery time requires harder pulling on the stretcher, which accelerates the boat more and increases the variation of its velocity.
- For the same reason, do not put the blade in too deep during the drive, which may 'break the force curve' and make drive time longer.

- A 'front-loaded' drive with quick force increase after the catch is the only way to accelerate the boat earlier during the drive and make its velocity more even.

It is difficult to estimate numerically the effect of the above methods, because it requires special experiments and/or complicated modelling. Some publications in this area[51] suggest that the effect should not be huge: only a few seconds could be saved in a 2km race by means of optimized recovery techniques.

2.4.3 Boat Acceleration

The boat acceleration could easily be measured and be a useful diagnostic tool for defining various aspects of rowing technique. Listed below are the definitions of the criteria of the boat acceleration curve and its interpretation for evaluation of the rowing technique (Fig. 2.21a).

1. '*Zero before catch*' defines the moment when the boat acceleration becomes negative during the recovery. At this moment, the crew changes the force application to the stretcher from pulling to pushing, which coincides with the peak seat velocity during the recovery and is followed by the seat deceleration towards the catch. At higher stroke rates and in better crews, this moment occurs later and closer to the catch, so its position relative to the oar angle and timing relative to the catch has a negative correlation with the stroke rate (r = − 0.35, Table 2.5).
2. '*Negative peak*' usually happens just after the catch (when the oar has changed direction) but before full entry of the blade. Its magnitude is highly dependent on the stroke rate (r = − 0.82, Table 2.5). The best crews show a deeper, but narrower negative peak

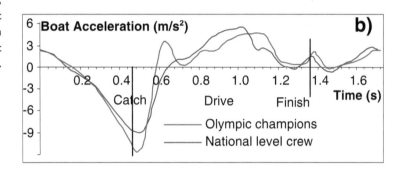

Fig. 2.21 A typical pattern of boat acceleration during the stroke cycle (a), comparison of boat acceleration with crews of different standards (b).

(Fig. 2.21b), which could be explained by a sharper 'catch through the stretcher'. Therefore, it is very unproductive to try to minimize this so-called 'boat check', which is one of the myths of rowing biomechanics. The negative peak has a slightly lower magnitude in eights, which could be explained by a heavier boat mass with a coxswain, in proportion to the rowers' mass.

3. '*Zero after catch*' occurs, when the boat acceleration becomes positive due to the gate/handle forces increasing faster than the stretcher force. This moment happens earlier in better crews and at higher stroke rates ($r = 0.37$).

4. '*First peak*' is caused by the fast increasing of the gate/handle forces ('front-loaded' drive) and defines 'the initial boat acceleration' sub-phase and 'the trampoline effect'[36]. It was not observed in about 30 per cent of crews at 20 str/min and in 6 per cent of crews at 36 str/min, so its magnitude has a moderately positive correlation with the stroke rate ($r = 0.41$). The best crews usually have a higher first peak, which can be close to or even greater than the second peak. No significant difference was found in the values of the first peak between various boat types.

5. '*Drive hump*' is explained by an increase of force on the stretcher during 'the main rower's acceleration' sub-phase[36], which is caused by shortening the leverage of the stretcher force relative to the hips at the placement of the heels onto the footplate. The best crews manage to maintain the value of the drive hump just above zero. Negative values of this variable are usually related to the hump of the force curve, which could be caused by one or more of the following:

   ■ 'Disconnection' of the legs and trunk due to a weak posture of the lower back;
   ■ 'Double trunk work', where the trunk opens early in the catch, causing a hump in the trunk velocity;

Table 2.5 Statistical values of the variables of the boat acceleration.

	Variable	Mean (n = 5248)	± SD	Correlation with Stroke Rate
Positions from Catch in per cent of Total Oar Angle	Zero Before Catch	33.5	8.9	-0.35
	Negative Peak	1.6	1.7	0.06
	Zero after Catch	12.1	3.7	0.12
	First Peak	16.8	6.6	0.18
	Drive	24.4	7.2	0.28
	Second	57.0	15.6	-0.07
	Finish	82.0	24.1	-0.16
Timing from Catch in per cent of the Stroke Cycle	Zero Before Catch	− 19.4	5.2	0.37
	Negative Peak	2.9	1.9	0.11
	Zero after Catch	9.7	2.0	0.37
	First Peak	11.9	3.0	0.40
	Drive Hump	15.8	3.4	0.60
	Second Peak	27.6	5.9	0.37
	Finish Hump	37.9	9.8	0.22
Absolute values (m/s^2)	Negative Peak (m/s^2)	− 7.42	2.57	− 0.82
	First Peak (m/s^2)	1.65	1.19	0.41
	Drive Hump (m/s^2)	0.50	0.88	0.01
	Second Peak (m/s^2)	3.88	1.19	0.23
	Finish Hump (m/s^2)	0.82	1.55	0.28

- Sinking the blade too deeply into the water, which causes a longer vertical leverage of the handle force relative to the stretcher;
- Too quick an increase of force at the catch: 'don't bite off more than you can chew'.

6. 'Second peak' occurs when leg velocity and stretcher forces start decreasing, while relatively higher handle/gate forces are maintained by fast movements of the trunk and arms. This causes the deceleration of the rower's CM and the transfer of his kinetic energy to the boat mass. The value of the second peak has a small positive correlation with the stroke rate ($r = 0.23$).

7. 'Finish hump' is related to the transition phase from the drive to recovery and blade removal from the water. In the best crews, this value does not drop below zero, which is achieved by an active arm-pull ('finish

through the handle') and clean blade work without feathering in the water.

The pattern of the boat acceleration should be considered as a resultant variable, a sort of 'indicator' of rowing technique. Therefore, it is not very productive to target the boat acceleration itself, but better to look into the movement of the rower and acceleration of his/her CM.

2.5 FORCES

Force is one of the most important variables in biomechanics, because it is the reason for any movement in the real world around us. To start a movement, any biological object has to produce a force with its muscles to overcome external forces: inertia, gravity and friction.

A force is a vector quantity, which means it has both magnitude and direction. A force F causes a free object of mass m to change its velocity, that is it creates an acceleration a, which is described by Newton's second law:

$$F = m\,a \qquad (12)$$

The unit of force is the Newton (N) = kg m/s², which means 1 N force changes the velocity of a 1 kg object by 1 m/s per s.

Rowing allows the measurement of forces at many points: at the oar handle and blade, at the gate and pin, at the stretcher and seat. Most of these forces are internal in the rower-boat-oars system. Though they are important for analysis of rowing technique, only the blade force is an external one which produces a propulsive reaction force in the water and moves the system forward.

2.5.1 Force Measurements at the Oar, Gate and Pin

In rowing, the oar works as a lever, so forces at the blade, handle, gate and pin are related each to the others. The blade force is difficult to measure directly because the point of its application is uncertain and varies during the drive. The most practical methods are measurements of the force at the oar handle, at the gate and pin[1,2,3]. These methods have the following features:

1. The handle force F_{hnd} (Fig. 2.22) can be measured perpendicular to the oar direction either with strain gauges applied directly on to the oar shaft or with detachable sensors. In fact, the sensor measures the oar bend, which is proportional to the torque M or moment of the force F_{hnd} and can be calibrated as a force applied at a known point on the handle. The rower's power production P can be derived as:

$$P = m * \omega = f_{hnd} * L_{in\text{-}a} * \omega \qquad (13)$$

where $L_{in\text{-}a}$ is the actual oar inboard lever, and ω is oar angular velocity, which can be derived from a measurement of the horizontal oar angle. In this case the calculated power is not affected by the point of application of the rower's force, which is unknown and may vary significantly especially in sweep rowing. Therefore, this is the most accurate method for measurement of rower's power with an estimated error of 1 per cent. The practical problem of this method is the necessity to calibrate every oar, which can be solved with modern technology[8].

The resultant force, $F_{hnd\text{-}res}$, which the rower applies to the handle, is not always perpendicular to the oar axis. Therefore, it can be resolved into the perpendicular F_{hnd} and axial $F_{hnd\text{-}ax}$ components. The last

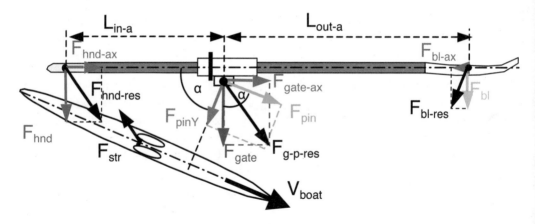

Fig. 2.22 Forces at the blade, oar handle, gate and pin.

is quite difficult to measure, but it does not produce any mechanical power at the oar. It is statically transferred through the oar shaft and creates an axial force at the gate $F_{gate-ax}$, which is a sum of vectors F_{hnd-ax} and axial force at the blade F_{bl-ax}. Then, the axial force $F_{gate-ax}$ is transferred through the gate, pin, rigger and statically balanced with the stretcher force F_{str}. Therefore, *a rower should apply only a small axial force to keep the button in contact with the gate and pull the handle as perpendicularly as possible.*

The torque of the blade force F_{bl} can be measured using the same method as was described above for the handle force and would produce the same accuracy in the calculation of the rower's power.

2. The gate rotates together with the oar and the perpendicular F_{gate} and axial F_{bl-ax} components of the gate force can be measured in the reference frame of the oar using instrumented gates. The rower's power can be derived using Equation 12, but F_{hnd} must be calculated as:

$$F_{hnd} = f_{gate} * (L_{out-a} / (L_{in-a} + L_{out-a})) \quad (14)$$

where L_{out-a} is actual outboard length from the pin to the centre of the blade force. We

do not know exactly L_{in-a} and L_{out-a} because actual points of force application during rowing are uncertain. We can only guess that they are located at the centres of the handle and blade. The estimated error in the rower's power calculation using this method could be up to 5 per cent. The sum of the normal F_{gate} and axial $F_{gate-ax}$ components gives a resultant gate force $F_{g-p-res}$, which is transferred to the pin.

3. The pin is fixed relative to the boat and the pin sensor measures force in the reference frame of the boat. Usually, it measures only the component of force F_{pin} parallel to the boat axis of the resultant gate-pin force $F_{g-p-res}$. The rower's power can be derived using Equations 12 and 13; however, gate force F_{gate} must be derived as:

$$F_{gate} = f_{pin} * \cos \alpha \quad (15)$$

In fact, only a part of the rower's force production can be measured using this method (for example only half when the catch oar angle is 60° as cos(60°) = 0.5). Also, the readings are affected by the axial gate force $F_{gate-ax}$, which, as was shown above, does not produce power. For this reason, the force measurements at the pin are

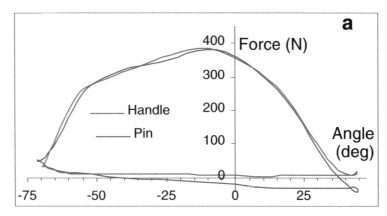

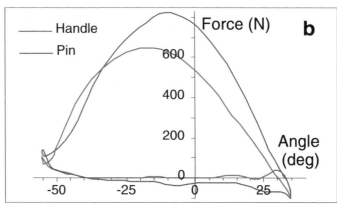

Fig. 2.23 Comparison of the force curves measured at the handle and at the pin (scaled using gearing ratio) in sculling (a) and rowing (b).

quite significant and variable during recovery (Fig. 2.23). The estimated error in the rower's power calculation is 10 per cent in sculling and up to 20 per cent in rowing. Accuracy of this method can be improved with 2D sensors of the pin force, which can also measure perpendicular to the boat component F_{pinY}. In this case, the accuracy would match the gate force sensors; the magnitude and direction of the resultant force $F_{g\text{-}p\text{-}res}$ could be determined and then the perpendicular component F_{gate} derived using the known gate angle α.

The situation with accuracy is the opposite if the purpose is a calculation of the balance of forces on the hull, which could be a target in some research studies. Usually, the stretcher force F_{str} is measured in these studies and

propulsive force F_{prop} can be derived for each rower:

$$F_{prop} = F_{pin} - F_{str} \tag{16}$$

If the force is measured at the handle, then F_{gate} must be derived from F_{hnd} using $L_{in\text{-}a}$ and $L_{out\text{-}a}$, and then F_{pin} is obtained using the oar angle α. In this case, measurement of the pin force F_{pin} is the most accurate method and its calculation from measurement of F_{hnd} can give up to 20 per cent error margins in sweep rowing.

2.5.2 Force Curve

When force is measured it is usually plotted against time or oar angle on the X axis and is commonly called the 'force curve'.

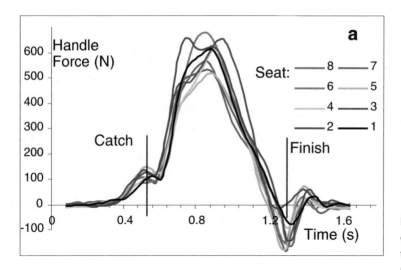

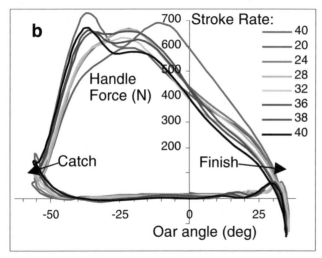

Fig. 2.24 Two types of representation of the force curve: (a) relative to the time on X axis, (b) relative to the oar angle on X axis.

The choice of X axis variable depends on what is intended to be analysed (Fig. 2.24). Time-based plots are useful for analysis of synchronization of the forces throughout the crew (a). Angle-based plots are better for comparison of the force curves at different stroke rates (b).

The force curve is a very important general indication of rowing technique: for example, gaps and double peaking (Fig. 2.24, right) reflect lack of coordination of large muscle groups, legs and trunk. The force curve shows the emphasis of the rower's efforts, which is related to the dynamics of the system and effectiveness.

What peak position of the force curve is the most effective: at the catch, the middle of the drive, or the finish? Let us use a very simple model with three types of force curve: F1 (back-loaded) slowly increases from 0 to 5N with simple arithmetical progression, F2 (front-loaded) jumps to 5N and then decreases, F3 is constant at average 3N. If each of these three forces acts on a body of mass 1kg, it is possible to derive the body's acceleration, velocity and applied power (Fig. 2.25):

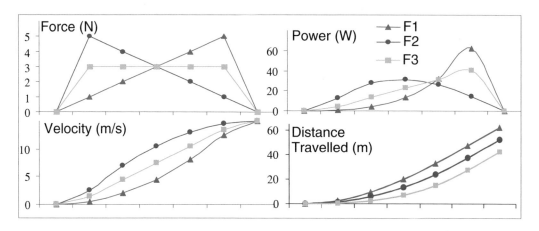

Fig. 2.25 Modelling of the force curve.

In all cases, the same total amount of force and power, and the same final velocity of the body were achieved. However, the front-loaded curve F2 increases the velocity earlier, so the total distance travelled and the average speed would be 46 per cent higher. Also, the back-loaded F1 requires double the peak power compared to the F2 curve. In rowing this late power peak would overload the trunk and arms, which are weaker body segments than legs. Therefore, *the front-loaded drive force curve is the most effective*: for the same effort it provides a higher average velocity and more even power distribution.

The following criteria were proposed for evaluation of the force curve (Fig. 2.26). The most obvious criterion is a maximum force *Fmax*, which is the highest point on the force curve. An average force *Faver* is equal to the height of a rectangle, of which the area is equal to the area under the force curve. The ratio of the average to maximal forces (*Ram = Faver / Fmax*) reflects 'fat' or 'slim' force curves:

- For a perfect rectangular shape, *Ram* = 100 per cent;
- For a perfect triangular shape, *Ram* = 50 per cent.

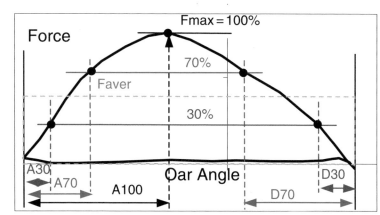

Fig. 2.26 Evaluation of the force curve.

This ratio in rowing was found to be in the range 38–64 per cent with average 50.9 ± 4.5 per cent (mean $\pm$ SD).

The term 'catch slip' was traditionally used as a definition of how quickly the force increases at the catch and 'release slip' was used to indicate its maintenance at the release. In fact, these parameters have very low correlation with a 'slippage' of the blade in the water (for vertical catch, see 2.3.2), so it is better to use the term 'gradient of force'. The slippage can be long, but the gradient is steep if the blade moves quickly on a shallow path through the water. At a higher stroke rate, it usually requires a shorter angle to achieve 30 per cent of the maximum force ($r = -0.44$), but a longer angle to bury the blade. (The vertical catch slip increases, $r = 0.20$).

Values of 30 per cent and 70 per cent of the maximum force were used as the criteria for the force gradient. The catch gradient was defined as an angle, through which the oar travels from the catch point to the point where the force achieves the criterion ($A30$ and $A70$). The release gradient is defined as an angle from the point where the force drops below the criterion to the finish of the drive ($D70$ and $D30$). Criterion $A100$ reflects the position of the peak force and can be used as a definition of the type of the force curve.

The purpose of the A30 criterion is to determine how quickly the blade grips the water. It was found that $A30$ has a correlation with the blade efficiency ($r = -0.34$). Ram also slightly correlates with the blade efficiency ($r = 0.32$), which means that a quicker force increase and a rectangular shape of the force curve reduces slippage of the blade in the water.

Contrarily, $A70$ has an insignificant correlation with the blade efficiency ($r = -0.13$), but $A70$ and $D70$ correlate with maximal legs velocity ($r = -0.28$ and $r = -0.38$), that is, quicker legs' activation produces steeper gradients of force. As the legs' velocity is related to the acceleration of rower's CM it could be speculated that $A70$ *relates to the effectiveness of rowing technique*. This difference between $A30$ and $A70$ could be explained by the mechanics of force increase: the 30 per cent level can be achieved by quick handling of the oar and using the small muscles of the arms and shoulders, but the 70 per cent level could be achieved only with acceleration of the rower's mass and involvement of the large leg and trunk muscles.

Values of the force gradients depend on the stroke rate: $A30$ and $A70$ getting shorter at high rates ($r = -30$ and $r = -43$), but $D70$ and $D30$ getting slightly longer ($r = 0.21$ and $r = 0.18$). This reflects changes in the force curve at higher rates. Table 2.6 shows average values of the above criteria in rowing and sculling at training and racing stroke rates.

2.5.3 Stretcher Force

The stretcher force is not easy to measure and analyse because its direction and centre of application vary throughout the drive: at the catch rowers push the stretcher with their toes and more vertically; during the second half of the drive, the force becomes more horizontal and located at the middle of the foot (Fig. 2.27).

The stretcher force F_S could be resolved into two components, which play very different roles in rowing biomechanics: the horizontal component F_{SH} involved in the propulsion of the rower-boat system, and the vertical component F_{SV} which brings about 'suspension' of the rower's weight and is discussed with the seat force (2.5.4). Therefore, it is not enough to measure just the 'stretcher force' F_S, but it is necessary either to define its direction as well, or measure horizontal and vertical components separately.

Criterion (deg)	A30		A70		D70		D30	
Rate:	T	R	T	R	T	R	T	R
Rowing	6.7	5.2	16.7	13.6	30.3	34.0	11.5	12.8
± SD	1.9	1.6	3.8	3.1	7.6	7.3	3.1	3.5
Sculling	5.8	3.8	17.2	13.4	35.6	38.2	14.5	15.7
± SD	2.0	1.5	4.8	4.6	7.0	6.6	3.3	3.3

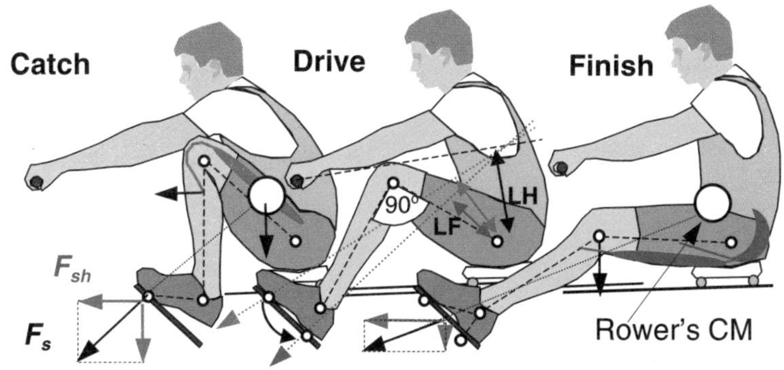

Table 2.6 Average values of force curve criteria at training T (below 30 str/min) and racing R (above 30str/min) stroke rates.

Fig. 2.27 Biomechanics of the stretcher force during the drive.

At the catch, the pressure must be applied at the toes, because it reduces the vertical lever of the handle force and increases the horizontal lever of the gravity force at the rower's CM, which allows higher handle force. If the torque at the handle exceeds the gravity torque, then the rower would lift himself, lose contact with the seat and have to stop rowing. At the catch, the lever of the gravity force is the shortest, so it is important to maximize it and minimize the vertical lever between the stretcher and the handle. Also, pushing with the toes reduces the lever at the knee joint, which allows more efficient use of the *quadriceps* muscles and quicker extension of the knee.

During the drive, the position of the rower, where the knee angle is passing 90 degrees and the heels settle down on the stretcher is a very important key point, which dramatically changes biomechanics of force production:

- Before this point, the rower pushes the stretcher with the toes, extends the knee using the quadriceps and should refrain from opening the trunk, because use of the muscles of the back of the thigh (hamstrings and glutes) would push the knee down and flex it;

- After this point, the heels are usually placed on the footboard, the centre of pressure is lowered and the rower can start using the trunk, emphasizing pushing the knee down with hamstrings and glutes, which mechanically extends the knee. Pushing with the heels is more effective because it reduces the lever of the stretcher force at the hip joint (*see* below).

At this transition, the lever of the stretcher force relative to the hip joint LF becomes shorter, while the lever of the handle force LH remains the same[21]. At constant muscle torque, the stretcher force increases and the handle force remains the same. This causes lower propulsive force and boat acceleration (Fig. 2.28a), but higher acceleration of the rower's CM. The ability to shift the pressure smoothly and coordinate it with the trunk movement depends on the rower's skill and is very important for effective rowing technique.

The horizontal stretcher force F_{SH} is a part of the balance of forces at the hull:

$$F_{PF} - F_{SH} = m_b\, a_b - F_D \qquad (17)$$

where F_{PF} ($= f_p \cos(A)$), the forward component of the pin force (A) is the gate angle, m_b is the active boat mass, a_b the boat acceleration, and F_D is the drag force. From this equation, F_{SH} appears to have a negative effect on the boat's propulsion, as it is in the opposite direction to the boat's velocity and plays the same role as the drag force; the higher the stretcher force, the lower the boat acceleration. Quite often, rowers and coaches attempt to minimize 'wrongly' directed stretcher force and maximize the handle force, which is applied in the 'right' direction, transferred through the rigger to the pin force F_{PF} and accelerates the boat forward.

However, this is correct only in regard to the hull, which contributes about 15 per cent of the total mass of the system. If the heaviest part of the system – the rower's mass m_R is considered, the balance of forces is:

$$F_{SH} - F_H = m_R\, a_R \qquad (18)$$

where F_H is the handle force and a_R is the

acceleration of the rower's CM. This means the stretcher (reaction) force accelerates the rower's mass forward, but the handle force pulls it backwards. Therefore, maximizing the horizontal stretcher force during the drive is a very important part of the effective rowing technique, and many successful coaches set it as the main target for the rower's efforts.

The pin/gate and horizontal stretcher forces have quite similar magnitude and pattern during the drive. The difference between them is the boat propulsive force, which is spent on overcoming drag F_D and boat inertia $m_b a_b$ forces (Equation 16), which are relatively lower.

The boat inertia force could be derived from the measured boat acceleration and known active boat mass (Fig. 2.28b), so the drag force at the hull $F_D(F)$ could be calculated from the equation 1. For comparison, the drag force $F_D(V)$ was also derived from the boat velocity Vb and drag factor DF:

$$F_D(V) = DF * Vb^2 \qquad (19)$$

The average drag forces over the stroke cycle were quite similar: $F_D(V) = 68.2N$, $Fd(F) = 66.9N$. Their curves during recovery were also close, but during the drive they were very different. The highest $Fd(F)$ peak 1 after the catch coincides with the highest seat velocity and could be explained by the friction force at the wheels, which looks like increased drag force. The smaller peak 4 could be related to the highest vertical seat force, which pushes the boat down and increases drag force. The nature of the negative peaks 2 and 3 is not clear yet. One of the possible reasons could be a small force at the rower's calves touching the hull, which is not measured, but affects the real balance of forces.

For better understanding, it is useful to compare propulsion mechanics in rowing and canoeing (Fig. 2.29).

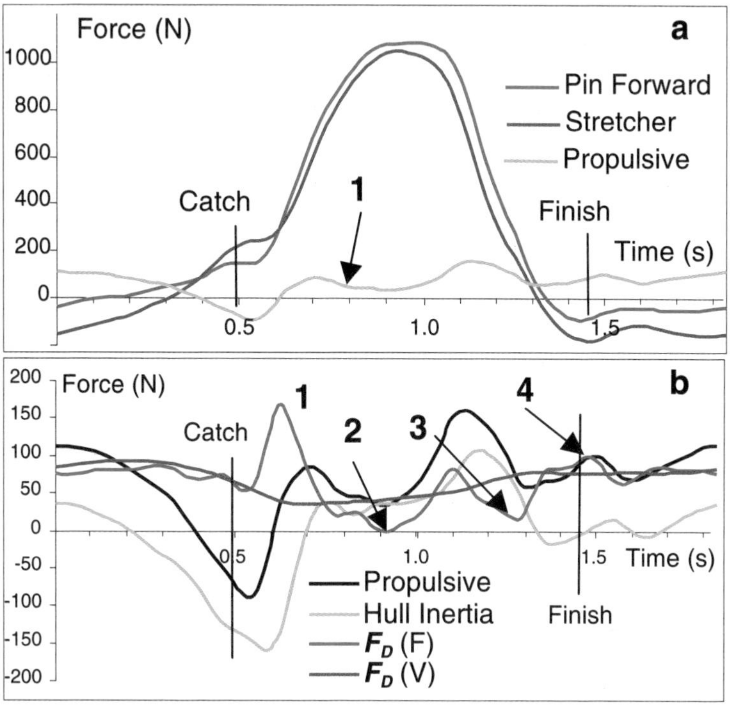

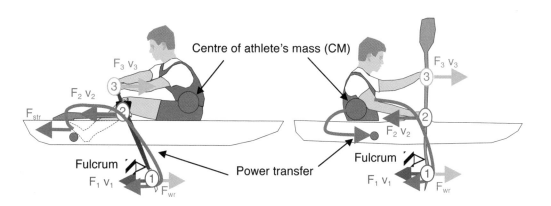

Fig. 2.28 Forces at the stretcher and pin in M1x measured with BioRowTel system at the stroke rate 32 min^{-1} (a), analysis of the propulsive force at the hull (b).

Fig. 2.29 Mechanics of propulsion in rowing (left) and canoeing (right).

In both cases, the oar could be considered as a lever of the second order with the fulcrum somewhere close to the blade (its exact position depends on the slippage of blade in the water). If we consider forces, then there are three points of force application at the oar:

1. Blade force F_1, which is directed backwards or creates water reaction force F_{wr} propelling the whole system forward;
2. Middle force F_2 (pulling arm in canoeing or gate in rowing) in the same direction as the blade force;

45

3. End force F_3 (pushing arm in canoeing or handle force in rowing) in the opposite direction to the above two forces.

Rowers do not apply the middle force F_2 directly (pin force F_{pf}), but transfer it through the stretcher, hull, rigger and pin. In fact, the stretcher and the blade forces work in the same direction, but the handle force is directed in the 'wrong' direction. The power applied by the rower to the stretcher is transferred to the blade and a part of it is spent on overcoming the boat inertia (see 2.6.2).

2.5.4 Seat Force and Dynamic Analysis in the Vertical Plane

Vertical seat force appeared to be quite a controversial issue among rowing coaches and scientists. Some of them believe that the rower's suspension decreases water displacement and drag and plays a positive role; others explain it only by a transfer of the rower's weight from the seat onto the stretcher, which increases oscillations of the boat and should be minimized.

There are six factors affecting the vertical force at the seat. The first three factors are internal ones and affect only the distribution of the rower's weight between the seat and the stretcher. They do not influence vertical movements of the boat and water displacement, but create pitch oscillations of the hull, which increases wave resistance.

1. *Static Weight Transfer* from the seat to the stretcher, when the line of gravity force Fg from rower's CM passes between them. At catch, about 30 per cent of the rower's weight is statically placed on the stretcher and only 70 per cent is left on the seat, which can be easily checked using scales on the seat.
2. *Legs Lift.* The hip joint H is located above the point of force application at the stretcher S, so the line of leg (knee) extension force is not horizontal. This creates a vertical component of the stretcher force F_{FV} and upward reaction force R_{FV}, which lifts the rower's weight from the seat.
3. *Hips Torque Lift.* When the glutes muscle is activated (even with legs straight), its torque τ_{hip} around the hip joint creates a vertical component of the stretcher force F_{FV} and reduces the seat force Fs.

   Factors 4 and 5 create vertical oscillations of the hull, but do not affect average water displacement of the system over the stroke cycle.
4. *Vertical accelerations* of the rower's mass. During the stroke cycle, the rower's body configuration changes, as well as the vertical

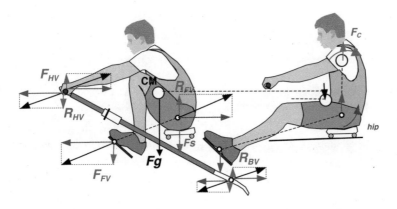

Fig. 2.30 Biomechanics of vertical seat force.

positions of body segments, which creates vertical accelerations. Also, the height of the total rower's CM slightly changes, because of the slides inclination, in which the fore end is 1–2cm higher than the aft end. During the drive, the vertical position of the legs' CM decreases, but the seat is going up on the slides, and vice versa during recovery. Therefore, the vertical inertia forces appear to be quite balanced during the stroke cycle and their resultant magnitude should not be high.

5. *Centripetal force F_c of the trunk swing*, which is directed upwards from the centre of rotation at the hips. It works in the same way during both the drive and recovery, but must be balanced by vertical acceleration of the trunk at catch and finish, so it affects only vertical oscillations of the hull, but not the average water displacement.

6. *Blade Pitch Lift* is the only external force, which affects the average water displacement of the system. The blade force is directed at some angle to the horizonal affected by the blade pitch, which creates a vertical blade force F_{BV} and its R_{BV} reaction force, which lifts the whole system upwards. As the rower pulls the handle slightly upwards, it creates a vertical component of the handle force F_{HV} and reaction force R_{HV}, which increases force at the seat Fs and stretcher F_{SV}, but is balanced at the gate, so these are internal forces.

A series of experiments was conducted to verify the balance of forces in the vertical plane (Fig. 2.31). On the water, the seat force, vertical and horizontal forces at the stretcher were measured (Fig. 2.31a,b) together with the standard measurements (oar angles, handle force, and so on.). A Concept2 erg was mounted on slides through three sensors measuring the whole weight force of the erg with a rower (d). The lift force was derived as the difference between static weight and measured vertical force during rowing. In a mobile rowing tank (c), two vertical force sensors were mounted between a trolley and a frame with the rower's workplace, so they measured the whole system weight, minus the buoyancy force.

On water, the vertical forces at the seat Fs and stretcher F_{SV} were summed and the sum was compared with the rower's weight Fg (Fig. 2.32d), so the suspension force $Fsus$ of the rower from the boat was found:

$$Fsus = Fg - (Fs + F_{SV}) \qquad (20)$$

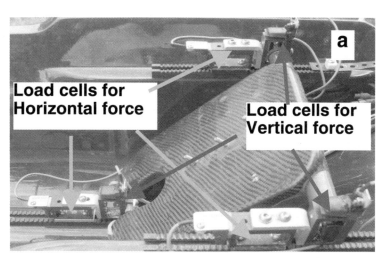

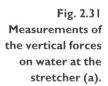

Fig. 2.31 Measurements of the vertical forces on water at the stretcher (a).

b

Load cells for
Vertical seat force

Fig. 2.31 (*cont.*)
Measurements of
the vertical forces on
water at the seat (b),
in a rowing tank (c)
and on an ergometer
(d).

c

Frame with rower's
workplace

Rails

Sensors

Trolley

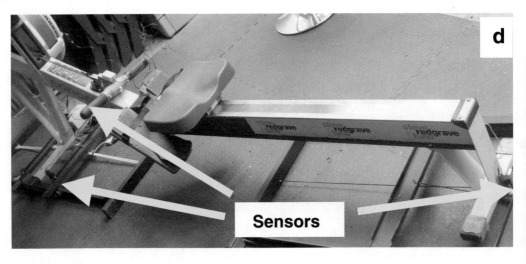

d

Sensors

The suspension was close to zero at the beginning of the recovery (1), when the rower's weight is placed on the seat and the vertical stretcher force is zero. Mid-recovery (2), the weight is transferring onto the stretcher and the suspension has a short peak up to 90N, which could be explained by negative vertical acceleration of the rower's CM descending on the slides. Before the catch (3), the suspension is close to zero again, but this balance of forces is very dynamic: the vertical stretcher force quickly increases, because the weight is transferring from the seat.

At the catch (4), 63 per cent of the rower's weight is located on the stretcher and only 37 per cent left on the seat, so the suspension is negative − 50N, which could be explained by upward acceleration of the arms and handles. Just after the catch (5), the suspension becomes positive, but the weight at this phase is transferring back onto the seat and the suspension has a little hump, which could be related to a rower's acceleration upwards on the slides and an increase of the vertical handle force, which pushes him down.

At the beginning of the drive, nearly the whole of the rower's weight is lifted from the seat (only 20N, ~ 2 per cent, left), but ~ 83 per cent of it is transferred onto the stretcher (6), so 15 per cent of the rower's weight is suspended and makes the rower-boat system lighter. Another 50N, ~ 4 per cent of the vertical component of the handle force, could be added (calculated at 4 degrees pitch), which pulls the rower down, so the real value of the suspension could be ~ 19–20 per cent of the rower's weight.

At the middle of the drive (7), almost all of the rower's weight remains lifted from the seat, and the stretcher force quickly decreases, so the suspension has a sharp peak of up to 230N, ~30 per cent of the rower's weight or 25 per cent of the system weight.

This could be an effect of the centripetal force F_c which is estimated as:

$$F_c = m_t \, v_t^2 \, / \, r \qquad (21)$$

where m_t is the mass-moment of the trunk with head, v_t is its instantaneous linear velocity and r is the radius of inertia from the centre at the hip joint. Approximating the data $m_t = 25$kg, $v_t = 1.25$ m/s, and $r = 0.4$ m (roughly 50 per cent of the height of the torso with head), $F_c \sim 100$N in the vertical direction, which is close to the magnitude of the bump during the drive.

At the finish (8), the F_{sv} is slightly negative, but Fs is high (125 per cent of Fg), so the Fsus is negative − 100N, which is related to vertical trunk acceleration.

On the erg, three samples were taken for various rowing techniques: a) legs only, b) trunk only and c) full length to make the effect of the centripetal force clearer. As was expected, the average lift force over the stroke cycle was zero in all samples. Lift force at 'trunk only' rowing was the most significant with a peak 350N, which happened at the maximal trunk velocity and confirmed the effect of the centripetal force.

Three similar samples were taken in the tank, and the results were similar to using the erg: the lift force had the highest magnitude 250N at 'trunk only' and its maximum coincides with the peak trunk velocity. The average lift force over the stroke cycle was above zero (30–40N), which equates to 9–13 per cent of the average handle force and can be explained by the vertical force at the blades at 6° pitch ($\sin(6°) = 10.5$ per cent).

Conclusions:

1. *Vertical blade force is the only external factor lifting the whole boat-rower system, but it is relatively small.*

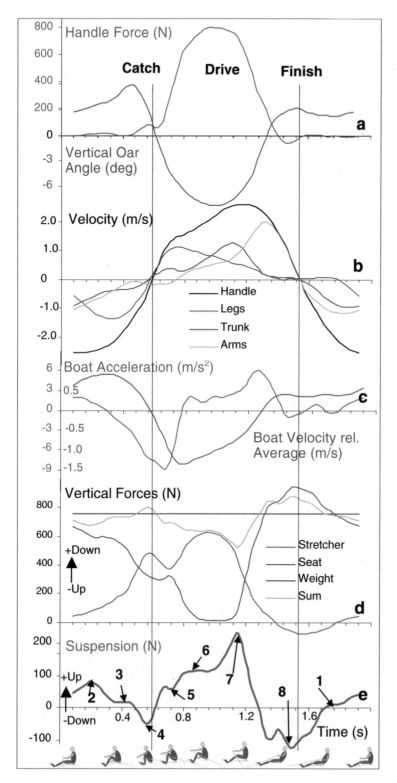

Fig. 2.32 Analysis of the vertical forces on water in M1x at 32str / min.

2. Centripetal force of the trunk rotation appears to be the most significant factor in vertical boat oscillations. Long and late trunk work at the drive and too fast return to recovery significantly increases the seat pressure (up to 150 per cent of rower's weight), the boat oscillations and wave resistance.

3. More horizontal stretcher force application reduces the boat pitch oscillations and, hence, the drag resistance. This could be achieved by a correct sequence of the segments (legs-trunk-arms) as well as with higher and steeper position of the stretcher (though the last could reduce the length of the drive).

4. At the catch, up to 60 per cent of the rower's weight is transferred onto the stretcher and only 40 per cent is left on the seat. Fast and early leg movement enables the achievement of a smoother weight suspension during the drive and a decrease in the pitch oscillations of the hull.

2.5.5 Dynamic Analysis in the Transverse (Horizontal) Plane

When a rower pulls the handle in a boat, the force is usually applied not exactly at the perpendicular direction to the oar shaft. This is one of the differences between on-water rowing and using an erg, where the force is always perpendicular to the axis of the handle. In rowing, at the catch, the angle between the oar and outside forearm is about 70 degrees, and for the inside arm it is 60 degrees (Fig. 2.33a), so the line of the resultant force should be directed at the angle 66–68 degrees (the outside arm pulls a higher force). In sculling, the angle between the oar and forearm is sharper; at the catch it is about 60 degrees (b).

The resultant handle force Fh can be broken down into two components: a normal (perpendicular) force $Fh.n$ and an axial force $Fh.a$. At the pulling angle $A = 60°$ the normal component $Fh.n$ should be equal to $\sin(A) = 86.7$ per cent of the total force Fh, and the axial component $Fh.a = \cos(A) = 50$ per cent of Fh.

When the axial component $Fh.a$ is transferred through the oar shaft to the gate, it creates the same axial gate force $Fg.a$ (ignoring a small axial force of hydrodynamic resistance from the blade). Ignoring inertia forces, to create the axial handle force the rower has to apply a force at the stretcher of the same magnitude, but in the opposite direction. As the stretcher is connected to the pin-gate through the rigger, these forces cancel themselves, that is they are internal forces and *the axial handle force does not contribute to the propulsion of the rower-boat system*. It does not create any power and energy losses, because there is no movement of the oar relative to the boat in this direction, but it works like a heavier gearing (see Chapter 6.2.1); the total force is higher (by 13.3 per cent at $A = 60°$), but could be applied at a proportionally slower speed.

The normal handle force $Fh.n$ is also transferred to the gate, where it is summed up with the normal blade force $Fb.n$, which is created by the reaction of the water. Therefore, the normal gate force $Fg.n$ is higher than the handle force:

$$Fg.n = Fh.n + Fb.n = Fh.n\ Lout.a\ /$$
$$(Lout.a + Lin.a) \qquad (22)$$

where $Lin.a$ is the actual inboard length and $Lout.a$ the actual outboard. The normal gate force can be resolved into forward $Fg.nf$ and side $Fg.ns$ components. On other side, the handle force creates an opposite reaction force Fs applied to the system through the rower's body. Its axial component $Fs.a$ is balanced at the gate, but the normal component $Fs.n$ can be resolved into forward $Fs.nf$ and side $Fs.ns$ forces. As the forward gate force

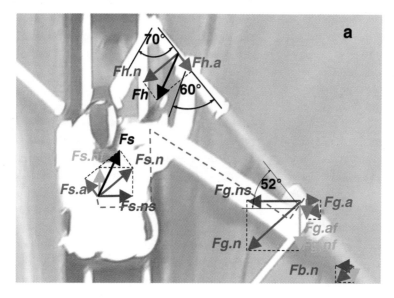

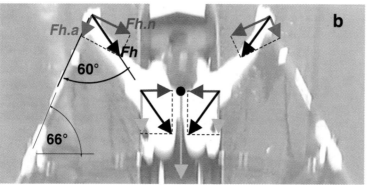

Fig. 2.33 Analysis of forces in the transverse plane in rowing (a) and sculling (b).

Fg.nf is greater than the handle reaction force Fs.nf, the difference between them makes a propulsive force, which is transferred from the blade in this way and accelerates the rower-boat system forward. Only the normal force Fh.n rotates the oar around the pin and creates velocity in this direction. The product of the force and velocity is the handle power, which is transferred through the leverage of the oar, applied by the blade to the water and spent on the propulsion of the rower-boat system and waste power of the blade 'slippage' in the water. *Only the normal handle force creates propulsion of the system. A rower should maximize the normal handle force applying minimal axial force to keep the oar in the gate.*

In sculling, the side components of the two handle forces cancel each other in the rower's body (Fig. 2.33b). Therefore, the resultant force has no side components and is applied in the direction parallel to the boat axis. This could be a reason why the forces in sculling are higher than in rowing and similar boat types are faster in sculling. Bringing the arms together at the beginning of the drive, that is, applying some inward torque at the shoulder using the pectoral muscles could be useful in sculling. This torque creates a tangential force at the handle Fh.t in the perpendicular direction to the arm.

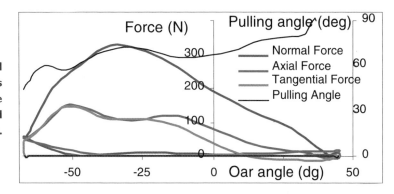

Fig. 2.34 Axial and normal forces measured at the gate and derived pulling angle.

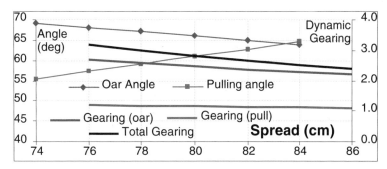

Fig. 2.35 Effect of the span / spread on dynamic gearing.

Fig. 2.34 shows the normal and axial forces in LM1x at 33 str/min measured with 2D instrumented gates[8], as well as the tangential force Fh.t required to make the pulling angle straight and completely eliminate the axial force Fh.a, which is very close to the measured axial force Fh.a.

How can the rigging be adjusted to make the pulling angle straighter and reduce the axial handle force? Longer arms and wider shoulders of a sculler make pulling angle *a* more acute and increase the oar angle *b*, which both make the 'dynamic gearing' heavier. Therefore, the arm span (sum of the shoulder width and arms' length) should be taken into account for rigging span adjustment. In rowing, arm span has no such effect.

With shorter inboard, the position of the handle moves outwards, which makes the pulling angle straighter and dynamic gearing lighter. However, it increases the oar angle and the dynamic gearing of the oar becomes 'heavier', which overcomes the effect of the pulling angle.

Wider span/spread (Fig. 2.35) makes the pulling angle straighter and also decreases the oar angle. This makes the effect of the spread very noticeable; *wider spread makes dynamic gearing significantly lighter in both rowing and sculling*. This could be a reason why, historically, the ratio of the outboard to the spread was used as a measure of gearing ratio. However, it works only at the catch and the beginning of the drive. At the middle of the drive and at the finish, the spread does not really affect the oar and pulling angles, and so the dynamic gearing. *Therefore, the only direct and valid measure of the oar gearing G is the ratio of actual outboard Lout to inboard Lin:*

$$G = lout / lin \qquad (23)$$

All other rigging variables, such as spread and position of the stretcher (affects oar angles) could be considered as indirect factors, which have gearing effects at various parts of the drive and so are called 'dynamic gearing'.

2.6 ENERGY VARIABLES

2.6.1 Definitions of Rowing Power

The power, P, produced by a rower is the most important variable, which is directly related to the boat speed v:

$$P = DF\,v^3 \qquad (24)$$

where DF is a drag factor. Power is a scalar quantity, which means it has only magnitude, but no direction. Power, P, is the rate of energy transfer per unit of time, T. In mechanics, energy usually means work, W, which is a product of the force F applied at the distance L, so:

$$P = W/t = F\,L/t = F\,v \qquad (24)$$

where v is the velocity of the object's movement. The unit of power is the watt (W) = j/s = kg m² / s³, where joule J = n m is the unit of energy or work. As stated by the law of energy conservation energy cannot be created or destroyed. It can only be transformed from one form into another; its amount is preserved. In rowing, a rower's metabolic energy is transformed into mechanical work (and the associated heat of the rower's body wasted), then into kinetic energy moving the boat-rower system, and finally, into heat dissipated by drag resistance. Contrarily, the amount of force can be easily changed with such a simple lever mechanism as an oar.

Coaches and rowers quite often mismatch the terms 'force' and 'power' and use 'power curve' to mean 'force curve'. Also, they say 'power strokes' meaning a drill with maximal applied force at low stroke rates, quite often with a water brake. In fact, the power during this drill is not very high because of the low stroke rate. The force and power curves in rowing look different (Fig. 2.36a,c): the force curve is more rectangular with an earlier peak

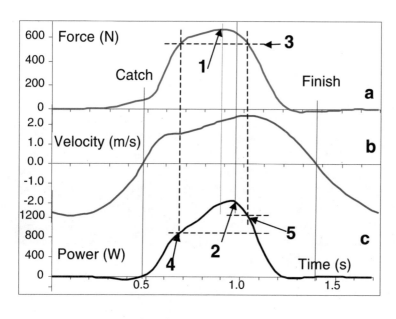

Fig. 2.36 The handle force, velocity and power in M1x at 36 str / min.

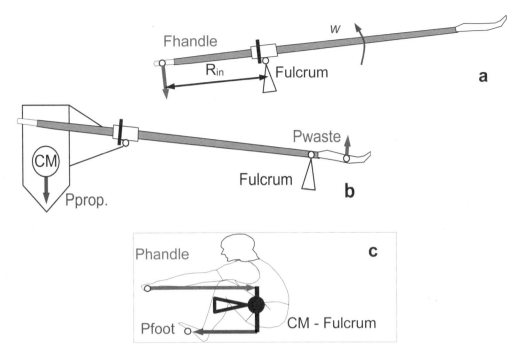

Fig. 2.37 Three definitions of rowing power.

(1), the power curve is more triangular with a later peak (2). As the handle velocity (Fig. 2.36b) more than doubles from catch to finish, with the same force applied (3) the power at the catch (4) is lower than power at the finish (5), so the same force at the catch 'costs' less energy than at the finish.

The method of power calculation in rowing is a quite complicated issue. It is very important though, because power production is the main characteristic of a rower's performance and the main component for calculation of rowing efficiency. Rowing power could be calculated in three ways:

1. *Traditional method* of power calculation (Fig. 2.37a) is based on the assumption that the rower applies power to the handle only. The oar works as a lever with a pivot point (fulcrum) at the pin. In this case, the power $Ppin$ equates to a product of the torque τ

and angular velocity ω, or to a product of the force applied to the handle Fh and the linear velocity of the handle Vh:

$$Ppin = \tau\,\omega = (\tau / r_{in})\,(\omega\,R_{in}) = fh\,Vh \quad (25)$$

where R_{in} is the inboard length. To be more accurate, R_{in} is the distance from the pin (+ 2cm = half of the gate width) to the middle of the handle (− 6cm for sculling, − 15cm for sweep).

2. *Propulsive-waste power (Ppw)*. In fact, the pin moves with the boat with quite irregular acceleration. Therefore, the boat is not an inertial reference frame in Newtonian mechanics. If we set the reference frame based on Earth (or water), we will find the oar fulcrum somewhere close to the blade (Fig. 2.37b). There are two components of the power here: propulsive power $Pprop$ on the inboard side from the fulcrum and

waste power *Pwaste* on the blade side. Propulsive power equates to the scalar product of the force vector acting on the rower-boat system *Fprop* and velocity of the system centre of mass *VCM*:

$$Pprop = fprop\ VCM \qquad (26)$$

This method is not very practical, because velocity of the system centre of mass *VCM* cannot be determined accurately and easily. The position of the centre of pressure on the blade is affected by the blade hydrodynamics, boat speed and oar angle and is also difficult to determine.

3. *Rower's power.* In fact, the rower is the only source of mechanical energy in rowing. The rower applies force and power only at two points (Fig. 2.37c): at the handle and at the foot-stretcher. In this case, it could be speculated that the fulcrum is the rower's centre of mass (CM). The rower's power *Prower* can be calculated as a sum of the handle and foot-stretcher powers and each of them equates to a scalar product of correspondent force and velocity vectors:

$$Prower = Phandle + Pfoot = Fhandle$$
$$Vhandle + Ffoot\ Vfoot \qquad (27)$$

A good correspondence between the traditional and the propulsive-waste power curves was found (Fig. 2.38). The average rowing powers were $P_{pin} = 462.9W$, $P_{pw} = 465.5W$ and $P_{rower} = 494.4W$. The reason for the more significant difference between the first two and the rower's power was the inertial component, which is required to move the boat relative to the rower. In this case, the inertial losses were 6.4 per cent of the total rower's power. The blade propulsive efficiency equates to a ratio of the propulsive to the total power, which was 80.4 per cent in this case.

2.6.2 Power Transmission

Power transmission can be understood better with the examples of two exercises:

- In squats, the feet are unmovable, so the velocity and power transfer through them are zero, because power is the product of force and velocity. The energy is transferred to the moving athlete's body and to the weight on his shoulders.
- In the leg press, the body is fixed, so its kinetic energy cannot be increased. Power is transferred through the feet and the stretcher to the weight.

In rowing on water or on a mobile ergo, both the rower's upper body and feet are mobile, and power is transferred through both the stretcher/boat and rower/handle. In the case shown in Fig. 2.38, the ratio of the handle/

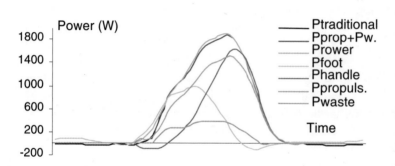

Fig. 2.38 Rowing power calculated using three methods, and their components: propulsive, waste, handle and foot-stretcher powers; (MIx, rate 32str / min).

Power (W)

1800
1400
1000
600
200
-200

——— Ptraditional
——— Pprop+Pw.
——— Prower
.... Pfoot
——— Phandle
——— Ppropuls.
——— Pwaste

Time

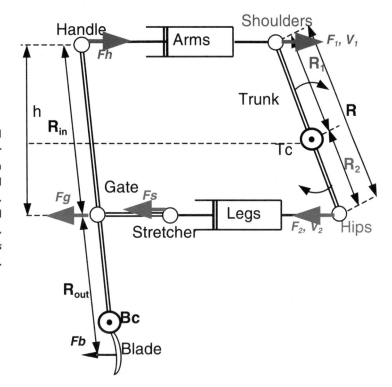

Fig. 2.39 Simplified model of power transmission (adopted from Dal Monte A., Komor A. 1989. 'Rowing and sculling mechanics'. *Biomechanics of Sport***).**

stretcher powers was found to be 60/40 per cent. This ratio depends on the shape of the force curve: the stretcher share increases at the 'front-loaded' force curve (see 2.5.2).

Contrarily, in rowing on a stationary ergo or in a tank the stretcher is fixed and power can be transferred only through the rower's body to the handle.

How does a rower manage to vary the ratio of forces applied to the handle and stretcher? This question has implications for deriving the body segments power and rowing styles.

Rower's hips are not fixed and move together with the boat and seat. Therefore the power generated by the trunk can be transferred through both ends (shoulders and hips) and, further, through the handle or stretcher (Fig. 2.39). The fulcrum of the trunk rotation could be a virtual point Tc. Similarly, the fulcrum of the oar rotation is a virtual point Bc on the shaft, the position of which

depends on the ratio of the boat velocity to the velocity of the blade slippage in the water. The position of the fulcrum of the trunk Tc is defined by a ratio of the levers R_1 and R_2, which are related to the ratio of the forces at the handle Fh and the stretcher Fs (ignoring inertia of arms and legs):

$$R_1 / R_2 = F_2 / F_1 = Fs / Fh = Fg / Fh = k \quad (28)$$

For a boat, the coefficient k is determined by the ratio of the actual oar length Loar = Rin + Rout to the actual outboard Rout:

$$k = (Rin + Rout) / Rout \sim 1.44 \quad (29)$$

If the ratio R1/R2 is expressed in percentages, then in the boat it approximates to 59/41. For an ergo, if again we disregard inertial forces, R1/R2 = 50/50. The stretcher/handle height

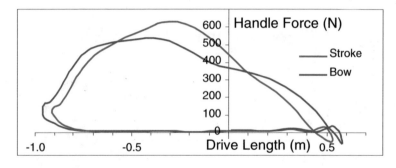

Fig. 2.40 Example of two force curves in a pair with equal work per stroke.

h is divided in the same proportion, so the difference 9 per cent at h = 22 cm gives the position of the fulcrum of the trunk as 2 cm higher for an ergo than for a boat.

The trunk power Pt could be derived from the measured handle and stretcher forces (*Fh, Fs*) and the linear velocity *Vt* between hips and shoulders. The force produced by the trunk was estimated as an average of the handle (*Fh*) and stretcher (*Fs*) forces, weighted in the proportions above, so:

$$Pt \sim Vt\,(0.59\,Fh + 0.41\,Fs) \qquad (30)$$

The practical implication of this analysis is the following: *in a boat, the trunk should work not only 'through the handle', but also 'through the stretcher'.* Power transferred through the stretcher can be generated not only by the legs, but also by the trunk.

2.6.3 Work per Stroke

Work per stroke (*WpS*) is an important biomechanical variable, which is not very often used yet by coaches and rowers. *WpS* can be defined as an integral (sum) of the products of the immediate force *F* and linear displacement *DL*, or the torque *M* and angular displacement $\Delta\phi$ over the drive time:

$$WpS\ 5D \int F\,\Delta L = \int M\,\Delta\phi \qquad (31)$$

The main determinant of the performance is rowing power *P*, which is *WpS* per unit of time *T* (s), or the product of *WpS* and stroke rate *R* (1/min):

$$P = WpS\,/\,t = WpS\ R/60 \qquad (32)$$

Therefore, the *WpS* combines two of the three main components of power: force and length, but excludes the third one – stroke rate. *As WpS does not depend on the stroke rate, it is a very useful indicator of the effectiveness of a rowing stroke at various training and racing intensities: from long steady-state rowing to short sprints.*

If the handle force is plotted relative to the drive length or oar angle, the *WpS* is equal to the area under the force curve. In Fig. 2.40, *WpS* of both the stroke and bow rowers is the same, but the force and length are quite different: the stroke rower has a higher peak force, but shorter length, than the bow rower.

Shortening the stroke length by, say, 1 per cent requires proportionally 1 per cent higher average force to maintain the constant *WpS*. At values of stroke length 1.6m and an average force of 350N (average target values in 14 Olympic categories), 1.6cm shorter length (about 1.1° in sculling and 0.9° in rowing) requires a 3.5N higher average force and 6.5N higher maximal force (at a constant shape of the force curve). This number varies depending on the rower's category (from

Table 2.7 Target *WpS* for Olympic boat types required to achieve prognostic boat speed. (The right-hand columns show 500m splits on a Concept2 erg, which corresponds to the target *WpS* at various rates.)

Boat type	Target time	Target rate	WpS (J)	500M erg splits					
				20	24	28	32	36	40
M1x	06:32.5	37	892	1:46	1:39	1:34	1:30	1:27	1:24
M2x	06:02.1	39	846	1:47	1:41	1:36	1:32	1:28	1:25
M4x	05:33.2	40	825	1:48	1:42	1:37	1:33	1:29	1:26
M2 −	06:08.0	38	789	1:50	1:43	1:38	1:34	1:30	1:27
LM2x	06:07.2	36	783	1:50	1:44	1:39	1:34	1:31	1:28
M4 −	05:37.0	40	750	1:52	1:45	1:40	1:36	1:32	1:29
M8 +	05:18.6	41	732	1:53	1:46	1:41	1:36	1:33	1:30
LM4 −	05:42.0	40	705	1:54	1:47	1:42	1:38	1:34	1:31
W1x	07:11.5	35	686	1:55	1:48	1:43	1:39	1:35	1:31
W2 −	06:52.9	36	667	1:56	1:49	1:44	1:39	1:36	1:32
W2x	06:39.5	37	649	1:57	1:50	1:45	1:40	1:37	1:33
W4x	06:08.5	38	632	1:58	1:51	1:46	1:41	1:37	1:34
W8 +	05:53.1	39	615	1:59	1:52	1:47	1:42	1:38	1:35
LW2x	06:47.0	36	550	2:04	1:57	1:51	1:46	1:42	1:38

5.5N in lightweight women to 8.5N in open men) and the shape of the force curve; it could be up to 10N at a 'slim' shape. Also, at a shorter length, it is quite likely that the force curve becomes 'slimmer' (correlation factor $r = 0.42$), because shorter catch angles make the dynamic gearing lighter, which requires faster movement at the catch, so it is more difficult to increase the force quickly. With very rough approximation: *1° shorter length would require up to 1 kg (10N) higher maximal force to keep the work per stroke constant, and vice versa.* There are two other factors to consider for selection of an optimal length/force ratio:

1. Rowing rhythm. Shorter length makes the drive time shorter and rowing rhythm lower, and vice versa, which gives more time on recovery, but shortens the propulsive phase. So the length is important, but it should not be too long, otherwise a rower has to rush on recovery.
2. Endurance factor. At long distances, it is more difficult to maintain high force than long length, while at sprints rowers usually shorten the length and apply higher forces.

To compare *WpS* at various stroke rates, our method could be used[35], which requires only speed and stroke rate inputs (Table 2.7).

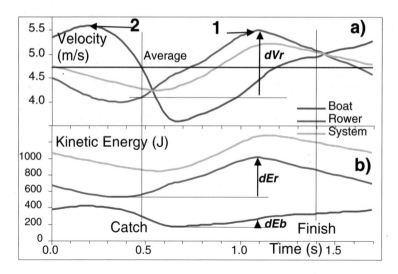

Fig. 2.41 Velocities of the boat, rower and the system's CM (a), kinetic energies of these three masses (b).

For different target speeds, corresponding percentages of the splits above could be used, but WpS values should be changed as a cube of the proportion to the target speed: for example a 10 per cent lower speed corresponds to about 27 per cent lower WpS ($0.9^3 = 0.73$). This table may help to find an optimal combination of the stroke length and force at various durations and intensities.

2.6.4 Impulse and Kinetic Energy

If force F acts on free mass m during time T, it creates an impulse or amount of movement J:

$$J = FT = m v \tag{33}$$

where v is final velocity of the object. Also, a force F applied at velocity v produces power P and increases kinetic energy E_k of the object:

$$E_k = 0.5\ m\ v^2 = W = pT \approx F L$$
$$\text{(simplified)} \tag{34}$$

In rowing, there is interference of two objects of different mass, where a boat is 5–8 times lighter than a rower. In fact, this difference is smaller because some parts of a rower's body (feet, partly shins and thighs) are connected to the boat and move with it. We estimate the active moving mass of the rower at about 88 per cent of the total mass, so the remaining 12 per cent is added to the active boat mass, which gives us the range of ratios 1:3–1:4.

During the drive, the velocity of the rower's CM (Fig. 2.41, point 1) increases much more than the boat velocity, which grows mainly during recovery and has its peak before the catch (2). As the rower is also heavier, his mass accumulates seven times more kinetic energy ($dEr = 478$J) than the boat mass ($dEb = 69$J). Then, at the end of the drive and during recovery, the impulse and kinetic energy is transferred from the rower's mass to the boat and spent in overcoming the drag resistance. Therefore, *the amount of impulse and kinetic energy accumulated by the rower's mass is the main determinant of the average boat speed and result in rowing.* In fact, there is nothing new in this conclusion. A great rowing coach and founder of the modern rowing style Steve Fairbairn said a long time ago[17]: 'Find out how to use your weight and you will have solved the problem of how to move the boat.'

Only the stretcher force can push the rower forward, while the handle force pulls him backwards. So, *the stretcher force must be emphasized during the drive, while the handle force only provides support through the oar – gate – rigger – stretcher*. Of course, the blade must be locked in the water to provide the support.

2.65 Power Transfer Between Rowers Through the Boat

During many years of testing, it was noticed that rowers on stern seats usually produced more force and power than rowers in bow seats, especially in pairs, fours and eights. Coaches usually put the strongest rowers at stroke, but this doesn't explain all of the observed differences in power of up to 30 per cent. The following experimental data sheds light on this phenomenon.

A top international-level four conducted the same $6 \times 5min$ step-test both on Concept2 stationary erg and on-water with power (P) and heart rate (HR) measurements. Because HR was slightly different during these two tests, second-order polynomial trends ($R^2 > 0.99$) were derived using P and HR data on erg for each rower:

$$P = a\,HR^2 + b\,HR + c \qquad (35)$$

Values of power were calculated for each rower using individual coefficients of the above function, where the argument was HR on water in each sample. These values were compared with on-water power and ratios were derived. Simply, ratios of power on-erg/on-water at the same heart rate were derived for each rower. This ratio was 85.8 per cent for the stroke, 79.3 per cent for the 3 seat, 82.2 per cent for the 2 seat and 77.7 per cent for bow, so the rowers in the middle of the boat apply 3–6 per cent less power than on

erg compared to the stroke rower, and for the bow this difference was 8 per cent.

To find the reasons for this phenomenon, measured patterns of handle force (Fig. 2.42a), seat and boat velocities (b) were analysed. Seat velocities for each rower (measured relative to the boat) were added to the boat velocity, so seat velocities relative to the Earth coordinate system were derived (c) and differentiated into accelerations (d). We assumed that these seat variables were quite close to velocities and accelerations of centre of mass (CM) of each rower.

At the catch, the stroke rower accelerates his seat/CM earlier (1) and achieves faster velocity (2) than his teammates. As the blades are at the entry stage and forces are low (3), it is quite easy for the stroke to do so. When blades go deeper into the water and forces increase to their maxima (4), it is the turn of other rowers to accelerate their masses (5). Therefore, they have to push the stretcher harder than the stroke, who is already moving fast. This extra force is transferred through the stretcher-hull-rigger-pin and applied to the gate of the stroke rower, so his measured handle/blade force becomes higher. In other words, *one rower can transfer power through the stretcher, boat and rigger to the gate and oar of another rower*.

Notice that only the acceleration of the CM plays a role in this effect, not the position of the rower in the boat. Bow rowers usually accelerate their CM later, probably because they focus on synchronization of handle movement and pay less attention to work through the stretcher. Also, higher efficiency of the stroke rower could be explained by better utilization of large leg muscles and faster single-motion movement, which is called 'rowing using the mass'.

Anecdotal evidence was obtained that a similar phenomenon also occurs on ergs. When a number of them are connected

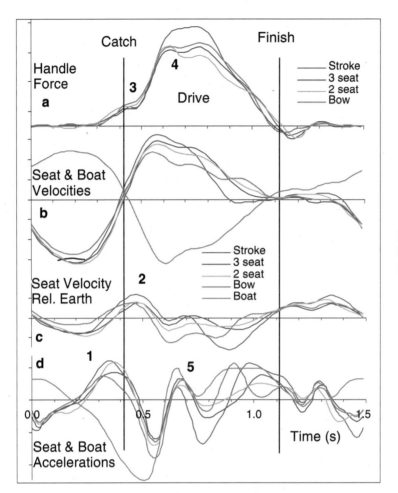

Fig. 2.42
Biomechanical data of
LM4 – at 40 str / min.

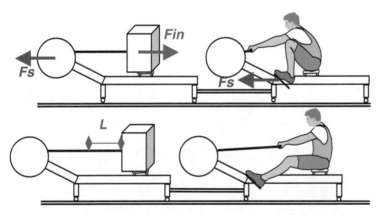

Fig. 2.43 Explanation
of the power transfer
between rowers.

on slides, the 'stern' rower usually shows a higher score than normal. This phenomenon can be illustrated with a simple model: two ergs on slides are connected together (Fig. 2.43). A rower sits on one of them, but the seat of another erg is occupied by a box of similar mass to the rower's mass. The box is connected to the handle of the erg. When the rower starts the drive and pushes the stretcher, this force Fs moves both ergs backwards. It creates a reaction inertia force at the box, which pulls the handle, increases the distance L between the box and erg and rotates

the flywheel. So, the box produces some erg 'score', which is explained by force/power transfer from the rower through the ergs.

Is this effect negative and should it always be avoided? Not necessarily. *The power transferred from the bow rower to the blade of the stern rower could help to keep the boat straight in pairs and fours* (see Chapter 4.2.4). The only problem for the bow rower is lower measured force and power. Therefore, method 3 with power detection at the stretcher (2.6.1) should be used for accurate testing of the rower.

CHAPTER 3

ANALYSIS

3.1 ROWING EFFICIENCY

The standard definition of the efficiency E of any mechanism is the ratio of power output $Pout$ to power input Pin:

$$E = pPout / Pin \qquad (36)$$

In rowing, three main efficiency components can be identified, which are linked by a chain of energy transfer (Fig. 3.1). The rower transforms a metabolic energy into mechanical power and transfers it to the blade propulsion; the blade transfers propulsive power into kinetic energy of the rower-boat system; the kinetic energy is spent on overcoming drag resistance, where some extra losses occur as well due to variation of the boat velocity. Therefore, the three components could be called 1) rower's efficiency $Erow$, 2) blade efficiency Ebl and 3) boat efficiency $Eboat$.

The rower's efficiency $Erow$ can be measured as the ratio of the total mechanical power $Ptot$ applied at the handle (and the stretcher) to the consumed metabolic power $Pmet$, which can be evaluated using physiological gas-analysis methods.

$$Erow = Ptot / Pmet \qquad (37)$$

The 'delta' rower efficiency was determined to be 22.8 ± 2.2 per cent (mean $\pm$ SD)[19].

The blade propulsive efficiency Ebl is the

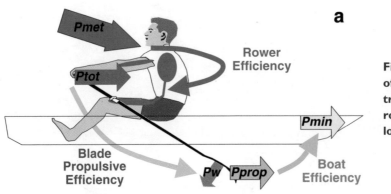

a

Pmet

Ptot

Rower
Efficiency

Pmin

Blade
Propulsive
Efficiency

Pw Pprop

Boat
Efficiency

Fig. 3.1 Schematics of energy transformation in rowing (a) and energy losses (b).

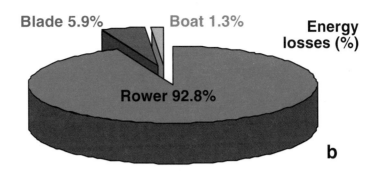

Energy losses (%)

b

Fig. 3.1 (*Cont.*) Schematics of energy transformation in energy losses (b).

ratio of the propulsive power at the blade *Pprop* to the total mechanical power *Ptot*, where *Pprop* can be calculated as the difference between *Ptot* and waste power *Pw*, which is spent on moving the water:

$$Ebl = Pprop \ / \ Ptot = (Ptot - Pw) \ / \ Ptot \qquad (38)$$

Ebl was determined to be in the range from 78.5 ±3.1 per cent in a single to 85.3 ± 3.5 per cent in an eight[28], so it depends on the boat speed.

Boat efficiency *Eboat* can be defined as:

$$Eboat = Pmin \ / \ Pprop \qquad (39)$$

where *Pmin* is the minimal power required for propelling the boat and rower with a constant speed equal to the average boat velocity. *Eboat* can be calculated using the variation of the boat velocity and was found on average to be 93.8 ± 0.8 per cent[28]. The standard deviation in *Eboat* is quite small and mainly affected by the stroke rate.

The above values of the efficiency components allow the modelling of the shares of energy losses caused by each of them. For example, in a single sculler at 5 m/s (6:40 for 2km) *Ptot* could be estimated at 544W. In this case *Pmet* must be 2386W, which requires 7.1 l/min oxygen (consumption plus debt). *Pprop* should be 427W and *Pmin* 400W. The absolute energy losses can be calculated by

subtracting each value from the previous one in the chain. The shares of energy losses can be determined by dividing each absolute value by their sum.

Most of the energy losses, 92.8 per cent, are related to the rower's efficiency (Fig. 3.1b). Blade slippage contributes 5.9 per cent and the boat speed variation only 1.3 per cent. These numbers suggest that the greatest scope for performance gain can be found in improvement of the rower's efficiency.

The standard deviation of each efficiency component could be used as a measure of variability between rowers, boats and various conditions, that is as a measure for changing the component. To model possible gain of boat speed, the efficiency value could be increased by its SD. In this case, 12.0s could be gained from improvement of *Erow* by 2.2 per cent, 4.9s from an *Ebl* increase of 3.1 per cent and only 1.1s from an *Eboat* increase of 0.8 per cent. Moreover, variation in *Ebl* and *Eboat* depends mainly on external factors (wind resistance and boat type), which are beyond the rower's control. Therefore, the main effort should be focused on improvement of the rower's efficiency.

3.1.1 Blade Efficiency

Between rowers and coaches, there is a quite widely spread idea that long catch angles

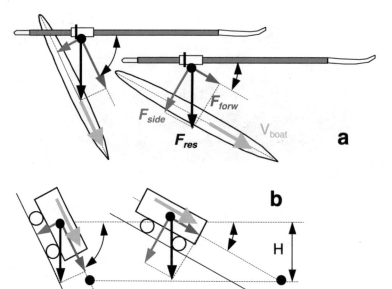

Fig. 3.2 Comparison of the pin forces at different oar angles (a) with similar forces acting on a cart on slopes with different inclination (b).

make the blade work inefficient, because 'the oar pushes the pin inwards, which is a waste of power, and so on…'. It was proved incorrect but is still very persistent so the following comparison of the blade work with a cart running down a slope may help to illustrate it better (Fig. 3.2).

In both cases, the resultant force F_{res} acts at an angle to the velocity vector and can be resolved into perpendicular F_{side} and parallel F_{forw} components. Power is the scalar product of the force and velocity vectors and equates to zero when these two vectors are perpendicular to one another. So, *sideward force does not produce any power and cannot cause energy waste itself*. In the case of the cart in conditions where there is no friction, at any slope angle the cart achieves the same velocity in the end, because the same amount of work is produced, which depends only on the height H of the centre of mass displacement. The differences are in acceleration and time. With a more orthogonal oar angle and steeper slope, F_{forw} is higher, which produces higher acceleration. With a sharper oar angle and flatter

slope, the acceleration is lower and it takes longer to achieve the final speed. Therefore, a longer catch angle makes the dynamic gearing heavier, but does not create energy waste and does not decrease the blade efficiency itself.

The correct definition of the blade efficiency is the following. During rowing, the blade slips through the water, which means it has some slippage velocity relative to the water *Vsl* and applies some force to it *Fbl* (Fig. 3.3). The scalar product of the force and velocity is waste power *Pw*, which is spent on moving the water at the blade:

$$Pw = Fbl * Vsl \cos\varphi \qquad (40)$$

where φ is the angle between the force, *Fbl*, and velocity, *Vsl*, vectors. The waste power, *Pw*, is subtracted from the total power *Ptot* produced by a rower. The remaining part is propulsive power *Pprop*, which moves the rower-boat system forward. The definition of the propulsive efficiency is the ratio of the propulsive power to the total power, so the blade efficiency *Ebl* can be defined as:

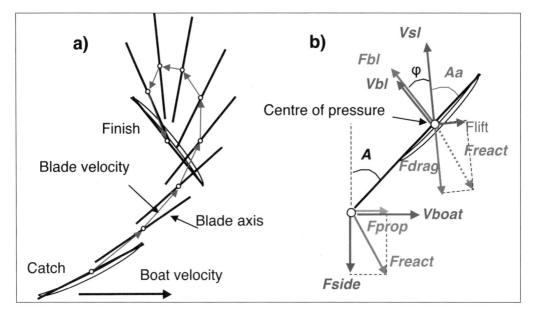

Fig. 3.3 Movement of the blade through the water (a), definition of forces and velocities used in calculations of the blade propulsive efficiency (b).

$$Ebl = Pprop / Ptot = (Ptot - Pw) / Ptot \quad (41)$$

Assuming the resulting force is applied at the centre of the blade and its vector has orthogonal direction relative to the oar axis, the blade efficiency Ebl can be determined using measurements of the boat velocity $Vboat$, the oar angle A and the handle force Fh. The force applied at the centre of the blade Fbl can be calculated using the measured handle force Fh and actual oar gearing (Equation 22). The velocity of the blade relative to the water Vsl can be determined using the oar angular velocity derived from the oar angle A, the acting outboard length (from the pin to the centre of the blade) and $Vboat$.

If the blade moves through the water at the angle of attack Aa different from 90 degrees it creates a lift force $Flift$ and the blade works as a hydrofoil. $Flift$ has orthogonal direction to Vsl and therefore it does not consume any power and has 100 per

cent efficiency. All energy losses depend on the drag force $Fdrag$, which has the opposite direction to Vsl. $Flift$ and $Fdrag$ are components of a total blade reaction force $FblR$, which has the same magnitude and opposite direction to Fbl. $FblR$ is transferred through the oar shaft to the boat and can be resolved into $Fprop$ mentioned above and $Fside$, which does not create any energy losses because it is perpendicular to the boat velocity. Fig. 3.4 shows the main variables above plotted relative to the oar angle.

The lift and drag factors were taken from Caplan and Gardner (2006)[13] for a flat plate, so they can be used quite approximately for a real blade. In this example $Flift$ contributes 56 per cent to the average blade force and $Fdrag$ contributes to the remaining 44 per cent. The total distance of the slippage of the blade centre was 1.7m and the minimal slippage velocity was 1.25m/s at the perpendicular position of the blade. Overall the blade

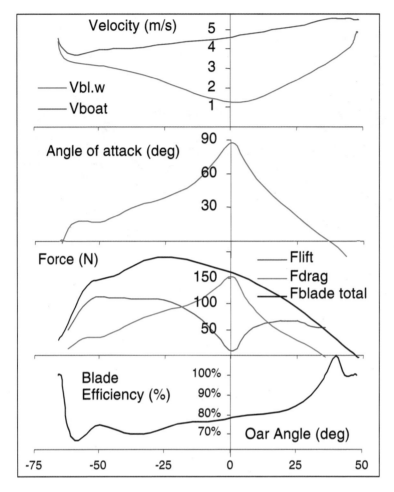

Fig. 3.4 Blade work variables in M1x at 36 str / min.

efficiency was found at 76.5 per cent; similar findings were made by Affeld et al.[3].

The angle φ between vectors of the blade velocity Vsl and force Fbl is the reversed angle of attack α (assuming the blade force is perpendicular to its surface), so:

$$cos\ \varphi = cos(90 - \alpha) = sin\ \alpha \qquad (42)$$

Combining Equation 41 with Equation 42 and moving Fbl out of the brackets, the blade efficiency Ebl can be expressed as:

$$Ebl = (Vbl - Vsl\ sin\alpha)/Vbl =$$
$$1 - (Vsl\ sin\ \alpha/Vbl) \qquad (43)$$

A general equation of the drag force created by any object moving in water is:

$$Fbl = k\ \rho\ A\ Vsl^2 \qquad (44)$$

where ρ is water density, A is the area of the blade and k is the combined drag factor of the blade, which depends on blade shape and angle of attack. (The last defines a ratio of the lift and drag factors). So, the blade slippage velocity Vsl can be defined as:

$$Vsl = (Fbl\ /\ (k\ \rho\ A))^{0.5} \qquad (45)$$

Substituting *Vsl* into Equation 43, the blade efficiency *Ebl* can be expressed as:

$$Ebl = 1 - ((Fbl / (k \, \rho \, A))^{0.5} \sin \alpha) / Vbl$$
$$= 1 - (\sin \alpha / (k \, \rho \, A)^{0.5})$$
$$(Fb \, l^{0.5} / Vbl) \qquad (46)$$

This equation can be useful for defining the following factors affecting the blade propulsive efficiency.

1. The blade efficiency is higher, when the angle of attack is sharper ($\sin \alpha$ is lower).
2. The blade efficiency is higher, when any of the multipliers $k \, \rho \, A$ increase: the blade shape is more efficient ($k\uparrow$), and/or the water is more dense ($\rho\uparrow$), and/or the blade area is bigger ($A\uparrow$).
3. The blade efficiency is higher, when the blade force decreases, but blade velocity increases (ratio *Fbl* / *Vbl* becomes lower). This usually happens at the end of the drive, which explains the rise of the efficiency curve. The efficiency is 100 per cent, when blade force is zero, that is, the rower does not pull at all, but the blade still moves in the water. When the blade force is negative (*Fbl* < 0), the blade efficiency cannot be defined using Equation 46. However, from Equation 41, *Ebl* can be higher than 100 per cent, if *Pw* is negative. This means that the energy is not spent on moving the water at the blade, but it is taken from it and added to the total power of a rower, that is when the rower takes the run off.

The first two points above could be used to decrease the amount of energy wasted due to slippage of the blade, though the water density is given by the conditions and the chances to improve the angle of attack, blade shape and area are quite limited. The third point is quite controversial:

- The ratio of the blade force and velocity can be changed with gearing: say, at two times longer outboard and the same inboard, the blade force is decreased twice, but its velocity is increased by the same factor. However, the force in Equation 46 is in square root, so the ratio $Fbl^{0.5} / Vbl$ decreases, which explains why *the blade efficiency is higher with heavier gearing*.
- For the same blade slippage velocity *Vsl* relative to the water, its velocity *Vbl* (relative to the boat) is proportional to the boat velocity *Vboat*. This explains why *the blade efficiency appears to be higher in faster / bigger boats*[28], though the real slippage of the blade could be the same, so the blade doesn't work better in the water.
- Increasing the blade efficiency by means of decreasing the blade force does not make sense, because it decreases the total and propulsive power, the main objective in rowing. *In a crew, the strongest rower usually has the lowest blade efficiency and vice versa*: a correlation between average force and blade efficiency within a crew is negative (r = − 0.48), which means the higher force creates more slippage of the blade of the strongest rower, but the boat velocity is the same for all crew members.

Conclusion: In its current definition, the blade propulsive efficiency can be used for limited evaluation of the equipment qualities and rower's oar handling skills, but only at a constant blade force and velocity.

To find a more representative measure for the evaluation of the blade work's effectiveness, it could be reasonable to model the oar blade like a jet engine, because it is not possible to create propulsion on the water without moving it backwards. In aviation and rocketry, a *specific impulse Isp* is the main factor to describe the efficiency of jet engines. It represents the thrust force *Fthrust* with respect to the mass of propellant *m* used per time unit *t*:

$$Isp = Fthrust / (g\, m / t) \qquad (47)$$

where *g* is the acceleration due to gravity. *Isp* depends on velocities of exhaust gases *Vg* and of the jet vehicle, *V*:

$$Isp = (Vg - V)\, m / t \qquad (48)$$

Efficiency, E, of the jet vehicle is also related to *Vg*:

$$E = 2 / (1 + Vg / V) \qquad (49)$$

Efficiency and specific impulse are inversely related. At the start of the runway, the efficiency of a jet plane is zero, because its velocity is zero, but the thrust and specific impulse are maximal. As the plane accelerates, its efficiency increases, and becomes 100 per cent, if the plane speed is equal to the speed of exhaust gases (Equation 49), but the thrust and specific impulse become zero then (Equation 48). Similarly in rowing, at the catch the velocity of the rower-boat system is at its lowest; then, it increases during the drive until the finish. Therefore, the propulsive power increases during the drive, as it is a product of propulsive force and velocity of the centre of mass system. Hence, the blade propulsive efficiency increases and becomes higher than 100 per cent when the system velocity is higher than blade velocity, but it doesn't mean the blade works better at the finish.

In rowing, the fuel flow can be substituted with the mechanical power produced by a rower, *Prow*, and the specific impulse *Isp* of the blade can be defined as:

$$Isp = Fthrust / Prow = Fthrust / Fh\, Vh. \qquad (50)$$

where *Fh* and *Vh* are the handle force and velocity. The blade thrust *Fthrust* can be expressed as:

$$Fthrust = Fh\, (Lin / Lout)\cos(\alpha) \qquad (51)$$

where *Lin* and *Lout* are the actual inboard and outboard lengths (from pin to centre of the blade) and α is the oar angle. Combining equations 50 and 51, the blade specific impulse could be derived as:

$$Isp = (Lin / Lout)\cos(\alpha) / Vh \qquad (52)$$

The blade specific impulse *Isp* appeared to be quite even during the drive (Fig. 3.5). Its higher

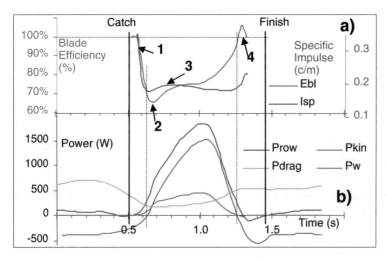

Fig. 3.5 Blade efficiency and effectiveness (*Isp*) in LM1x at 32 str / min (a), and corresponding rowing power *Prow*, gain of kinetic energy of the system *Pkin*, drag power *Pdrag* and waste power *Pw* of the blade slippage in the water (b).

values were found at the beginning and the end of the drive and the lowest one at the perpendicular position of the oar. The average *Isp* of underwater blade work was 0.19 s / m in this example. It decreases at higher stroke rates and boat speeds from 0.27 s / m at a rate of 20 str / min down to 0.17 s / m at 41 str / min.

At the catch (Fig. 3.5a, point 1), both blade efficiency and effectiveness are high because the power production *Prow* is less than drag power *Pdrag*, and *Pkin* is negative, so kinetic energy of the system is spent on overcoming the drag and, partly, on moving the blade forward through the water together with the boat. Then, the power production starts increasing, but the system CM velocity is still close to its minimum, so the blade efficiency has its lowest value (2). During the drive, it increases together with the system velocity and *Pkin*. Contrarily, the specific impulse is quite constant during the drive and has only a small maximum (3) at the oar angle of 40–45 degrees at catch, *which could be considered as the most effective position for the force application.*

At the finish, the velocities of the boat and system CM increase together with the drag power, but the rower's power production decreases. At a +30–35 degrees oar angle *Prow* becomes lower than drag power *Pdrag* (4), the system starts decelerating and *Pkin* becomes negative. This means kinetic energy

of the system is spent on moving the boat forward together with the blade, while there is still some backward force on it. It could probably be explained by the hydro-lift effect. The product of this forward blade velocity (with the boat) and backward force creates negative 'waste power' *Pw* and *Ebl* > 100 per cent. *At the finish, the blade efficiency becomes higher than 100 per cent, but this doesn't indicate more effective blade work.*

The specific impulse can be used together with blade efficiency for evaluation of the blade work. A higher specific impulse is generated at a lighter gearing ratio, but at a lower handle velocity at the same time. Obviously, this is possible only when the blade has significant resistance in the water, which could be achieved either by using a bigger blade area, or by more effective thrust production using a better shape and / or utilization of the hydro-lift effect, which happens at the beginning and the end of the drive.

3.1.2 Rower's Efficiency

To produce maximal power, a muscle must contract at an optimal velocity, because movements with very slow or fast speed are less efficient. Fig. 3.6 illustrates a Hill principle of muscle mechanics, discovered in the 1920s by

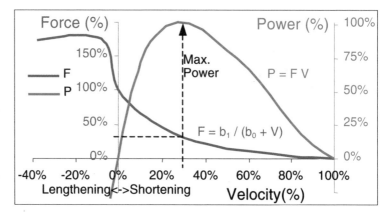

Fig. 3.6 Relationships between velocity, force and power of a muscle contraction (Hill principle).

$$F = b_1 / (b_0 + V)$$

$$P = F V$$

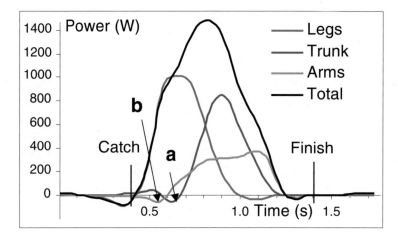

Fig. 3.7 Examples of negative power in trunk (a) and arms (b).

the famous physiologist Archibald Vivian Hill. The hyperbolic relationship between velocity and force was obtained from a study of frog muscle tissue, but a number of recent researches confirmed that it can be valid for complex multi-joint movements, which can be measured as velocities of body segments. According to the Hill principle, the maximal power can be achieved in a movement at about 30 per cent of both the maximal static force and near 30 per cent of the maximal unloaded velocity of a muscle contraction.

Static (isometric) muscle contraction does not produce any mechanical work and power, because its velocity is zero, and power is a product of force and velocity. This means no energy is added into the propulsion of the rower-boat system, but an athlete has to spend metabolic energy for static effort. This wasted energy decreases rower's muscle efficiency and the total power production. In rowing, it is not possible to completely eliminate static muscle contractions: for example, trunk muscles and glutes must be activated in order to maintain posture.

In eccentric muscle contraction, the velocity is negative: it has opposite direction to the force (a muscle extending under external force), so the power is negative. This means the muscle is not producing mechanical energy but consumes it for its stretching. In fast-impact movements like sprint running and jumps, eccentric contraction may play a positive role, because the muscle works as a spring and returns most of the energy into propulsion. In rowing, it may happen at the catch, when kinetic energy of relative movement of the rower and boat masses could stretch leg muscles and be returned during the drive. However, during the drive, any eccentric muscle contraction must be avoided because it consumes the energy produced by other muscles and reduces propulsive power production. Technical faults are usually related to negative power production in the trunk and arms-shoulders segments. Negative trunk power is a technical fault called 'slide-shooting' or 'bum-showing', when stretching of the back muscles consumes power produced by the legs (Fig. 3.7, point a). If a rower uses 'grubbing' of the arms and shoulders before the catch, they may extend the muscles at the beginning of the drive, produce a negative power (b) and decrease the total muscle efficiency.

In rowing, the total force / velocity ratio could be adjusted using the oar gearing ratio: heavier gearing makes muscle contractions slower, but produces a higher force; lighter

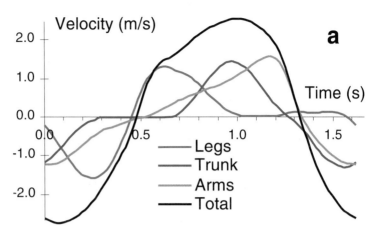

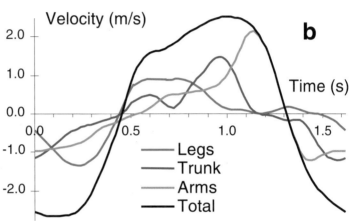

Fig. 3.8 Examples of two rowing styles in the same M2x at 36 str / min: a) consecutive activation of legs and trunk; b) simultaneous legs and trunk at catch.

gearing allows faster rower's movements, but makes it more difficult to produce high forces. Too heavy or too light gearing could affect the force / velocity relationship and thus decrease the muscle efficiency Historically, the more or less optimal human body gearing in rowing was found empirically, simply by adopting that gearing which produces the highest speed. Also, it changes with new equipment development: for example, after the introduction of bigger blades in the early 1990s, the gearing was significantly lighter, because rowers felt it heavier and less efficient. More accurate modelling of an optimal muscle contraction velocity could be done by means of extensive isokinetic testing for every individual athlete.

A correct rowing technique is very important for maximizing rower's muscle efficiency. Here a few main principles are outlined illustrating the effect of rowing technique on muscle efficiency.

1. Effective utilization of big muscle groups (glutes and hamstrings). In experiments with legs and arms ergometry, it was found that bigger muscles have higher efficiency than smaller muscles.

2. An optimal body sequence (rowing style) matched to the rower's characteristics and boat speed plays the most significant role in rowing efficiency. Fig. 3.8 shows two examples of rowing styles with (a) consecu-

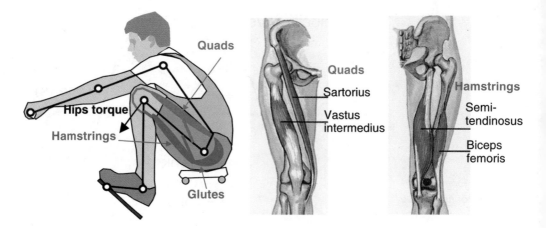

Fig. 3.9 Schematics of utilization of biarticular (two joints) muscles in rowing.

tive and (b) simultaneous activation of legs and trunk. In the first case, the maximal leg velocity was nearly 30 per cent higher, and this difference was achieved in the same boat by means of rowing technique only.

3. Effective coordination of muscles-antagonists activities. The thigh has biarticular muscles both at its front (quads) and back (hamstrings), which are connected across two joints: hip and knee. In the quads muscle group, the *rectus femoris* and *sartorius* are connected to the shins and (partly) to the pelvis at the front. In the hamstrings, the *biceps femoris* long head and *semitendinosus* are connected to the shins and to the pelvis at the back (Fig. 3.9). An attempt to simultaneously extend both knees and hips joints (use legs and trunk at the same time as in the rowing style in Fig. 3.8b) may lead to a situation where quads and hamstrings work against each other; the quads pull the pelvis forward with the upper end of the *sartorius* and flex the hips, while hamstrings and glutes try to extend it; hamstrings pull the shins with the lower end of the *semitendinosus* and collapse the knee, while quads try to extend it. Also, activation of the glutes creates a torque around the hips,

which pushes the knee down and collapses it. Therefore, simultaneous activation of legs and trunk at the beginning of the drive could be inefficient for this reason.

3.1.3 Inertial Efficiency

In rowing on water or a mobile erg, the two significant masses of the rower and boat or machine move in relation to one another[11]. Erg rowing is the simplest case; the on-water model is similar, but affected by the acceleration of the whole rower-boat system, so it will be discussed later. From a stationary position at the catch or finish, some energy has to be spent to achieve a velocity V between the rower's centre of mass (CM) and the machine, which is a sum of rower's V_{row} and ergo V_{erg} velocities:

$$V = V_{row} + V_{erg} \tag{53}$$

Accelerations of the components and, therefore, velocities V_{row} and V_{erg} are inversely proportional to their masses:

$$V_{row}/V_{erg} = M_{erg}/M_{row} \tag{54}$$

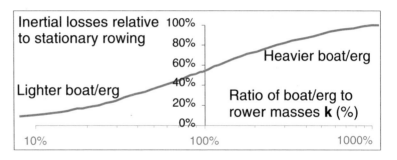

Fig. 3.10 Dependence of inertial losses on the boat / erg mass relative to the rower's mass.

where M_{row} is the rower's mass and M_{erg} is the erg mass. This energy is transferred into kinetic energy, E_k, which can be expressed as:

$$E_k = (M_{row}V_{row}^2 + M_{erg}V_{erg}^2)/2 \qquad (55)$$

A rower will also expend metabolic energy on the deceleration of the masses at the end of the drive or recovery. These losses can be minimized using the elastic properties of muscles and ligaments, and kinetic energy can be transferred into propulsion (see 3.1.2). Therefore, the decelerations could be removed from the equation and E_k should be multiplied by two, bearing in mind that the acceleration happens twice during the stroke cycle (during the drive and recovery). Combining all three equations above, the total inertial losses P_{in} can be expressed as:

$$P_{in} = (M_{row}(V/(1+1/k)^2) + M_{erg}(V/(1+k))^2) = v^2(M_{erg}M_{row}/(M_{erg}+M_{row})) \qquad (56)$$

where k is the ratio of the masses, M_{erg}/M_{row}. The higher the mass of the ergo or boat, the higher the inertial losses (Fig. 3.10), which have the maximal value on a stationary ergometer (M_{erg} = infinity):

For example, a 90 kg rower at a stroke rate of 36 str / min is spending 32W on a mobile Concept2 erg on slides (35kg erg mass), which is nearly 50 per cent more compared to a boat or RowPerfect (21W).

What could be done to decrease inertial losses? The velocity V in Equation 56 is the maximal velocity between CM-s and defined by an average velocity V_{av} and a pattern of instantaneous velocity curve. The most efficient is a rectangular pattern with constant $V = V_{av}$, but it is not achievable in practice. A triangular pattern with a constant acceleration and deceleration gives $V = 2V_{av}$ and increases the inertial losses by a factor of four ($2^2 = 4$). A sinusoidal pattern, which is the most typical in rowing and was used in our model here, gives $V = 1.65V_{av}$ and 2.7 times less efficient than the rectangular curve.

The average velocity V_{av} is defined by the drive and recovery times (T_{dr} and T_{rec}) and amplitude of travel L of the rower's CM relative to the machine: $V = L/T$. T_{dr} and T_{rec} depend on the stroke rate R and rhythm Rh ($= T_{dr}/T_{cycle}$).

Absolute inertial losses P_{in} significantly increase at higher stroke rates and longer travel of the rower's CM. However, the rower's power production P_{row} also grows, so inertial efficiency E_{in} ($= P_{row}/(P_{row}+P_{in})$) does not decrease dramatically. Fig. 3.11 shows E_{in} at various combinations of R, L and Rh (M_{row} = 90kg and M_{erg} = 18kg).

Between stroke rates of R = 20 and 40 str / min the efficiency E_{in} decreases only by 3.1 per cent (from 96.9 per cent down to 93.8 per cent), but then the curve goes down increasingly steeply, which means further increasing cadence is getting more

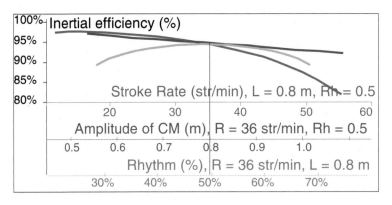

Fig. 3.11 Dependence of inertial efficiency on the stroke rate, amplitude of CM movement and rhythm.

and more expensive in term of inertial losses, so 42–44 str / min could be an inertial limit of the stroke rate.

The amplitude affects efficiency linearly: a twice longer L (0.5–1m) decreases E_{in} by 3.3 per cent (from 96.5 per cent down to 93.2 per cent). It is difficult to determine the amplitude of CM travel, so it was assumed it was a half of the handle travel. An opinion was expressed[46] that the rower should minimize the CM travel to decrease inertial losses and maximize the handle travel to increase power production, which is correct mechanically. However, it is likely that it would lead to lower utilization of the big muscles of the legs and trunk in favour of smaller muscles of the arms and shoulders and could decrease the rower's overall effectiveness.

Efficiency E_{in} is the highest at the rhythm Rh = 50 per cent (drive / recovery = 1 / 1). Deviation of rhythm by 10 per cent changes E_{in} only by 0.7 per cent, but another 10 per cent gives a loss of 3.7 per cent.

Conclusion: the inertial losses can be decreased by means of quick acceleration between the rower's CM and ergo / boat at the beginning of the drive and recovery and maintaining a constant velocity between these masses as long as possible. This is one more argument in favour of a front-loaded drive and fast leg extension at the catch. An optimal balance of stroke rate,

length and rhythm needs to be found to maximize the power and minimize inertial losses.

3.1.4 Case study on Inertial Efficiency in Two Different Rowing Styles

In rowing on water, the whole system accelerates during the drive and decelerates during recovery, contrarily to rowing on a stationary erg. A rower can shift emphasis either on acceleration of his CM, pushing the stretcher harder and using his legs more or on the acceleration of the boat, pulling the handle more strongly and using the upper body more. To compare inertial efficiency of these rowing styles, their main biomechanical variables were compared (Fig. 3.12).

At the catch, the legs velocity of Sculler 1 is increasing faster and earlier than the handle velocity. Sculler 2 uses his trunk at the same time for initial acceleration at the blade entry. At the middle of the drive and finish, Sculler 1 is using the trunk more actively and returning it earlier (negative trunk velocity) by means of a faster arms pull.

At the catch, Sculler 1 develops both accelerations of the boat and his CM earlier, which leads to a smaller magnitude of negative velocity of his CM (Fig. 3.13). During the drive, the maximal positive velocity of his CM also has

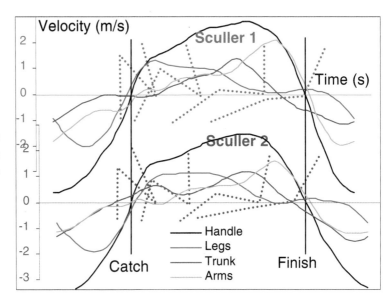

Fig. 3.12 Comparison of two rowing styles in M1x at 36 str / min.

Table 3.1 Kinetic energy of the boat and rower's CM, inertial losses and efficiency (ratio of the rowing power to its sum with the inertial losses).

Rower	Rower's Inertia			Inertia of the Boat			Total		
	Ekin Recovery (J)	Ekin Drive (J)	Inertial Power (W)	Ekin Recovery (J)	Ekin Drive (J)	Inertial Power (W)	Total Inertial Losses (W)	Inertial Efficiency (per cent)	
1	37.4	26.2	44.2	34.6	33.0	47.0	91.1	88.0 per cent	
2	45.1	36.1	56.1	32.1	30.5	43.2	99.3	86.3 per cent	

a smaller magnitude because of more active utilization of his upper body at that moment. As a result, there are peaks of kinetic energy and, therefore, his inertial losses are lower than for Sculler 2.

Sculler 2 has to expend 9 per cent more power to overcome inertia of his CM (Table 3.1), being 3kg lighter than Sculler 1. The inertial efficiency is 1.7 per cent lower, which alone would decrease speed by 0.43 per cent or by 1.7s over a 2km race. The other problem of Sculler 2's style is a less effective catch, caused by ineffective utilization of muscles-antagonists, which creates a disconnection, a hump on the force curve (Fig. 3.13d). As a result, at even higher relative force per kg of body weight the speed of Sculler 2 is 8.3 per cent slower than Sculler 1 (30s per 2km, this could also be affected by an 8 degrees shorter length of the stroke).

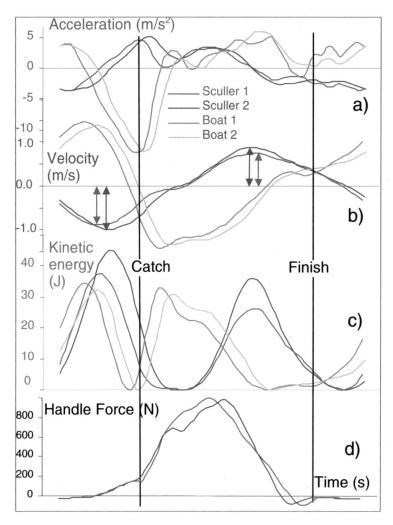

Fig. 3.13 Acceleration, velocity, kinetic energy of the boat and rower's **CM** and force curves in two scullers with different rowing styles.

It is still widely believed that the target of efficient rowing technique is maintenance of the most even boat velocity, with avoidance of the boat 'check' or 'disturbing'. However, it appeared to be that even velocity of the rower's CM is more efficient and important.

3.1.5 Boat Deadweight

Boat deadweight is a very practical issue, which is important for the selection of the boat and coxswain. There are three factors of deadweight influencing rowing speed, which affect it in different ways.

1. Higher drag resistance force caused by higher mass of the system and consequently greater water displacement;

2. Higher inertial losses, which decrease propulsive power because the rowers have to move a heavier mass back and forth;

3. Lower energy losses caused by reduced fluctuations of the hull velocity in the water.

Table 3.2 Effect of each 1kg extra deadweight per rower on the boat speed.			
Factor	Effect on speed (per cent) '−' slower, ' + ' faster	2km race in 5:20	2km race in 7:10
Drag factor	− 0.06	+ 0.20s	+ 0.26s
Inertial losses	− 0.24	+ 0.77s	+ 1.03s
Speed fluctuations	+ 0.11	− 0.35s	− 0.47s
Sum	− 0.19	+ 0.61s	+ 0.82s

The drag factor depends on the amount of water displaced by the hull, which is equal to the total mass of the system. Using the basic relationship of power and speed (Equation 3), the ratio of the speeds could be calculated using values of the drag factors:

$$V_1/V_2 = (DF_1 / DF_2)^{1/3} \qquad (57)$$

Using an empirically obtained equation for the average of all boat types, the drag caused by 1kg of extra deadweight per rower decreases the boat speed by 0.061 per cent.

The inertial losses could be derived using mathematical modelling with sinusoidal movement of two known masses relative to each other (see 3.1.3). It was found that at a stroke rate of 36 str / min and relative displacement 0.6m, each 1kg of extra deadweight per rower decreased the boat speed by 0.33 per cent (1.13s over a 2km race). However, this value depends on the rowing technique and could be decreased by means of transferring kinetic energy to blade propulsion at the finish of the drive. Using the analysis of experimental data it was taken to be 0.24 per cent (0.81s over a 2km race).

Modelling of the boat velocity fluctuations revealed that each 1kg of extra deadweight per rower would make the boat speed smoother and increase its average value by 0.11 per cent (0.37s over a 2km race). However, if rowers rush the recovery and increase velocity fluctuations in hull, this value will be reduced (see 2.4.1).

Every 1kg of extra deadweight per rower would decrease the boat speed by 0.19 per cent. The effect determined above corresponds quite well with findings of other authors[6,16]. However, they only analysed the drag factor component, which represents 30 per cent of the total effect of the deadweight.

These findings could be verified by comparing the speed of similar boat types with and without a coxswain. In fours, 55kg of extra deadweight (13.75 kg per rower) should make the coxed boat 9.5s slower over a 2km race in 6:00. Similar analysis for pairs (27.5kg extra per rower) gives 21.3s difference in speed over 2km at 6:40.

The results of the 1992 Olympics, where the coxed four and pair events were last contested, has shown 4.3s difference between the winners in M4 − and M4 + and 6.4s as an average for the finalists, which is lower than the above value. In M2 + and M2 − these differences were 22.1s and 20.5s respectively, which is very close to the predicted value.

3.2 TEMPORAL ANALYSIS OF THE STROKE CYCLE

Temporal or phase analysis divides a movement into a sequence of phases and sub-phases. Each phase has a clearly defined biomechanical function and strictly identified phase boundaries often called 'key events' or 'key moments'[8], which must be represented by momentary snapshots with zero time duration, otherwise accurate timing would not be possible. A temporal analysis is a very versatile method of biomechanical analysis and could play an integrating role for other biomechanical techniques, for example by linking kinetic and kinematic measurements obtained using various instruments (such as force sensors with video analysis). It should reduce the complexity of a sporting technique, and help a coach's and athlete's understanding of biomechanical principles.

Temporal analysis is a well-developed technique in a number of cyclic locomotion sports such as running, cycling, swimming, skating and skiing. The most common definition uses two main phases in the cycle: the 'propulsive' phase ('drive' or 'stroke' phase), when an athlete actively interacts with the support substance (ground, water, snow or ice) and executes an effort to propel the centre of mass (CM) of the athlete-equipment system forward; and the 'non-propulsive' phase ('glide' or 'recovery' phase), where resistance forces act alone to decrease the speed of the system CM[59]. These two phases may be further divided into sub-phases. For example, in running the propulsive phase has been divided into 'foot strike', 'mid-support' and 'take-off' sub-phases, and the recovery phase has been divided into 'follow-through', 'forward swing', and 'foot descent' phases[24].

In rowing, oar movement clearly defines two main phases: drive and recovery, which are separated by two moments: catch and finish, where the oar changes direction. However, accurate definition of smaller sub-phases is more difficult. Attempting to use blade work to define 'water phase' and 'air phase' won't be accurate, because blade entry and exit are not momentary points in time. What should be taken as the start of 'water phase'? The moment when the bottom blade edge touches water level? Or when the centre of the blade crosses it? Or when the blade is fully immersed? For the same reason, there were unproductive attempts to use muscular activity and body segment sequencing to define sub-phases ('legs push', 'trunk drive', and 'arm pull') during the drive phase[15,51].

To solve the above problem, it was proposed to use accelerations of the boat, rower's CM and the whole system to define the main sub-phases of the stroke cycle[36]. This approach has a number of advantages: acceleration is clearly related to propulsion, velocity and performance in rowing; boat acceleration can easily be accurately measured with the modern technology.

Typical patterns of boat acceleration have one period of negative acceleration (that is reducing boat velocity) at the catch, and two periods of positive acceleration during the drive and recovery[57]. The negative acceleration at the catch and the positive acceleration during the recovery were explained by the transfer of momentum between the rower's mass and the boat mass (which can move significantly relative to each other). Positive acceleration during the drive phase was explained by the propulsion forces produced by the oars. Boat acceleration during the drive phase is usually not constant: it typically has a first peak, then a short gap, and finally a longer positive peak (see 2.4.33). The main purpose of the analysis below is to relate the temporal structure with the effectiveness of rowing,

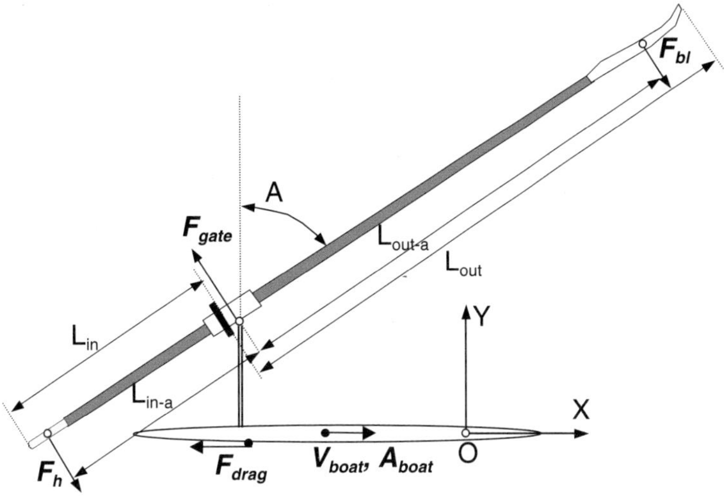

Fig. 3.14 Coordinate system and forces acting on the boat and oar.

which may help to understand it better and improve performance.

3.2.1 Method to Define Acceleration of the Rower's CM

While the boat acceleration is easy to measure directly, acceleration of the rower's CM is difficult to determine because the shape of a rower's body is always changing and it is not possible to firmly relate its CM to any of its components. The following method was proposed to define accelerations of a rower's CM and the CM of the whole system.

The total blade force of the crew, F_{bl}, was derived from the sum of the measured handle forces, F_h, times the ratio of the actual inboard length, L_{in-a}, and outboard length, L_{out-a} (3.14).

Neglecting oar inertia (which is very small during the drive) the total blade force is given by Equation 58:

$$F_{bl} = F_h \left(L_{in-a} / L_{out-a} \right) \qquad (58)$$

where the effective inboard length L_{in-a} was calculated from Equation 10, and effective outboard length L_{out-a} was calculated from Equation 59:

$$L_{out-a} = (L_{oar} - L_{in}) - L_{sp} / 2 - W_g / 2 \qquad (59)$$

where L_{oar} is the overall oar length, and L_{sp} is the length of the blade spoon. We assumed that this point is the centre of water pressure on the blade, which is a limitation of the method.

The drag force F_{drag} acting on the boat shell was derived from Equation 60:

$$F_{drag} = DF V_{boat}^2 \qquad (60)$$

where drag factor DF was derived as the ratio of the integral of the blade propulsive force and the integral of the square of boat speed over the stroke cycle interval T in Equation 61:

$$DF = \left(\int_{t=0}^{t=T} F_{bl} \cos \theta \, DT \, / \left(\int_{t=0}^{t=T} V_{boat}^2 \, DT \right) \right) \qquad (61)$$

The propulsive force F_{sys} acting on the rower-boat system was defined as:

$$F_{sys} = F_{bl} \cos (Ah) + F_{drag} \qquad (62)$$

81

The system CM acceleration, A_{sys}, was calculated as:

$$A_{sys} = F_{sys} / M_{sys} = F_{sys} / (M_{boat} + M_{row}) \qquad (63)$$

where M_{sys}, M_{boat}, and M_{row} are the masses of the system, boat, and rower, respectively. The acceleration of the rower's CM, A_{row}, was calculated as:

$$A_{row} = F_{row} / M_{row} \qquad (64)$$

Where the force F_{row} applied to the rower was derived from:

$$F_{row} = F_{sys} - F_{boat} = F_{sys} - A_{boat} M_{boat} \qquad (65)$$

The deviations of instantaneous velocities V_d of the system, boat, and rower's CM from the average velocity of the system (and each component) during the stroke cycle were calculated:

$$V_d = \int A \, DT \qquad (66)$$

where A is the corresponding acceleration (A_{sys}, A_{boat}, and A_{row}). This means the frame of reference used moves with a constant velocity equal to the average speed of the rower-boat system. The X axis was aligned parallel to the boat longitudinal axis towards the bow of the boat.

Velocities of the body segments were derived for the purpose of qualitative analyses of sub-phases (see Chapter 4.1.4). Leg velocity V_{leg} was derived as a rate of the measured seat position L_s. Velocity of the trunk relative to the boat $V_{trunk/b}$ was derived in the same way using trunk position L_t. Trunk velocity V_{trunk} relative to the seat was calculated subtracting V_{leg} from $V_{trunk/b}$. Arms velocity V_{arms} was derived as the difference between handle velocity V_h and the velocity of the trunk relative to the boat, $V_{trunk/b}$, where

V_h was derived from the measured horizontal oar angle and actual inboard.

$$V_h = DA_h / DT \, L_{in-a} \, (\pi / 180) \qquad (67)$$

3.2.2 Definition of the Sub-Phases of the Stroke Cycle

Accelerations of the CM of the boat, rower, and the whole system (A_{boat}, A_{row}, A_{boat}) were used to define the sub-phases of the stroke cycle. These variables were chosen because they are related to the accumulation of kinetic energy in the two major components of the rower-boat system, and hence to the effectiveness of rowing technique. Handle velocity V_h was used to define the overall drive phase boundaries (Fig. 3.15).

Six sub-phases of the drive phase (D1–D6) and three sub-phases of the recovery phase (R1, R2, R3) were defined. Table 3.3 presents the sub-phase definitions, descriptions, and the key events, which define their start and end points.

It was found[36] that sub-phases D1, D2, and D3 were slightly longer in sweep boats than in sculling boats, and sub-phases D4, D5, and D6 were slightly shorter. The longer duration of D1 in sweep rowing might be due to the greater width of the sweep oar blade, which requires more time to insert into the water. The shorter duration of D2 and D3 in sculling might be due to the longer catch angles, which create heavier effective gearing (see Chapter 6.2.1). A heavier gearing produces a lower ratio of handle-to-gate forces, which creates higher acceleration of the boat compared to the rower's CM.

There were no significant differences found in the durations of the D1, D2, D3 and D6 sub-phases among boats of different sizes. D4 was significantly longer in big boats (eights and quads) and D5 was longer in small boats

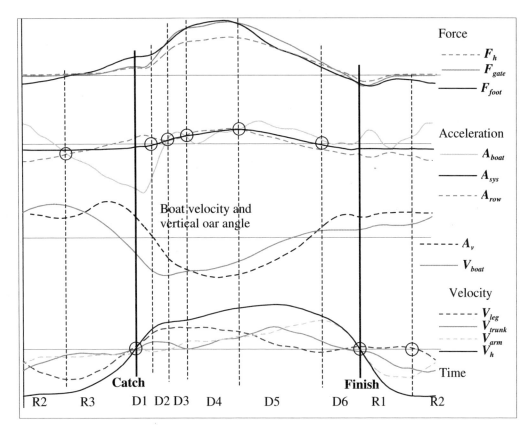

Fig. 3.15 Typical biomechanical variables and sub-phases of the stroke cycle (M1x, rate 32 str / min). Key events are marked with circles.

(singles and pairs), but the reasons for these differences are not yet known.

Male crews had a longer D3 sub-phase than female crews, which is probably due to their more rapid generation of forces. Differences in other sub-phases between genders were not statistically significant.

The absolute duration of all sub-phases, except for D3, tended to decrease at higher stroke rates, so the correlation coefficients ranged from − 0.10 for D4 to − 0.70 for D1. This decrease in duration was strongly cor-related with a decrease in total drive time at higher stroke rates ($r = -$ 0.87). The relative share of the D1 sub-phase within the drive phase tended to decrease at higher stroke

rates ($r = -$ 0.49), whereas the relative share of the D6 sub-phase tended to increase. Sculling crews tended to exhibit an absolute maximum in the relative share of the D3 sub-phase at stroke rate 30 str / min and sweep crews at 36 str / min.

To analyse the relationship between sub-phase proportions and the force curve profile, times were derived from the catch until the moment when the force V_h achieved 10 per cent, 20 per cent, …100 per cent of its maximal value. The following statistically sig-nificant relationships were found (Fig. 3.15):

- D1 period had the strongest positive correlation with the time of achieving

Table 3.3 Biomechanical definitions of sub-phases of the stroke cycle.

ID	Sub-phase	Start event	Description
D1	Blade Immersion	Catch, beginning of the drive. V_h changes sign to positive	A_{sys} and A_{boat} are negative, but A_{row} is positive. Fast increase in handle and leg speed
D2	Initial rowers' acceleration	A_{sys} becomes positive. The centre of the blade crosses the water level downwards	Handle force and A_{boat} increase, but A_{boat} is still negative and lower than A_{row}
D3	Initial boat acceleration	A_{boat} becomes higher than A_{row}	First positive peak of A_{boat}, which becomes higher than A_{row}. Maximum of V_{leg}
D4	Rowers' acceleration	A_{boat} decreases and becomes lower than rower's acceleration	F_h, A_{row} and A_{sys} increase slowly. V_{leg} decreases
D5	Boat acceleration	A_{boat} again becomes higher than A_{row}	F_h, F_{foot}, A_{row} and A_{sys} decrease, but F_{foot} decreases faster than F_h which produces the highest A_{boat}
D6	Blade removal	A_{sys} becomes negative. The centre of the blade crosses the water level upwards	A_{row} is negative and A_{boat} is close to zero. V_h is still positive. V_{arm} is maximal
R1	Arms and trunk return	Finish, end of the drive. V_h changes sign to negative	A quick positive peak of A_{boat} and negative A_{row}, caused by transfer of moment of inertia from rower to boat
R2	Legs return	Seat starts moving towards the stern. Increasing of A_{boat} and decreasing of A_{row}	A_{boat} is positive, but A_{row} and A_{sys} are negative. V_{leg} increases towards the stern
R3	Catch preparation	A_{boat} becomes negative and A_{row} becomes positive	F_{foot} increases, which causes a decrease in V_{leg}, the boat deceleration and the rower acceleration

30 per cent of maximal force ($r = 0.91$, $p < 0.001$);

- D3 had the strongest negative correlation with the time of achieving 70 per cent ($r = -0.45$, $p < 0.05$) and 80 per cent ($r = -0.46$, $p < 0.05$) of maximal force;
- D6 had negative correlation with the time taken to achieve 30 per cent of maximal force ($r = -0.46$, $p < 0.05$).

3.2.3 Case Study: the Importance of the D3 Sub-Phase

The data samples were taken in two crews of international level at a stroke rate 32 str / min. The first crew were Olympic champions and considered by experts to be highly technically effective. The second crew were the world championship finalists, and had very good physiological work capacity, but could not achieve excellent performance on the water. The first crew produced a much quicker rise in the handle force (Fig. 3.16a), achieving 70 per cent of their maximal force at 23.1 per cent of the drive time. The second crew had a relatively flatter force curve (70 per cent of maximal force at 29.1 per cent of the drive time), but higher maximal and average forces.

The faster rise of the force in the first crew coincided with a faster increase in leg speed V_{leg} (Fig. 3.16d), so the peak leg velocity was achieved at 22.4 per cent of the drive time, which was accompanied by a steady increase in the trunk speed V_{trunk} (Fig. 3.16f). The second crew had slower leg velocity during the first half of the drive (peak leg velocity at 32.2 per cent) and a double-peaked trunk velocity profile. Consequently, the handle velocity V_h of the first crew increased faster during the first half of the drive (Fig. 3.16b).

The boat acceleration A_{boat} of the first crew had a deeper and later negative peak at the catch (8.4m / s² compared to 7.3m / s² in the second crew), but a much quicker increase afterwards (Fig. 3.16c). The first peak of A_{boat} was 2.7m / s² in the first crew, but only 0.3m / s² in the second crew, which had A_{boat} drop below zero after the first peak.

The first crew had a higher acceleration of the rower's CM A_{row} at the catch, but the second crew accelerated their body mass more intensively during the middle of the drive (Fig. 3.16e). As a result, the second crew did not have sub-phase D3 (initial boat acceleration) at all (Fig. 3.16g), but it had a much longer D4 (main rowers' acceleration).

3.2.4 Temporal Analysis and the Effectiveness of Rowing Technique

The main measure of rowing performance is the average speed of the rower-boat system.

The drive phase is the only time when rowers can increase the system velocity; more precisely, only that part of the drive when the propulsive force is higher than the drag force. The system accumulates kinetic energy during the drive phase and loses it during the recovery phase, so a higher acceleration of the system CM during the drive phase means a higher average speed and hence better performance. The gain of kinetic energy of a body, dE, can be defined as:

$$dE = (m\ v_2^2\ /\ 2) - (m\ v_1^2\ /\ 2)$$
$$= (m\ /\ 2)\ (v_2^2 - v_1^2) \qquad (68)$$

where m is the mass of the body and v_1 and v_2 are the start and end velocities of the body's CM. The mass of the rower is significantly greater than that of the boat (the ratio ranges from 400 per cent in lightweight women to 600 per cent in heavyweight men). To maximize the average speed, the rowers must maximize the gain of kinetic energy, which is the most effective with acceleration of the heaviest part of the system (that is the rower's CM). Therefore the effectiveness of rowing technique is related to the magnitude and timing of the acceleration of the rower's CM.

The acceleration of a body depends on the force acting on it. The force, F_{row}, applied to the rower's CM (Fig. 3.17) is equal to the sum of foot-stretcher reaction force $F_{r.foot}$, which is positive (pushes the rower's CM forward), and handle reaction force, $F_{r.handle}$, which is negative (pulls the rower backwards). Both these reaction forces have the same magnitude and the opposite direction to the action forces: F_{foot} and F_h.

$$F_{row} = F_{r.foot} + F_{r.handle} \qquad (69)$$

The force applied to the boat hull F_{boat} is equal to the sum of the gate force F_{gate}, the stretcher

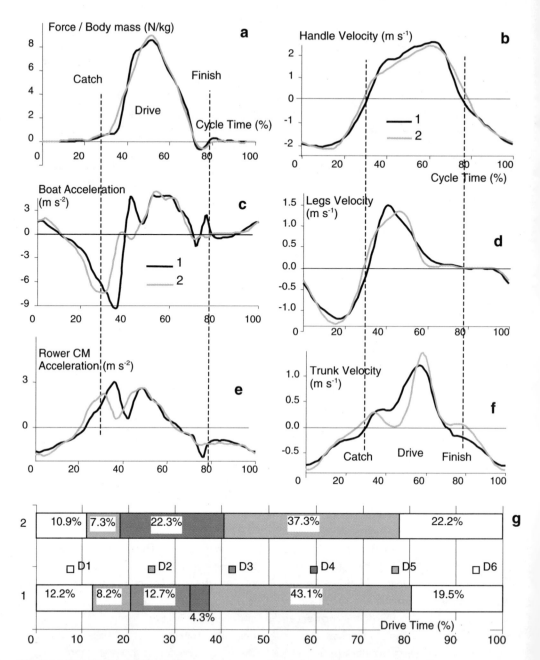

Fig. 3.16 Biomechanical variables and temporal structure of the drive phase for two examples of rowing technique.

force F_{foot} and drag force F_{drag}, (ignoring small seat friction force):

$$F_{boat} = F_{gate} + F_{foot} + F_{drag} \qquad (70)$$

Therefore, emphasis on the boat acceleration requires rowers to produce a higher gate force F_{gate} (and a correspondingly higher handle force F_h) and to push on the stretcher

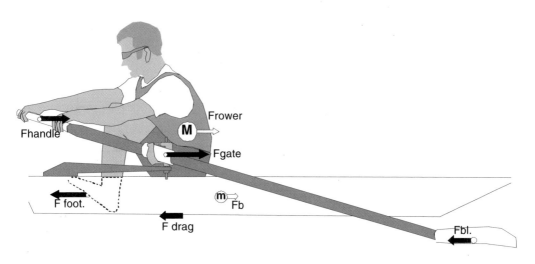

Fig. 3.17 The main forces in the rower-boat-oar system.

less. Vice versa, emphasis on accelerating the rower's CM requires a higher stretcher force F_{foot} and lower handle force F_h. The charts of the gate and stretcher forces in Fig. 3.15 confirm that this switching of the emphasis happens twice during the drive.

The stretcher force F_{foot} is the primary focus during the drive because it increases the acceleration A_{row} of the rower's CM, which provides the most significant accumulation of kinetic energy, and hence increases the system's average speed.

However, the effectiveness of the rower's push on the stretcher is affected by the boat velocity at that time. If the stretcher (and the boat) has a higher velocity then the rower can accelerate his CM more effectively than when the boat is moving more slowly It could be speculated that using the elastic energy stored in the rower's tendons and muscles can play some role at the beginning of the drive. The use of elastic energy is similar to jumping on a trampoline: the point of support moves in the direction of the acceleration of the athlete's CM and adds its velocity to it, which makes the acceleration more effective. Therefore, the presence of D3 could be called a 'trampolining

effect' and regarded as an important indicator of the effectiveness of the rowing technique (see 3.2.5).

The practical implications of the sub-phases of the drive phase are as follows.

During sub-phases D1–D2 a rower emphasizes pushing with his legs, because he has to change the direction of movement from the stern to the bow. This accelerates the rower's CM and decelerates the boat. At the same time, the blade obtains a grip on the water.

During D3 the handle pull is emphasized. This accelerates the boat and creates a faster moving support on the stretcher. This sub-phase is important for performing an effective drive phase. It was found that in 43 per cent of the crews this sub-phase was absent, but a longer duration of D3 does not mean better technique because D3 was the longest in some low-level crews.

During D4 the stretcher push is emphasized again, which accelerates the rower's CM and hence the accumulated kinetic energy. The effectiveness of this sub-phase depends on the degree of boat velocity gained during the previous sub-phase D3, and on a fast, powerful leg drive.

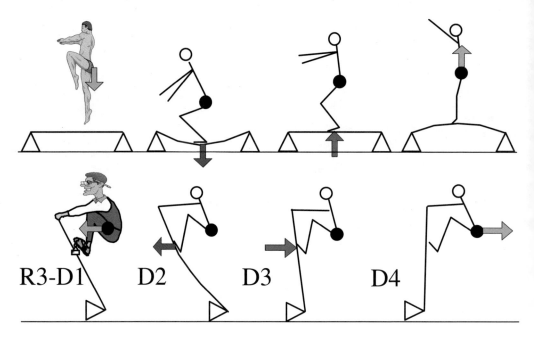

Fig. 3.18 The 'trampoline effect' in rowing.

The sub-phases D5 and D6 occur after the legs are substantially extended, so the trunk and arms are utilized instead. The level of the forces and the total system acceleration decreases, but the stretcher force decreases more quickly and becomes negative (pull on the stretcher), which puts the emphasis on the boat acceleration again. The rower's CM acceleration becomes negative, which means transferring kinetic energy from the rower's mass to the boat.

The phenomenon of a double peak in the boat's acceleration during the drive phase can be explained by a double switching of the emphasis from pushing the stretcher (more rower's CM acceleration) to pulling the handle (more boat hull acceleration). The presence of the sub-phase D3 (initial boat acceleration) is an important indicator of the effectiveness of a rower's technique. The initial boat acceleration creates a faster moving platform for the stretcher to allow better acceleration of the rower's CM.

3.2.5 'Trampoline Effect'

Of course, biomechanical conditions in trampoline jumping are very different from rowing, where there is no firm ground support and force of gravity is perpendicular to the movement. Rowers have to create support on the stretcher for themselves by placing the blade in the water and applying handle force. However, a model of the 'trampoline effect' could be useful for a better understanding of rowing biomechanics and its practical implications. Rowing can be considered as a series of jumps, where the drive phase is similar to the takeoff and the recovery is similar to the flight phase. The longer the jumps are and the higher their frequency, the higher the rowing speed.

The 'trampoline effect' can be modelled as in Fig. 3.18:

1. Before the catch (R3 and D1 sub-phases), a rower quickly approaching the stretcher

creates an impact push on the stretcher at the moment of the blade immersion.

2. This impact force is transferred though the rigger and pin to the oar sleeve and bends the oar (D2 sub-phase). The oar shaft accumulates elastic energy, which could amount to 25 per cent of the total power at the catch (*see* Chapter 6.2.4), and also the elastic properties of the rower's muscles and ligaments may be utilized.

3. In the D3 sub-phase, the handle force quickly increases, transferred through the oar shaft, pin and rigger and creates a high positive boat acceleration called the 'first peak'.

4. A rower uses the faster moving boat-stretcher as a support for effective acceleration of their CM during the D4 sub-phase.

5. When the forces decrease during D5–D6 sub-phases, the oar shaft recoils and returns accumulated elastic energy into propulsion at the blade. At this time, velocities are higher than at the beginning of the drive, when the oar is bent, so this recoil energy works more effectively.

The 'trampoline effect' model could have a number of practical implications:

1. Fast approach to the stretcher before the catch is beneficial. This contradicts some theories, which propose a slower approach to the catch.

2. Precise timing of the stretcher and handle work is very important. In the best crews, the seat changes direction 0.04–0.08s before the handle, which is the most effective for the 'trampoline effect'.

3. In crew boats, all rowers have one common trampoline because their stretchers are connected through the hull. Therefore, they must take off synchronously. Otherwise, the boat acceleration created by one rower with higher handle force would be cancelled out by a higher stretcher force in another rower and the 'trampoline effect' won't work.

4. Rowing on stationary ergometers does not allow practising the 'trampoline effect', so mobile machines are preferable.

5. The best drill to practise the 'trampoline effect' is rowing using legs only with emphasis on fast explosive work through the stretcher. It should be done with the whole crew together, but not by seats, because the large passive mass of sitting rowers would significantly decrease the boat acceleration and cancel the 'trampoline effect'.

3.3 VARIOUS ASPECTS OF BIOMECHANICAL ANALYSIS

3.3.1 Frame of Reference

The choice of the frame of reference is important for valid biomechanical analysis. In rowing biomechanics, the following frames of reference (FoR) could be used:

- FoR related to the boat hull;
- FoR related to the CM of the rower-boat system;
- FoR related to the ground of Earth or water;
- FoR moving with the constant velocity equal to the average speed of the rower-boat system.

To determine the internal kinetic energy fluctuations it is very common to use the FoR, which is related to the CM of the system. Using a FoR which moves with constant velocity absorbs the speed fluctuation of the system CM into the equations of the speed fluctuation of the rower and boat

(Vboat-Vrower). However, the speed fluctuation of the CM of the system does not involve energy losses due to internal kinetic energy fluctuations. Therefore, the physical interpretation of the two representations is different. The one using kinetic energy as determined from the FoR which does not move with constant velocity more purely reflects the internal kinetic energy losses. A way to relate the two different paradigms or representations is:

$$E_{kinetic\ total} = E_{rower} + E_{boat} = E_{sys} + E_{in} \quad (71)$$

$$E_{row} + E_{boat} = \tfrac{1}{2}\,M_{row}\,V_{row}^{2} + \tfrac{1}{2}\,M_{boat}\,V_{boat}^{2} \quad (72)$$

$$E_{sys} + E_{in} = \tfrac{1}{2}\,M_{sys}\,V_{sys}^{2} + \tfrac{1}{2}\,M_{in}\,V_{in}^{2} \quad (73)$$

Equations 72 and 73 are equal, if:

$$M_{sys} = M_{row} + M_{boat} \quad (74)$$

$$V_{sys} = V_{row}\,M_{row}\,/\,(M_{row} + M_{boat}) + V_{boat}\,M_{boat}\,/\,(M_{row} + M_{boat}) \quad (75)$$

$$M_{in} = M_{row}\,M_{boat}\,/\,(M_{row} + M_{boat}) \quad (76)$$

$$V_{in} = V_{row} - V_{boat} \quad (77)$$

The difference between the two representations is that E_{in} determines the internal fluctuation inside the rower-boat system (internal inertial losses) and E_{sys} determines fluctuation of CM of the whole system in the external environment (external inertial losses). Modelling of experimental data revealed that internal and external inertial losses are split nearly equally. In fact, the external losses are not 'losses' by their nature: this is the amount of kinetic energy that the system accumulates during the drive and spends during recovery to overcome the drag resistance. In this case, the choice of FoR does matter because more power is required to create propulsive force F_{prop} and increase kinetic energy at higher velocity V_{prop} relative to the environment:

$$P = F_{prop}\,V_{prop} = \tfrac{1}{2}\,M_{sys} \\ (V_{cm2}^{2} - V_{cm1}^{2})\,/\,dt \quad (78)$$

It is similar to the acceleration of a car, which requires more power of the engine at a higher speed. Therefore, the FoR based on the substance used to create propulsive force, the water in this case, should be chosen for the whole system. Internal inertial losses could be calculated relative to a FoR moving with the constant velocity equal to the average speed, which makes the analysis very similar to the one on an erg.

3.3.2 Sculling Versus Sweep Rowing

'Why are sculling boats faster than rowing boats with the same number of athletes?' This question is discussed quite often on rowing forums. Using a database of experimental data, four categories of boats 2 × versus 2 − and 4 × versus 4 − were compared (n = 2738). Stroke length (Table 3.4) cannot be compared directly because sculling and rowing use different inboard lengths, which create different oar angles. Comparison of the length of the arc derived using the standard method (see Chapter 2.3.1) at 6cm from the top of the handle in sculling and at 15cm in rowing gives very similar numbers between rowing and sculling.

Both male and female scullers have higher use of their legs than rowers (Table 3.5). Male scullers use relatively longer arms drive and produce more power by arms than sweep rowers. In females this difference was less

Table 3.4 Stroke length in sculling and rowing.

	Oar angle (deg)		Arc Length (m)		Arc / Height (per cent)	
Gender	M	W	M	W	M	W
Rowing	86.9	85.0	1.56	1.54	83.7	85.2
Sculling	107.9	105.8	1.58	1.56	83.5	89.2

Table 3.5 Shares of amplitudes of body segments in doubles and pairs.

	Legs (per cent)		Trunk (per cent)		Arms (per cent)	
Amplitude	M	W	M	W	M	W
Rowing	35.1	35.3	30.7	32.4	35.1	33.8
Sculling	34.1	34.0	27.4	32.4	39.0	34.9
Power						
Rowing	42.7	42.1	34.3	35.2	22.8	22.4
Sculling	43.6	44.4	30.2	33.8	26.3	21.7

Table 3.6 Applied force in sculling and rowing.

	Max.Force (N)		Aver.Force (N)		Av.F / Weight (N / kg)	
	M	W	M	W	M	W
Heavyweight Sweep	664.9	503.3	332.8	255.6	3.78	3.48
Lightweight Sweep	576.0		291.5		4.02	
Heavyweight Sculling	739.8	529.2	388.0	274.9	4.43	3.70
Lightweight Sculling	699.4	465.2	370.9	250.0	5.06	4.25

significant. The possible reasons could be the specifics of sculling geometry and rowing style.

Applied force was found to be significantly higher in sculling (Table 3.6). The possible reasons could be:

- Sculling symmetry is more comfortable for a higher applied force.
- The inside arm in sweep rowing has much shorter leverage and, therefore, produces much less torque and oar bend, which is used to measure force.

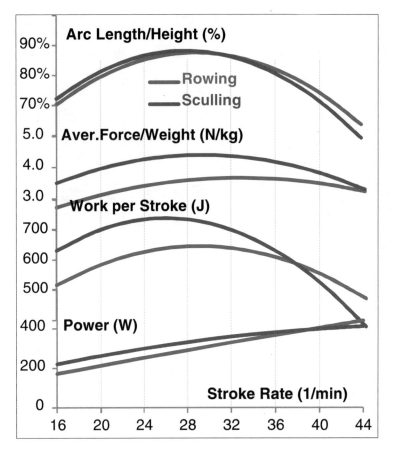

Fig. 3.19 Stroke-rate-based trends of the main biomechanical variables in sculling and rowing.

Rowing power is highly dependent on the stroke rate, so rate-based trends should be analysed as well as trends of other variables (length, force and work per stroke). Both relative length and force achieve their maximum at 28–30 str / min in sculling and at 32–34 str / min in rowing (Fig. 3.19). At higher stroke rates they both drop down but this decrease is more significant in sculling. Consequently, the work per stroke and power are higher in sculling at stroke rates below about 38 str / min where they are equal. Above this stroke rate the work per stroke and power are higher in sweep rowing. This is probably the reason why the racing stroke rate is usually higher in sweep rowing than in sculling (see Chapter 7.3); on average it was

38.9 str / min in pairs and fours compare to 37.8 str / min in doubles and quads.

Fig. 3.19 explains why forces were significantly higher in sculling in Table 3.6, where the data was averaged over the whole range of the stroke rates. At the racing stroke rates of 36–40 str / min and higher, the forces are only slightly higher in sculling, but the length became shorter. It could be concluded that *power production at the racing stroke rates does not differ significantly between sculling and rowing.*

The blade efficiency was 4.1 per cent higher in sculling boats (on average 84.6 per cent in doubles and quads) compared to similar rowing boats (80.5 per cent in pairs and fours). This makes them 1.4 per cent faster than similar rowing boats. The reasons could be:

- a bigger total area of sculling blades, which causes lower relative pressure and less slippage in the water;
- longer angles at catch in sculling, which cause better utilization of the hydro-lift effect;
- a better manoeuvrability of sculling blades, which cause shorter catch and release slips (see Chapter 2.3.2).

With the difference in speed between similar rowing and sculling boats being 3.3 per cent on average (see Chapter 7.1.2), the rest of the 1.9 per cent difference could be related to the following factors:

- Sweep oars produce a higher air drag during recovery because they are longer. This loss could be estimated as 0.3 per cent.
- Rowing boats are usually asymmetrical, which causes a wiggle and additional losses in speed (see Chapter 4.2.4).
- Rowing boats have a rudder creating an extra drag. This is why speed differences between doubles (no rudder) and pairs (with a rudder) are usually more significant than between quads and fours (both have a rudder).

Finally, *the remaining difference in speed between sculling and rowing can be explained only by higher efficiency of sculling blades and boats.*

3.3.3 Stability and Variability of Rower's Motions

Rowing is a cyclic sport. That means it requires repeating a similar cycle of motions many times. Usually, 200–250 stroke cycles are performed in covering the standard racing distance of 2km and many more have to be done in training. Visually, all strokes look similar and only experts would see some small differences. Biomechanical equipment allows very accurate measurements of rowing motions and software allows the determination of how consistent or variable the motions of each rower in a crew are.

The simplest measure of consistency is variation of the stroke rate: the higher variability, the lower consistency or stability and vice versa. Usually, a coach sets a task for rowers to row a piece of certain duration at a certain stroke rate. If all stroke periods are recorded, it is possible to derive an average stroke rate *AV* over the piece and its standard deviation *SD*. The common measure of consistency is variation *VAR* which is equal to the ratio of *SD* to the average:

$$VAR = SD / AV \qquad (79)$$

With software, this operation is performed every time before processing the typical patterns over the sample. Then, the data is filtered and all strokes with duration outside a certain range (usually $\pm$ 2SD) are rejected to produce reliable average patterns.

International-level crews usually maintain variation of the stroke rate within 1 per cent, but with beginners it could be up to 4–5 per cent. To convert it into absolute numbers, we can use a statistical rule, saying that 99.7 per cent of the data remains within a $\pm$ 3SD range (assuming a normal distribution of the data). At 32 str / min a variation of 1 per cent means that practically all strokes are within the range 31–33 str / min, but for 5 per cent variation this becomes 27–37 str / min.

Usually, the source data for biomechanical analysis is implemented as arrays of *average* values of each biomechanical variable (angles, forces, accelerations, and so on),

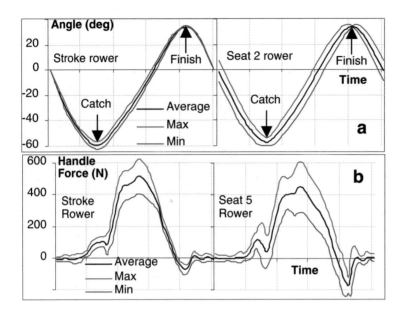

Fig. 3.20 Average curves of the oar angle (a) and handle force (b) and their maximal (+ 3SD) and minimal (− 3SD) curves in a collegiate eight at a stroke rate of 36 str / min.

which represent typical patterns (curves) of rowing technique over the sample period. Also, BioRowTel software allows the derivation of SD values for each variable at each moment of the stroke cycle, which represents the *variability* of rower's motions.

Fig. 3.20 illustrates rowing variability analysis. Analysing angles (a), the stroke rower had the lowest variation in the crew (average SD over stroke cycle is 0.7° = 0.8 per cent VAR relative to the angle amplitude), while the seat 2 rower had the highest variation (SD 2.1° = 2.3 per cent VAR). At the catch, all rowers had higher variation of the oar angle (average SD = 1.1°) than at the finish (SD = 0.5°). This fact illustrates the point that *the catch is more difficult for coordination of rower's motions than the finish*, where the oar position is quite firmly defined by rigging and rower's posture.

Variation of the handle force was found to be at a much higher level than it was for the oar angles (Fig. 3.20b). The stroke rower in this crew also had the lowest variation of the force in the crew (average SD 16N = 5.7 per cent VAR), the seat 5 rower had the highest variation (SD 29N = 12.6 per cent VAR). This fact could be explained by the point that *crew rowers have higher complexity of their motions, because they have to coordinate them with the stroke rower, who sets the timing for the crew.*

Variation of the vertical angle (Fig. 3.21a) was also high, but it was randomly distributed in the crew, where seat 7 had the lowest variation (SD 0.7° = 5.3 per cent VAR) and seat 2 had the highest variation (SD 1.0° = 10.1 per cent VAR).

The boat acceleration is a resultant variable, which reflects consistency of rowing technique of the whole crew and was found to be much better in elite rowers. Fig. 3.21b shows variation of the boat acceleration at 36 str / min in an Olympic single sculler (SD 0.31m / s² = 1.9 per cent VAR) and in a club sculler (SD 0.59 m / s² = 4.1 per cent).

There are many open questions in this area, which require further work: for example, how to define consistency near zero values of the average, where the variation goes to infinity; normative values and functions.

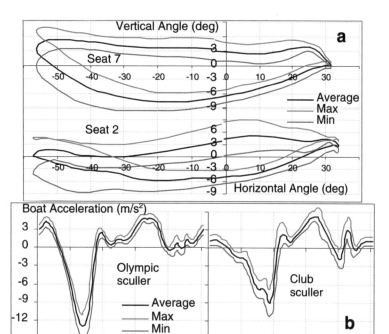

Fig. 3.21 Variation of the oar vertical angle (a) and boat acceleration (b).

CHAPTER 4

TECHNIQUE

4.1 BIOMECHANICAL DEFINITIONS OF EFFECTIVE STROKE CYCLE

The purpose of these definitions is twofold:

- to clarify rowing biomechanics terminology
- to describe a model of effective rowing technique.

This model is based on the temporal analysis of the stroke cycle (see Chapter 3.2) and can be defined as eight moments M1–M8 – momentary snapshots, and eight phases Ph1–Ph8 – transitions between the moments. Figs 4.1 to 4.8 illustrate the rower and / or positions at each moment and the text between them explains the rower's actions between them.

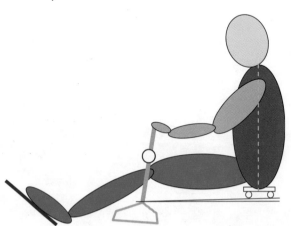

Fig. 4.1 M1. Stroke cycle start. During recovery, the oar is perpendicular to the boat (zero oar angle). The handle is on top of the knees; the trunk is nearly vertical.

Ph1. Trunk Preparation. The trunk together with the pelvis continues rotation ('pivoting') around hips, and the hamstrings and glutes are stretched. Knees gradually rise and the seat accelerates towards the stern. The rower smoothly pulls the stretcher according to the stroke rate (faster at higher rate).

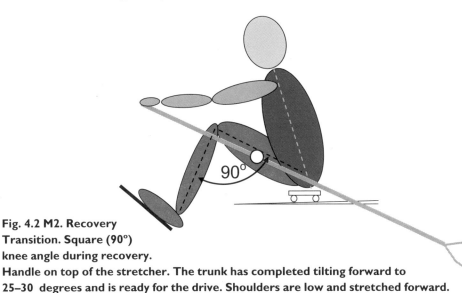

Fig. 4.2 M2. Recovery Transition. Square (90°) knee angle during recovery. Handle on top of the stretcher. The trunk has completed tilting forward to 25–30 degrees and is ready for the drive. Shoulders are low and stretched forward.

Ph2. Final Recovery. Heels are rising from the footboard and toes start pushing the stretcher, which leads to deceleration of the boat and legs / seat velocity decreasing. Then, the blade is squared and the handle is pushed away towards the stern and upwards. At the last moment (0.02–0.04s), the legs are 'catching' through the stretcher to create counter-movement of the blade into the water.

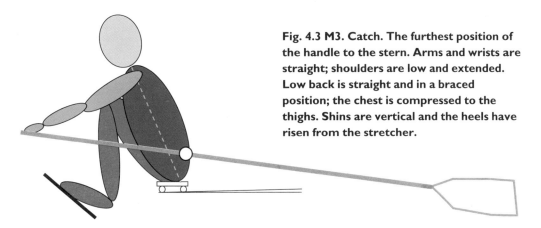

Fig. 4.3 M3. Catch. The furthest position of the handle to the stern. Arms and wrists are straight; shoulders are low and extended. Low back is straight and in a braced position; the chest is compressed to the thighs. Shins are vertical and the heels have risen from the stretcher.

Ph3. Blade entry. The blade sharply enters into the water with a small splash towards the stern, which is achieved by 'kicking' the stretcher through the toes, and the knees are extended by means of fast, but 'light' work of quads muscles.

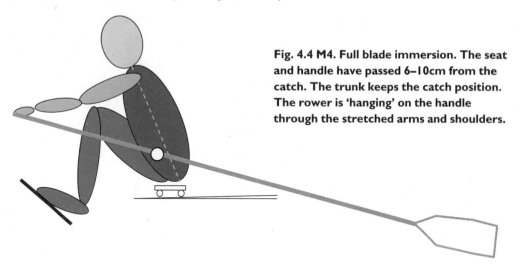

Fig. 4.4 M4. Full blade immersion. The seat and handle have passed 6–10cm from the catch. The trunk keeps the catch position. The rower is 'hanging' on the handle through the stretched arms and shoulders.

Ph4. Initial boat acceleration. The direction of blade movement becomes horizontal. The handle force quickly increases and the boat acceleration becomes positive. The rower's weight is lifting from the seat and suspending between handle and stretcher.

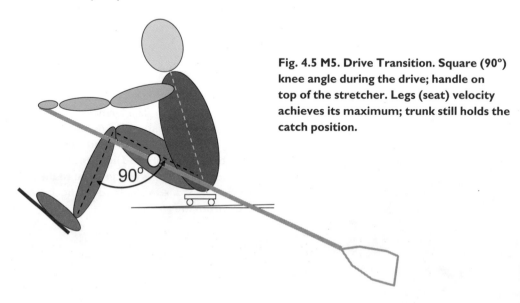

Fig. 4.5 M5. Drive Transition. Square (90°) knee angle during the drive; handle on top of the stretcher. Legs (seat) velocity achieves its maximum; trunk still holds the catch position.

Ph5. Rower's acceleration. Heels are placed onto the footboard and pushing it. The muscle activation is sharply switched from quads to glutes and hamstrings, from knees to hips extension, which 'opens' the trunk, pushes the knees down and 'automatically' extends it. The force and power achieve their maximums by use of the biggest muscles of the body. Acceleration of the rower's CM increases, but the boat acceleration decreases.

Fig. 4.6 M6. Middle of the drive. The oar is close to the perpendicular to the boat and the handle is on top of knees. Legs are nearly straight; trunk is vertical, shoulders and arms are beginning to pull.

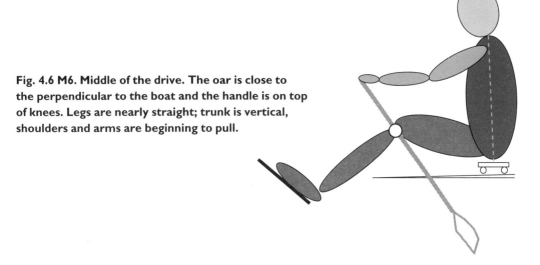

Ph6. Boat 'roll out'. The handle continues acceleration by means of a fast extension of the trunk as well as pulling with the shoulders and arms. Forces are decreasing, and the stretcher force decreases faster than the handle force, which causes significant boat acceleration.

Fig. 4.7 M7. Late drive. Legs are straight, trunk is close to its final position, handle has 5–7cm to travel (the less the better). Elbows are level with the handle. Upper edge of the blade surfaces.

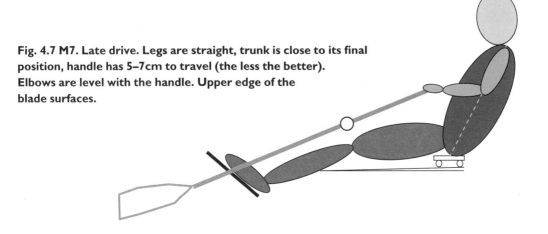

Ph7. Blade extraction. The stretcher force is sharply cut, but the arms continue a fast drive of the handle forward-down. This causes the trunk to begin return movement to the stern. The rower's weight is fully transferred onto the seat. The blades are quickly and cleanly extracted from the water.

Fig. 4.8 M8. Finish of the drive. The handle is in the furthest position towards the bow. Legs are straight, the trunk angle is 20–25°. In sweep rowing the outer hand 'brushes' the trunk.

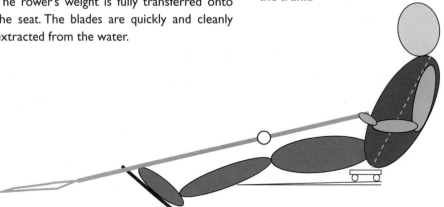

Ph8. Early recovery. The handle starts moving towards the stern and the blade is feathered. The hands, arms and shoulders are smoothly extending and 'follow' the handle. Then, the pelvis and trunk together are 'pivoting' around flexing hips.

M1 Cycle End / start of the next one (see Fig. 4.1).

The most important phases and moments are explained below in more detail.

4.1.1 Catch

Here, the definition of the catch is extended to a period of time immediately before and after the moment when the oar movement changes its direction at the furthest position of the handle to the stern. During this time, the blade should quickly finish the recovery and accelerate to drive velocity, which overcomes the boat speed and produces propulsion. The most common questions about the catch are:

■ What should be the main target of the rower's efforts at the catch?

■ What is the most efficient coordination between pulling the handle and pushing the stretcher at the catch?

The catch can be modelled in two ways (Fig. 4.9):

1. **'Catch through the handle'** – changing direction by means of pulling the handle and leaving the pin as a fulcrum. This is the most traditional understanding of the catch.
2. **'Catch through the stretcher'** – changing direction by means of pushing the stretcher and holding the handle as an artificial 'fulcrum'. The power is transferred through the stretcher – boat – rigger – pin – swivel, pushes the oar sleeve and accelerates the blade. Obviously, the handle is always mobile and, theoretically, cannot be considered as a real fulcrum (stationary centre of rotation). The sense of this model is only practical coaching, the most effective emphasis of the rower's efforts at the catch. The handle in this case could be considered as an artificial 'fulcrum', which is stationary relative to the rower in the

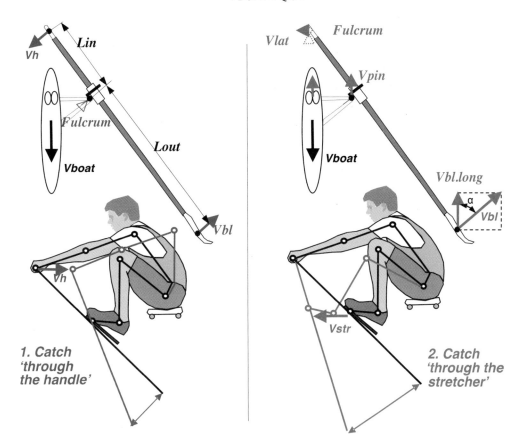

Fig. 4.9 Schematics of two methods of implementing the catch.

longitudinal direction but moves in the lateral direction.

Using the simplest flat model in the frontal and horizontal (transverse) planes, in the first case of 'catch through the handle', the blade velocity Vbl could be defined as:

$$Vbl = Vh \, (Lout \, / \, Lin) \qquad (80)$$

where Vh – handle velocity relative to the stretcher, $Lout$ – active outboard length, Lin – active inboard length.

In the second case of 'catch through the stretcher', Vbl is:

$$Vbl = Vstr \, ((Lout + Lin) \, / \, Lin) \qquad (81)$$

where $Vstr$ – stretcher velocity relative to the handle. In fact, Vh and $Vstr$ are the same velocities between the stretcher and handle so, if they are modelled as equal, the second method of 'catch through the stretcher' would produce *46 per cent higher blade speed* Vbl (at a common gearing, say, at an oar length of 2.88m and inboard length of 0.88m).

The difference in the ratio of handle and blade velocities is not the only advantage of the 'catch through the stretcher' technique. It also benefits by utilization of the most power-ful leg muscles (see Chapter 3.1.2), engage-ment of the 'trampoline' effect (see Chapter 3.2.5) and effective acceleration of the rower's centre of mass (see Chapter 2.5.3).

Therefore verbal coaching expressions like:

'pull the handle at the catch before the stretcher push to prevent disturbing the boat run' should not be considered as effective. Instead, a rower should concentrate on a fast kick on the stretcher, while holding the handle ('hanging on the handle') in the longitudinal direction and allowing its movement in the lateral direction.

4.1.2 Case study: Catch 'through the Stretcher'

Experimental data was obtained from two single scullers at 36 str / min (Fig. 4.10). Sculler 1 (Olympic medallist) changes the direction of the seat movement (1) 0.26s before the handle changes its direction (catch), so at the catch his seat is already moving to the bow at a speed of ∼ 0.4m / s. Sculler 2 (Olympic B finalist) changes the direction of the seat (2) practically at the same time as the handle (only 0.003s before) and his seat achieves a speed of only 0.06m / s at the catch. Instead of his legs, Sculler 2 uses his trunk (3) after the catch.

The maximal leg speed during the drive (Fig. 4.11, point 1) was very similar in these two scullers (1.22 and 1.20m / s), but was achieved much earlier by Sculler 1. Also, he had much faster approach to the catch: his maximal leg speed during recovery was − 1.95m / s (2) compared to − 1.68m / s in Sculler 2. Therefore, boat 1 receives a much higher acceleration during recovery (3) and achieves higher maximal velocity before the catch (4).

The negative peak of the boat acceleration was deeper in Sculler 1, occured earlier and coincided with the catch (5), which is related to an earlier 'kick' to the stretcher to change the direction of the seat movement. Sculler 2 has a later and shallower negative peak (6). The boat speed 1 at the catch was relatively slower, which helps to make changing the direction of the oar movement easier and insertion of the blade into the water earlier (7) without a back splash.

Acceleration of the rower's mass was also earlier and higher in Sculler 1 (8), which meant his CM moved much faster after the catch (9). This helped Sculler 1 to increase the force much more quickly (10): it grew up to 70 per cent of the maximum in just 10 degrees of oar travel, while it took more than 16 degrees for Sculler 2. This force was then transferred through the gate to the boat and created the first peak in the boat's acceleration (11), which rapidly increased the boat velocity (12) and

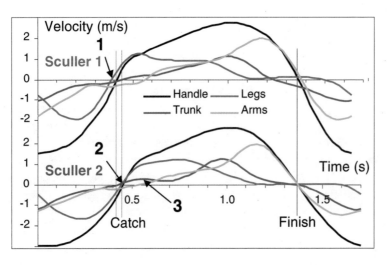

Fig. 4.10 Handle and body segment velocities of two single scullers at 36 str / min.

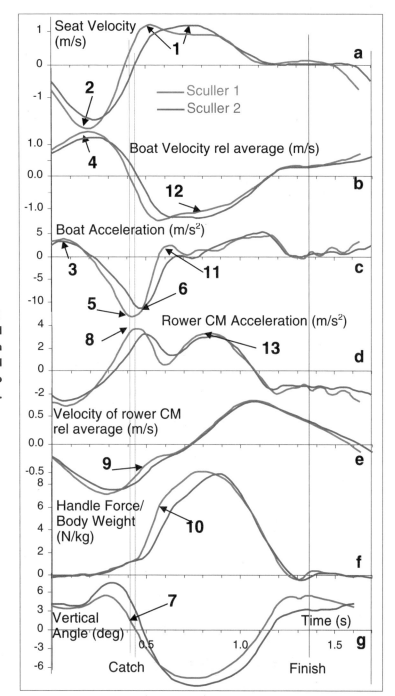

Fig. 4.11
Superimposed
data of the main
biomechanical
variables for two
scullers.

is called the 'trampoline effect' (see Chapter 3.2.5).

The rower's 'main acceleration' was also more significant in Sculler 1 (13). His leg velocity was slower during this sub-phase. This caused the accumulation of more kinetic energy in Sculler 1's mass (737J), even though he was lighter (95kg) than Sculler 2 (660J and 100kg mass). As a result, Sculler 1 produced 10.5 per cent more power and his boat speed was 3.9 per cent faster. This was despite the weather conditions being worse.

Conclusion: the 'catch through the stretcher' technique has the following positive features:

- *The rower approaches the catch faster and then has earlier and sharper 'bounces' from the stretcher, which makes the catch and blade insertion more effective.*
- *The rower's mass accelerates earlier and more effectively, which causes a quicker force growth using the most powerful muscle groups.*

4.1.3 Blade Entry

During the catch (in its extended definition) and immediately after it, the blade must be accelerated downwards to enter the water. Gravitational acceleration is not enough to insert the blade quickly enough, though some coaches believe that the rowers should just take the weight of the arms off the handle and 'let the blade go' into the water.

The free-falling angular acceleration of a standard sculling oar (2.90 / 0.88m, centre of mass (CM) at 1.42m from the handle top) was found about 240° / s², and for a sweep oar (3.77 / 1.15m, CM at 1.80m) it was 200° / s². At the catch the oar has to change its vertical angle from + 5 degrees (positive indicates the centre of the blade above water level) down to − 5 degrees; that is, it has to travel about 10 degrees. At free-falling angular acceleration this would take about 0.3s, which is nearly one third of the drive time. In our measurements, the best athletes achieve the peak vertical oar accelerations of more than 400° / s². This means they apply an upward vertical force to the handle, increasing the acceleration to nearly double that of gravity.

Using only free-fall acceleration at the catch nearly doubles the vertical catch slip (see Chapter 2.3.2). This increases the slippage of the blade in the water, decreases the blade propulsive efficiency and creates energy losses. To achieve effective blade entry, rowers have to apply quite a significant upward kick to the handle before the catch.

The maximal vertical acceleration at the catch is highly dependent on the stroke rate (Fig. 4.12). On average, the vertical acceleration exceeds the free-fall value at stroke rates higher than 30str / min. This means rowers

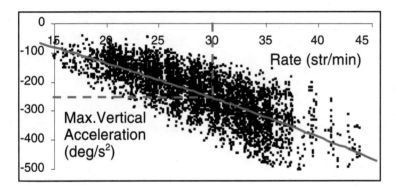

Fig. 4.12 Statistical dependence of vertical oar acceleration on stroke rate (n = 5222, r = − 0.76).

Table 4.1 Normative data for blade work.					
Catch Slip (deg)					
	Very Good	Good	Average	Bad	Very Bad
Sweep	6.9	10.1	13.4	16.6	19.8
Scull	4.3	7.1	9.9	12.7	15.5
Release Slip (deg)					
Sweep	3.6	9.0	14.3	19.7	25.1
Scull	7.7	13.2	18.7	24.2	29.7
Effective Angle (per cent) = (Total Angle) − Slips					
Sweep	82.5 per cent	75.4 per cent	68.3 per cent	61.3 per cent	54.2 per cent
Scull	86.3 per cent	79.7 per cent	73.0 per cent	66.4 per cent	59.7 per cent

can 'let the blade go' at a low rate, but have to apply upward force at a higher rate. Usually rowers can't compensate for a higher speed of horizontal movement of the oar at a high rate with a faster vertical movement. Evidence of this fact is the positive correlation of the stroke rate with the catch slip ($r = 0.24$) and release slip ($r = 0.38$). Statistics revealed the catch slip is shorter in scullers, but the release slip is shorter in sweep rowers (Table 4.1).

An upward force should be applied to the handle to achieve adequate vertical acceleration of the oar. This handle force F can be defined through its moment M and lever L relative to the centre of rotation (oarlock), where M is related to the angular acceleration ω and moment of inertia of the oar I by:

$$F = M / L = I \omega / L \qquad (82)$$

The moment of inertia I was determined experimentally as 3.2kg.m for a standard scull and 6.6kg.m for a sweep oar. Lever L was taken as the common inboard length of 0.88m for a scull oar and 1.15m for a sweep oar. From Equation 82, a sculler needs to apply upward force of 10N (in addition to gravity) at each handle to achieve the oar acceleration of $400° / s^2$ required for effective blade entry. A rower needs to apply twice that force, 20N, for the same acceleration.

The following practical methods can be used to achieve fast vertical acceleration at blade entry. Before the catch the blade should not be raised too high, which is called 'skying the blade'. It was found that the catch slip had a positive correlation ($r = 0.21$) with the highest vertical oar angle before the catch.

The most complicated coordination is combining the vertical push upwards with squaring the oar. It is much easier to separate these two movements and to do the squaring first and then to place the blade into the water. This method should be recommended for beginners and young rowers. However, early squaring dramatically increases the aerodynamic resistance of the blade (see 4.1.8). Also, rough water conditions do not allow early squaring. Therefore, elite rowers very often practise a combination of squaring

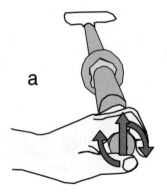

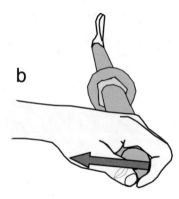

Fig. 4.13 Using the thumb at the blade entry.

with simultaneous upward acceleration of the handle.

Effective use of the thumb is important in sculling, where it also has to push the handle outwards to keep the oar button in contact with the swivel. So the thumb should be placed at the outer-bottom edge of the grip and hold it with the base of the distal phalange (Fig. 4.13). During recovery, the thumb controls the vertical position of the handle and pushes it forward. Before the catch the thumb quickly switches to kicking upwards in combination with bending backwards (Fig. 4.13b), which allows a quick squaring of the oar followed immediately by placing it in the water. This upward kick must be very quick, otherwise the blade would be inserted too deeply into the water, which is not effective.

The simplest drill for better blade entry is a short stroke movement at the catch position targeting the shortest possible slip of the blade. As the ratio of handle to boat speed is lowest at long angles (see Chapter 6.2.1), rowers can practise a good catch quite comfortably. It is more difficult to achieve a good catch at shorter angles, when the oar is close to perpendicular to the boat. So the vertical kick at the catch must be emphasized during the 'arms-only' and 'quarter-slide' drills.

4.1.4 Rowing Styles and Sequence of Body Segments

The most popular classification of rowing styles was introduced in 1977 by Klavora[25], who defined three rowing styles: the Adam style; the DDR style; the Rosenberg style:

- *Adam* – Comparatively long leg drive and limited amplitude of the trunk. Simultaneous activity of legs and trunk during the stroke;
- *DDR* – Large, forward declination of the trunk, which begins the drive, followed by simultaneous activity of the legs;
- *Rosenberg* – Large, forward declination of the trunk at the beginning of the stroke, then strong leg extension without significant trunk activation. At the end of the cycle the trunk stops in the deep backward position.

Definition of these styles was made based on the sequence of the two biggest body segments, legs and trunk, their simultaneous or consequent activation, as well as on their amplitude and emphasis in power production. These two factors can be presented as a quadrant, where the X axis represents the sequence and the Y axis the emphasis on the legs or trunk (Fig. 4.14).

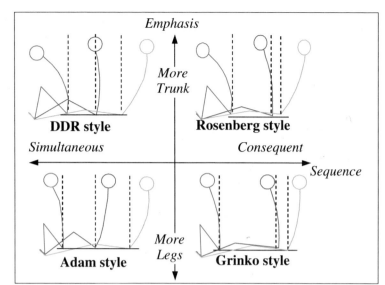

Fig. 4.14 Quadrant of rowing styles.

It was found that the three styles correspond to three quarters of the quadrant, but the bottom-right corner was empty. It was hypothesized that there should be a fourth rowing style with consequent timing and emphasis on the leg drive. It was found that this style was practised by talented Russian coach Igor Grinko. Grinko coached many world champion scullers in the USSR, USA and China. One of them was world champion and silver Olympic medallist in M1x Jueri Jaanson. Positive feedback was received from Igor Grinko in regard to this rowing style classification. He said: 'I remember when my guys won the first gold medals in 4 × in 1986–87, the coaches' comments were: "I don't understand how they could win with this technique". However, a few years later coaches understood this style better and tried to copy it. Three times Olympic champion in single scull Viacheslav Ivanov told me in 1987 that he likes the style I was teaching. He said that it is very close to what he thinks about good rowing technique.'

Pure examples of these styles cannot be seen very often. Most rowers have a style

somewhere in between these four extremes. Force curve and rowing style (segments sequence) are not functionally related; with any rowing style it is possible to increase force quicker or slower, achieve peak force earlier or later. Therefore, the models below have observational background rather than strict experimental verification.

The total power (product of force and velocity) was modelled as a sum of segment powers (Fig. 4.15). The following characteristics of rowing styles could be identified:

Simultaneous work of the legs and trunk (both DDR and Adam styles) produces a more rectangular shape of the power curve, but the peak power is lower than in the other styles. More even pressure on the blade may improve its propulsive efficiency. However, slower and more static movement of the legs and trunk does not allow the delivery of the optimal power.

Sequential work of the legs and trunk (Rosenberg and Grinko styles) produces a triangular shape of the power curves with higher peaks of force and power curves.

Emphasis on the legs or trunk affects the

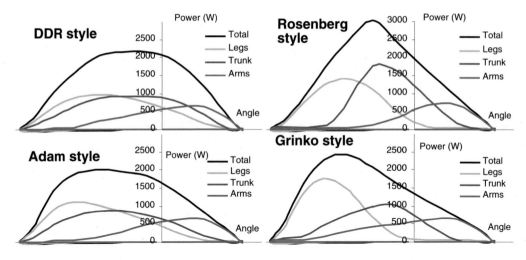

Fig. 4.15 Modelling of power curves in four rowing styles.

position of the force and power peaks. Styles with leg emphasis (Adam and Grinko styles) allow a quicker increase of the force and earlier peak of the force curve. This improves the initial boat acceleration sub-phase D3 (*see* Chapter 3.2.2) and makes the drive timing more effective.

Styles with trunk emphasis (Rosenberg and DDR styles) produce more power owing to better utilization of big muscle groups (*gluteus* and *longissimus* muscles). These muscles are quite slow by nature as they are intended to maintain body posture in humans, so the force and power usually increase more slowly in these styles. However, rowers with these styles have to pay a significant price for higher power production: large amplitude of heavy trunk mass increases inertial losses and creates more significant hull oscillations, which increases drag resistance.

The above classification of rowing styles was made in the 1970s when a very high diversity in techniques was observed at inter-national regattas. These days we still can see in some rowers the distinctive features of the four styles classified above (Fig. 4.16). However, most winning crews use styles

somewhere in between these four types, so it is possible to describe their convergence into something which could be called 'modern international rowing style'[45].

4.1.5 Case study: Consecutive and Simultaneous Rowing Styles.

Experimental data was obtained at 36 str / min from two male single scullers (Fig. 4.17), whose styles could be defined as consecutive (a) and simultaneous (b).

At the beginning of the drive, sculler a has an emphasis on the legs extension and stretcher push (1), while the simultaneous style of sculler b utilizes more upper body work and handle pull (2). The handle force grows similarly for the two scullers up to 50 per cent of the maximum force level (3), but then the slope of the force curve becomes much flatter for sculler b, which coincides with decreasing of his trunk velocity (4). As a result, sculler a achieves a much earlier peak force (5), which makes his style more effective (see Chapter 3.2.4). This was a quite typical example with a similar correlation of the

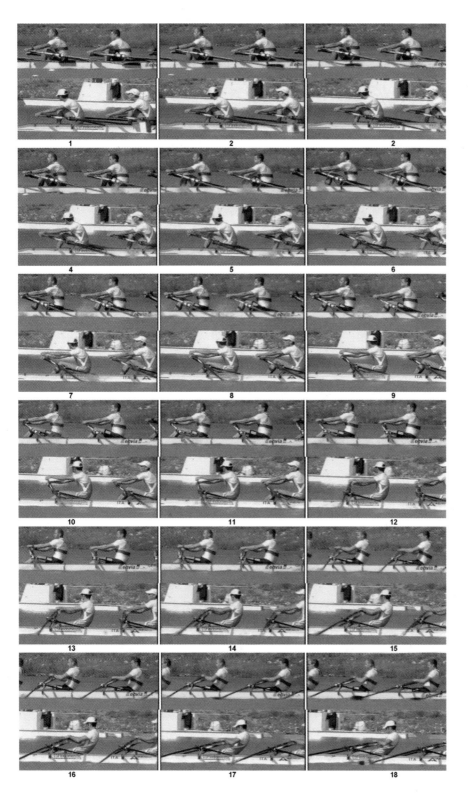

Fig. 4.16 Examples of the simultaneous and consecutive rowing styles in two boats – both world champions, 2003: Top: simultaneous style, M4x GER; Bottom: consecutive style, LM2x ITA.

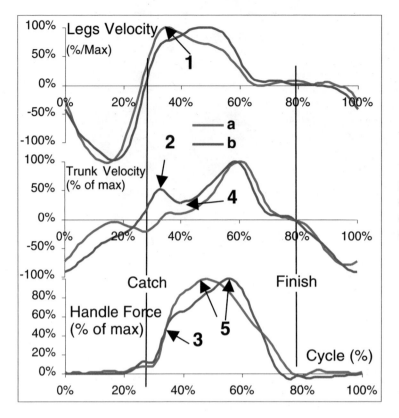

Fig. 4.17 Experimental data of consecutive (a) and simultaneous (b) rowing styles.

rowing style and force curve found in many other rowers.

4.1.7 Body Segments Work

With the BioRowTel system, the movements of the seat and the top of the trunk can be measured with string transducers in singles, doubles and pairs (the seat is only measured in big boats). For the trunk measurements, the sensor is mounted on a mast (Fig. 4.18) and a string is connected to the trunk at the level of the clavicle-sternum joint (between C7–T1 vertebrae), so it measures movement of the spine but not the shoulders. Therefore movement of the shoulders was included with the arms and called simply 'arms' for conciseness.

The legs' amplitude and velocity V_{legs} was assumed to be equal to the seat movement. Trunk velocity V_{trunk} was derived as the difference between the top of the trunk V_{tt} and seat velocities. 'Arms' velocity V_{arms} was derived as the difference between handle velocity V_h and V_{tt}. The handle velocity V_h was derived from oar angular velocity ω and actual inboard length $L_{in.a}$ (see Chapter 2.3.1):

$$V_{h\,s}\,\omega\,L_{in.a} \tag{83}$$

Statistical analysis (n = 5437) reveals that all three body segments contribute nearly equally to the stroke length, about one third each: legs 33 per cent, trunk 31 per cent and arms 36 per cent. However, most of the leg and trunk movements occur during the first two-thirds of the drive, when forces are high,

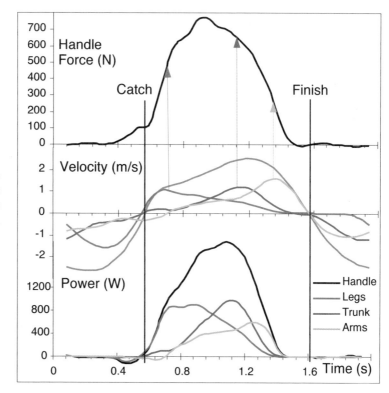

Fig. 4.18 Measurement of the trunk position with the BioRowTel system.

Fig. 4.19 Force curve, body segments velocities and powers in M1x at 32 str / min.

whereas work by the arms is mainly at the finish and at low forces (Fig. 4.19). Therefore, the average shares of the total power production were higher for legs (43 per cent) and trunk (33 per cent), and lower for arms (24 per cent). This depends on rowing style and shape of the force curve (see Chapter 2.5.2): consequent segments activation and front-loaded drive increases the legs' share; simultaneous style and late peak force increases the arms' (with shoulders) share. The first style is more effective, as it was proved that the

Fig. 4.20 Measurement of the trunk angle using video analysis.

bigger muscles of the legs and trunk are more efficient and powerful. Therefore, *the segment's power of the world's best rowers have a higher trunk share and less arms: legs 43 per cent, trunk 36 per cent, arms 21 per cent.*

The above instrumented measurements were related to joints angles, which were analysed using video. From footage of the twenty-five best rowers in small boats during the World Championship, 2014, in Amsterdam, trunk angles were analysed relative to the vertical axis at the catch α_1 and finish α_2 (Fig. 4.20).

It was found that the average trunk angle at the catch α_1 was 22.5° ($\pm$ 4.6, min 12°, max 31°) and α_2 at finish was 25° ($\pm$ 6.2, min 8°, max 35°), so the total angular displacement of the trunk was on average 47.5° ($\pm$ 6.5, min 32°, max 60°). Assuming the length of the trunk from hips to shoulders (C7–T1) is about 0.6m gives us 0.50m linear displacement at the top of the trunk, which corresponds to about one third of the average stroke length 1.52m measured with telemetry, so a good agreement of two methods was found.

Longer amplitude of the trunk movement allows better utilization of glutes and hamstrings, the two biggest and strongest muscle groups, which helps to increase power production. However, it creates significant movement of the heavy trunk mass, increases inertial losses and vertical oscillations of the boat (see Chapter 2.5.4), and therefore the drag resistance. Therefore, *the trunk amplitude must be optimal. The average numbers of the world's best rowers ($\pm$ 25 degrees from the vertical) could be a good guidance.*

4.1.7 Finish

During the finish of the drive, the movement of rower's mass towards the bow should decelerate and then accelerate towards the stern of the boat. The finish may be performed in two ways: by means of pulling through the stretcher (1), or through the handle (2).

Some coaches believe that the first method is more efficient because it requires less effort when the force is transferred through straight legs. They argue that in the second case the inertia force goes through bent arms that require some muscle energy.

The following five arguments can be presented in favour of the finish through the handle (*FH*), and none were found in favour of finish through the stretcher (*FS*).

Fig. 4.21 Schematics of forces at the finish.

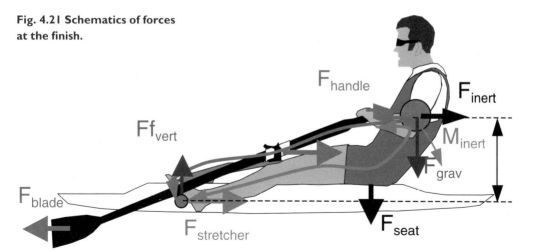

1. *FH* creates a propulsive force on the blade (Fig. 4.21), which is the only external force moving forward the whole rower-boat system. *FS* works as an internal transfer of kinetic energy from rower to boat and does not create any external propulsive force. Moreover, if the blade is still in the water, pulling the stretcher creates braking force and slows down the rower-boat system, which is familiar to rowers when paddling backwards.

2. *FH* does not push the boat down. At the finish, the legs are practically stationary relative to the boat, and the upper body moves pivoting around the hips, so its higher parts have a greater velocity. The centre of inertia (imaginary point where resultant inertia force is applied) is located about 2/3 of trunk height; that is, the centre of a moving rower's mass is very close to the level of the handle. Therefore, with *FH* action and reaction forces act nearly in one line and do not create a rotating moment. In comparison, the stretcher force acts at a significant vertical distance *H* from the centre of trunk inertia. This creates a torque $M_{str} = F_{inert} \times H$, which must be balanced with the seat force and could increase it

up to 140–150 per cent of the rower's body weight (*see* Chapter 2.5.4). The extra vertical force pushes the boat down and increases its water displacement and drag resistance force. Another contributor to the seat force is the moment of the weight of the trunk. At *FS* this force is balanced by an upward vertical force on the stretcher and this pair of forces increases the pitching movement of the boat and wave resistance of the shell.

3. *FH* works more efficiently using oar leverage. At *FS* the forces applied to the rower and boat CM are equal:

$$F = m_{boat}\, a_{boat} = m_{rower}\, a_{rower} \qquad (84)$$

At *FH* the force acting on the boat is:

$$F = m_{boat}\, a_{boat} = m_{rower}\, a_{rower}\, (L_{oar} / L_{out})\, cos(\alpha) \qquad (85)$$

This creates 25–15 per cent higher boat acceleration at the common oar angles $\alpha = 30$–$40°$ at the finish.

4. *FH* allows earlier relaxation of the leg muscles (quads) and better recovery of these muscles working hard during the

drive. The *quadriceps* are two-joint muscles, which are connected to the shins and pelvis and go across the knee and hip joints. At *FS* these muscles must be used in static mode to prevent the knee from bending and flexing the trunk.

5. *FH* has less risk of injury to the hip, stomach muscles and tendons, which can be overloaded at fast *FS* at a high stroke rate.

Conclusion: the only effective rowing technique at the finish is returning the trunk by means of pulling the handle.

The drill for developing the finish using the handle is quite simple: rowing with the feet out of the stretcher shoes. It should be practised at different stroke rates, and the stretcher push during the drive should not

be compromised. The rower should push the stretcher as long as possible during the drive and then perform quick counter-movements with the arms providing an impulse to the trunk for recovery.

4.1.8 Body Segments During Recovery

It was very often found that the sequence and velocities of the segments on recovery mirrors the sequence on the drive. The plot of the segments' velocities relative to oar angle (Fig. 4.22) show that the curves look like mirror images relative to the X axis, where the negative part (recovery) resembles the positive part (drive).

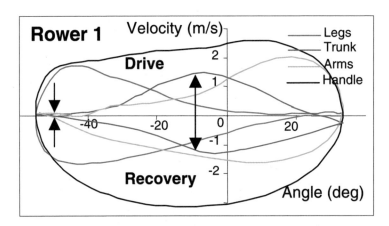

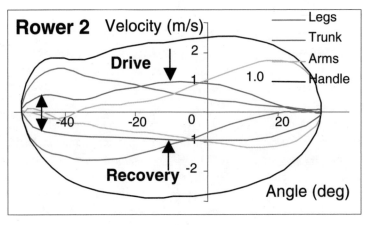

Fig. 4.22 Examples of the mirror sequence of body segments on recovery.

Rower 1 prepares his trunk earlier during recovery and approaches the catch with legs only. The trunk is ready for the drive and its velocity is close to zero. Naturally, this rower has a fast legs drive after the catch and an increased trunk velocity later, during the second quarter of the drive. This 'consequent' rowing style (see 4.1.4) produces higher relative maximal force and power.

Rower 2 spreads his trunk velocity across the recovery and continues its movement until the last moment before the catch. As a result, this rower 'opens the body' early during the drive and spreads its movement across the drive. This 'simultaneous' rowing style produces lower maximal force and power, but the shape of the force curve is more rectangular.

There are no mechanical reasons for these phenomena, and, of course, a rower could practise different sequences during the drive and recovery, if it were specifically targeted. However, observations show that this regularity is very consistent and exceptions are very rare. Probably, the explanation is based on neural motor control principles, which is not clear yet.

A simple practical application of this principle could be the following: for achieving a certain sequence of the segments during the drive (legs-trunk-arms), the mirror sequence should be practised during recovery (arms-trunk-legs). The trunk should have quite a

fast distinctive movement at the middle of recovery ('pivoting around hips') and archive its catch angle at the position of the handle on top of the stretcher and at square knee angle (moment M2, see 4.1). After this point the trunk should be completely prepared for the drive and its angle should stay unchanged and only the legs continue its movement to the catch.

4.1.9 Blade Squaring During Recovery

During recovery, the technique of the blade squaring / feathering is important. The blade moves in the air with a speed of up to 14 m / s (50 km / h), which is the sum of the boat velocity (it has the highest value during recovery and could be up to 7 m / s in M8 +) and the handle velocity (up to 3 m / s) multiplied by a gearing ratio 2.3–2.4. The air drag of the blade is very significant because it increases with the square of the speed. If a rower squares the blade early during recovery, it increases the area affected by wind, which creates extra loss of the boat speed (Fig. 4.23).

Conclusion: If the blade is squared early, at the middle of recovery, a crew can lose up to 10 s over a 2km race in calm conditions and up to 30 s with a headwind of 5 m / s.

Fig. 4.23 Speed losses at various shares of recovery passed with squared blades.

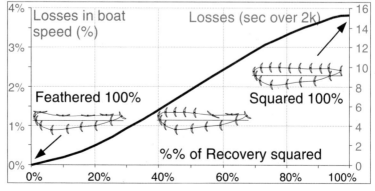

4.2 CREW SYNCHRONIZATION

4.2.1 Definition

For a number of reasons, time synchronization of rowers' movements and force application is a very important condition for effective rowing. The rowers in a crew are mechanically connected to each other through the stretcher and boat hull. The importance of synchronization can be illustrated using the concept of 'the trampoline effect' (see Chapter 3.2.5), which explains the summation of accelerations of the boat and rowers' mass. Imagine two jumpers hit the same trampoline board at different times: when it recoils to accelerate the first jumper, the second one arrives. Acceleration of the

board would be stopped by impact of the second jumper and the first one couldn't jump high. The second jumper would receive a jolt from the board, which moves fast towards his feet, and he could be injured. Therefore, rowers have to move and apply forces synchronously, otherwise the effectiveness of the crew would be diminished.

The simplest method to measure synchronization is to check the time of catch and finish, when the oar changes direction of movement. This could be done with frame-by-frame video analysis (high-speed video is recommended for accuracy) or, better, with biomechanical equipment (telemetry system). A detailed method of quantitative evaluation of the synchronization in a crew is based on velocities of the handle and seat, handle force and vertical oar angle, which is illustrated in Fig. 4.24.

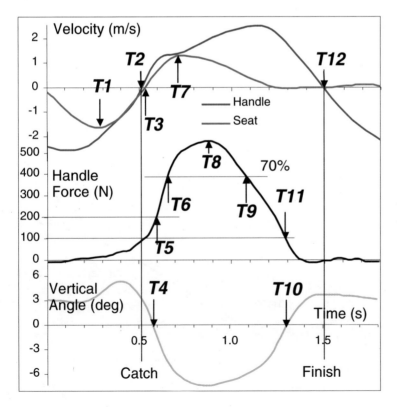

Fig. 4.24 Definition of the synchronization criteria.

Twelve key moments of the cycle were defined:

T1. *Peak seat velocity* (negative) during recovery, when the rower is switching from pulling the stretcher to pushing it;

T2. *Catch* – Zero handle velocity, when the oar changes direction from recovery to drive;

T3. *Zero seat velocity* at the catch, when the seat changes direction;

T4. *Zero vertical angle* at the catch, when the centre of the blade crosses the water level;

T5. *Entry Force* 200N at catch (sum of left and right forces in sculling), when the blade grips the water. The threshold was chosen to distinguish force in the water from oar inertia force;

T6. *Force up to 70 per cent*, which indicates engagement of large muscle groups;

T7. *Peak seat velocity* during the drive, which indicates acceleration of rower's mass;

T8. *Peak Force* – emphasis of efforts;

T9. *Force down below 70 per cent* shows maintenance of the force during the second half of the drive;

T10. *Zero vertical angle* at the finish shows 'washing out' of the blade;

T11. *Exit force* 100N (sum in sculling) at the finish – end of the propulsive phase;

T12. *Finish* – Zero handle velocity, the oar changes direction from drive to recovery.

For evaluation of synchronization, the time differences from the stroke rower at each of these twelve moments were derived for each member of the crew. Then, the following values were calculated:

1. Average difference of all rowers from the stroke. This value could be zero if some rowers overtake the stroke (negative dif-ference) and others are late (positive difference). Therefore, this value could be used only for defining a direction of general trend in a crew.

2. Standard deviation SD of the differences defines magnitude of synchronization, but not direction (it is always positive) and should be used as a primary measure of synchronization. For simplicity, it can be assumed that synchronization of all rowers in a crew lies within the range ± 3SD.

The data was collected for eights (Table 4.2) and divided into three groups:

J – Junior rowers in clubs, schools and universities (n = 338 boat samples at various stroke rates);
B – Seniors B, adult rowers of national level (n = 161);
A – Seniors A of international level (n = 170).

As expected, general synchronization in seniors A eights was better (average SD for 12 moments was 46.2ms), than in B group (61.4ms) and in Juniors (55.9ms). The average direction was close to 0 in A and negative in B and Juniors but in all moments around the catch, T1–T5, it was negative in all groups. This means that rowers, in general, tend to overtake the stroke. It was found that the *synchronizations at the catch and finish are significantly better at higher stroke rates*: average SD of T2 and T12 decreases from 25–30ms at 20 str / min down to 10–15ms at 40 str / min (correlation r = − 0.46 and r = − 0.42).

4.2.2 Case Study on Synchronization

The data obtained with the BioRow telemetry system (Fig. 4.25) illustrates the importance of synchronization. Two junior quads (A and B) were measured at 33.5–34 str / min, where

Moment	Sen.A	± SD	Sen.B	± SD	Jun.	± SD
T1	− 9.8	62.5	− 17.2	34.3	− 11.2	41.6
T2	− 13.8	15.2	− 2.7	17.0	− 12.9	20.2
T3	− 14.3	55.3	− 11.6	21.4	− 13.2	27.7
T4	− 0.1	34.4	− 1.5	38.9	− 23.2	44.0
T5	− 4.9	18.1	− 0.9	42.6	− 0.3	31.7
T6	6.0	33.3	2.1	67.4	6.4	46.6
T7	11.3	71.6	− 4.5	47.6	− 4.9	58.5
T8	16.4	51.6	− 9.3	85.8	− 3.4	67.9
T9	4.1	39.8	− 4.5	77.4	− 1.2	51.7
T10	5.9	131.5	− 21.3	216.4	− 52.0	219.4
T11	2.7	23.6	− 9.1	65.4	− 11.2	36.3
T12	5.2	17.6	6.5	22.2	− 4.9	25.3
Average	0.7	46.2	-6.2	61.4	− 11.0	55.9

Table 4.2 Average direction and magnitude of synchronization in these three groups in ms (1 ms = 0.001s).

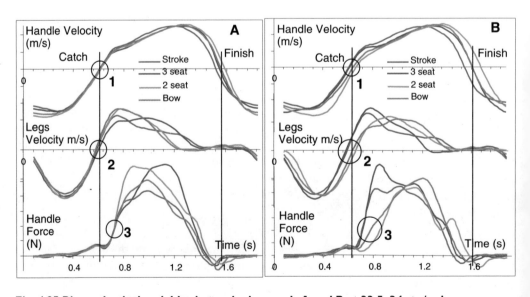

Fig. 4.25 Biomechanical variables in two junior quads A and B at 33.5–34 str / min.

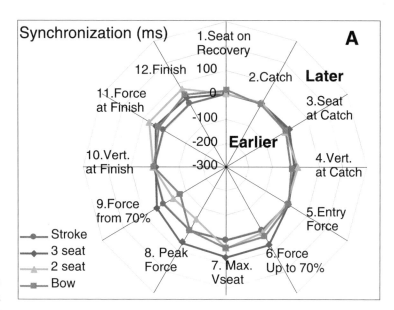

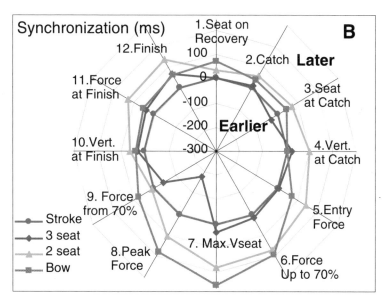

Fig. 4.26
Synchronization data in two junior quads A and B presented as radar charts.

crew A had much better synchronization at the catch in the handle (1) and seat (2) movements, and in the force increase after the catch (3).

An effective presentation of synchronization data is a radar chart (Equation 3), where 12 axes indicate corresponding criteria moments. As the synchronization is defined as the time lag (in milliseconds) relative to the stroke rower, his data is always zero and presented as a perfect red circle on the charts. Negative values are located inside the red circle and indicate earlier timing, overtaking the stroke. Positive values are outside the red circle and indicate later than the stroke.

	Criteria	Crew A	Crew B	Correlation with DF
Table 4.3 Magnitude of synchronization in two quads, ms, and their correlations with DF.				
T1	Seat on Recovery	20.4	36.1	0.60
T2	Catch	5.9	25.7	0.64
T3	Seat at Catch	11.7	41.4	0.65
T4	Vert. at Catch	23.1	50.2	-0.25
T5	Entry Force	4.7	69.7	0.42
T6	Force up to 70 per cent	66.4	95.1	0.52
T7	Max.Vseat	101.9	110.3	0.31
T8	Peak Force	123.9	191.0	0.31
T9	Force from 70 per cent	58.1	57.9	0.38
T10	Vert. at Finish	4.6	17.0	0.48
T11	Force at Finish	22.5	47.0	0.36
T12	Finish	20.8	41.0	0.27
	Average	38.7	65.2	0.60

Three of the rowers were the same in both crews; only one athlete was replaced and the other two changed seats. However, *the speed in crew A with better synchronization was 2.1 per cent faster (7s over 2km) with the same weather and water conditions,* even though their total power was slightly lower. Therefore, the calculated drag factor DF (Equation 3) was lower in crew A, which is related to lower internal energy losses due to better synchronization.

Table 4.3 shows the magnitude of synchronization (standard deviation of time lags of three crew members, excluding the stroke) for twelve criteria in these two crews and their correlations with DF (based on 16 data samples at constant weather and various stroke rates in these two crews). On average, crew A had more than twice better synchronization: its magnitude was 38.7ms compare to 65.2ms in crew B. The most important criteria (the highest correlation with DF) were even better in crew A: at the catch, they had more than four times better handle synchronization (5.9 and 25.7ms), their seat changed direction nearly four times more synchronously (11.7 and 41.4ms), and forces achieved at their entry level were nearly twelve times better together (4.7 and 69.7ms).

The correlation between DF and average synchronization over the 12 points was found to be very high (r = 0.60). *This confirms the high importance of good synchronization in a crew for achieving the best result.*

4.2.3 How can Synchronization be Improved?

If a rower is consistently earlier or later than the stroke (average difference is significant, but SD is small), it can be improved with video or biomechanical feedback. (All the above criteria T1–T12 were recently included in BioRowTel reports.) If mistiming is inconsistent (direction is small, but SD is high), then the rower's feeling of the rhythm should be targeted, which could be improved through various means of real-time feedback, or pace-makers[38]. Quite an effective tool is synchronous rowing on ergs on slides, where the mobile frames of the ergs are connected to each other.

Synchronization at the catch depends completely on the skills of every crew member, and usually improves with experience of rowing together. Uniformity of the rhythm of movement of each rower during recovery is important. Every rower in a crew should pay special attention to the forces on the stretcher, which form a specific 'feeling' of the boat and other crew mates. Using drills could accelerate improvement[61].

Synchronization at the finish depends on that at the catch and the duration of the drive time Td. Theoretically, Td depends on the following factors:

- Longer angles, less force, deeper blade path, heavier gearing increase the duration of the drive time;
- Shorter angles, more force, shallower blade path, lighter gearing make the drive time shorter.

To analyse the effect of the above factors, absolute values should not be used because they are significantly affected by the variation in various boats and rowers' categories. Therefore, deviations of each variable from the average in a crew were analysed in the same data sample. It was found that the total oar angle and arc length has significant correlation ($r = 0.59$) with the drive time within a crew. Applied force and blade depth have shown very small and statistically insignificant correlations ($r = -0.09$) with deviation of the drive time in a crew. This means that *drive time is defined mainly by its length.*

The drive time Td can be related to the length of the arc L and average handle velocity $Vh.av.$ as:

$$Td = L / Vh.av. \tag{86}$$

The instantaneous handle velocity Vh depends on the gearing (ratio of the actual outboard $Lout$ to inboard Lin), boat velocity Vb, oar angle θ and velocity of blade slippage Vbl in the water.

$$Vh = (Lout / Lin)(Vb \cos(\theta) + Vbl) \tag{87}$$

Combining these equations and assuming the same boat speed Vb and very similar blade slippage Vbl in a crew, it can be concluded: *To achieve the same drive time, difference in the drive length can be compensated for by an inversely proportional difference in gearing ratio.* For example a 1 per cent shorter drive length (about 1 degree or 1.5cm), could be compensated for by a 1 per cent heavier gearing ratio (about 2cm longer outboard or 1cm shorter inboard) and vice versa. However, it could be better to work on the rowers' technique to achieve similar time and length of the drive.

4.2.4 Synchronization in Sweep Boats

In a pair, the measured force of the stroke rower is usually applied earlier at the catch, while the bow rower is pulling harder later at the finish (Fig. 4.27a). Empirically, it was

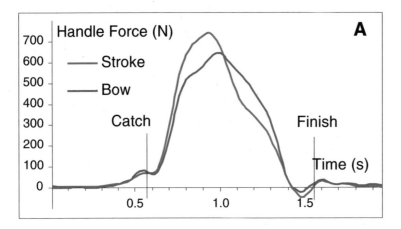

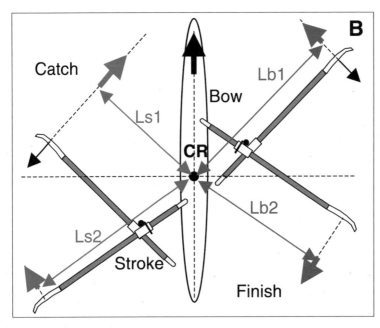

Fig. 4.27 Measured forces in Olympic champions pair (A), mechanics of torques applied to the boat hull in a pair (B).

found that this synchronization of efforts helps to keep the boat straight on the course and avoid wiggling. The reason for this phenomenon could be explained through different leverage of the blade forces in stroke and bow rowers. The blade force is the only external force produced by rowers. All other forces (on the handle, stretcher, pin and seat) are internal, so their torques applied to the boat hull should be balanced inside the system. Therefore, torques of the blade forces

relative to the geometrical centre of the hull (centre of rotation CR) were analysed (Fig. 4.27b).

The actual outboard (from pin to the middle of the blade) was used to calculate the blade force. The lever for the blade force is equal to the length of the perpendicular from the line of the blade force to the centre of the boat. At the catch, the bow has an advantage (Lb1 is longer than Ls1), so the stroke has to apply more force to produce the same

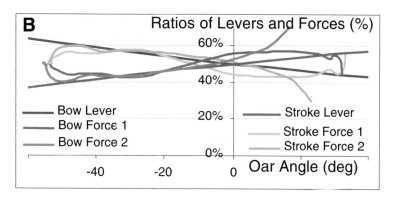

Fig. 4.28 Comparison of the ratios of the levers and forces in two pairs.

rotating moment. At the finish, the opposite is the case (Lb2 is shorter than Ls2).

As the catch angle is longer than the finish angle, the stroke has to produce a higher average force. At angles of 56 degrees at the catch and 34 degrees at the finish, the contribution made by the stroke must be 52.5 per cent and by the bow 47.5 per cent, that is a 5 per cent difference. Fig. 4.28 compares the ratios of calculated levers and forces measured in two international-level pairs (World Champions and Bronze medallists). The ratios of forces were very close to the inverse ratio of the levers, which helps to keep the boat straight on the course. The ratios of average forces were 51.5 : 48.5 per cent for the first crew and 52.1 : 47.9 per cent for the second, which is also close to the model.

What can be done to reduce the difference in the leverage? A longer spread / outboard could be used for the stroke rower. However, the difference must be very significant to make the ratio even (4cm difference in spread + 10cm in outboard makes the average leverage only 3 per cent different). Alternatively the same 3 per cent difference in leverage can be achieved if the bow rower moves his arc 5 degrees closer to the bow.

A similar model could be applied for analysis in bigger sweep boats: fours and eights. However, various positioning of crew members (rigging) in big sweep boats could

be considered in order to avoid a sideways wiggle at simultaneous force application. The levers of the blade forces were calculated for the most common range of oar angles from − 55 degrees at the catch to 35 degrees at the finish. In the four with traditional rigging the sum of the levers was found non-zero and equal to 0.47m (Fig. 4.29a), which turns the bow to the port side. In the Italian rigging (Fig. 4.29b), the sum was zero, so the boat should go straight for an equal application of force. Similarly, in the eight with normal rig the sum of the levers was found 0.93m. In the eights with the Italian and German rigs the sum was zero[7].

What sort of boat wiggle could be created by the above non-zero levers? The blade force Fbl was modelled as a typical front-loaded curve with maximum magnitude 350N (800N at the handle). The rotational torque T was calculated for each rower as:

$$T = Fbl * L \tag{88}$$

Where L is a lever calculated with the model above. This torque creates angular acceleration a

$$a = T / I \tag{89}$$

where I is the mass moment of inertia of the boat with rowers, which could be defined

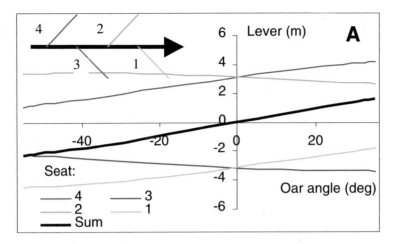

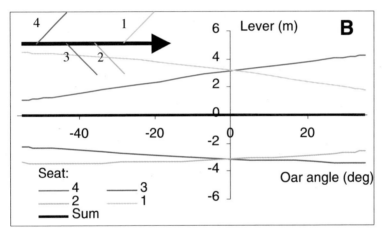

Fig. 4.29 Levers of the blade force in fours with the normal (A) and Italian (B) rigging (positive lever turns the boat towards the bow side, clockwise on the pictures, and vice versa).

approximately using the boat length and mass plus a product of rower's mass and the square of the distance between their CM from the centre of the boat (Table 4.4). The angular acceleration a was integrated twice and it was found that *each stroke with synchronous force application creates a boat yaw angle of 0.37 degrees in a pair, 0.076 degrees in a normally rigged four and 0.015 degrees in an eight.* This yaw must be compensated for by a side force applied by the fin and rudder, which creates the wiggle of the boat. In bigger boats the wiggle is smaller, which is explained by the square increase of the mass moment of inertia.

Table 4.4 Mass moments of inertia in various boat types (kg m^2).

	Boat	Rowers	Total
Pair	15	88	103
Four	243	882	1125
Eight	3360	7400	10760

How can rowers compensate for the wiggle? It was shown above that a pair could be kept straight if the stroke rower applies a 5 per cent higher average force. Similar modelling in big sweep boats revealed that this difference should be similar in fours and eights. Stroke-side rowers (closer to the stern, it doesn't matter which side) in both the four and eight should apply force earlier, so the average value should be about 5 per cent higher. *It is preferable to put the stronger stroke-side rowers closer to the bow* because these seats have the longest levers: 5 per cent higher force (at the same curve) of 2 seat of the eight makes the wiggle 10 per cent smaller, 4 seat, 7.5 per cent; 6 seat 5 per cent; and the stroke seat can make it only 2.5 per cent smaller.

Alternation of the oar length, inboard and span could have a very small effect on the wiggle. For example, in the normally rigged four the stroke side must have 55cm longer oars and proportionally 18cm longer inboard and span to compensate for the wiggle at the same forces.

Zero-moment rigging (Italian and similar) is the optimal solution for crews with rowers of similar strength. Boats with the normal rig can be kept straight if stronger rowers are placed on the stroke side closer to the bow.

4.3 ASYMMETRY IN SCULLING

Asymmetry in sculling is defined by the overlap of the scull handles, which is com-

monly set to 18–22 cm (Fig. 4.30). Overlap itself is defined by the inboard length and necessity to scull long angles of 100–120 degrees. At inboard 88cm, span 160cm and an overlap 20 cm (+ 4cm of swivel width), the distance between handles is about 100cm at catch angle 70 degrees and 30cm at finish angle 44 degrees. If the overlap was set to zero, then the above distances would be 20cm wider, which is too wide for a normal sculler.

If a sculler pulls the handles symmetrically in the horizontal plane, then the vertical distance between them at the middle of the drive must be 6–7 cm. To achieve this, the difference in height of the gates must be set at 4–5 cm, if a boat is kept level and the blades move at the same depth in the water. At the finish, however, a sculler must pull the handles the same 6–7 cm apart, which is very difficult in terms of balance and could negatively affect an athlete's posture.

The usual difference in height of the gates is set to 1–2 cm, which allows pulling the handles at the finish to more or less the same height. Therefore, at the middle of the drive, a sculler has to separate the handles in the horizontal plane (pull one handle in front of another) and / or tilt the boat and / or move the blades at different depth in the water. Usually, a combination of all these options is used (Fig. 4.31).

As the most common sculling style is 'left handle above right', the right handle is

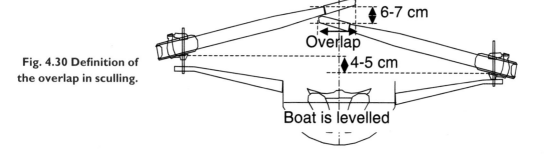

Fig. 4.30 Definition of the overlap in sculling.

6-7 cm
Overlap
4-5 cm
Boat is levelled

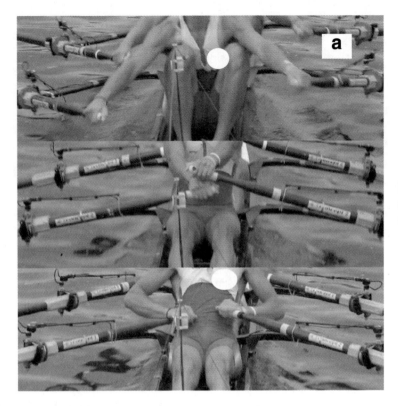

Fig. 4.31 Video analysis (a) on asymmetry in sculling.

usually pulled in front of the left (Fig. 4.29a). The left catch angle is about 1 degree longer and this difference in the angles increases up to 4 degrees at the middle of the drive, then decreases again down to 1 degree at the finish. To do this, the sculler must apply forces asymmetrically: the right handle force increases faster at the catch, which creates higher velocity and allows the right handle to take position in front. At about 30 degrees oar angle, the left force increases and becomes higher than the right one, which allows the left handle to catch up the right one at the finish of the drive. This asymmetry in forces creates a small (0.5–1 degree) wiggle of the hull during the drive, which increases the drag resistance losses. In fact, this particular sculler put the right blade deeper at the catch, which makes the forces asymmetry worse. During the first half of the drive, the boat also tilts about 2 degrees right side down. At the finish, the tilt decreases down to zero, which helps to keep the balance.

With the intention to minimize losses caused by asymmetry, a sculler should adopt the following:

- Handles should be pulled with even forces to reduce the boat wiggle.
- Reasonable boat tilt at the catch and the middle of the drive is not a problem, as it doesn't create energy losses itself.
- Recommended overlap is 18–20 cm and the difference in height of gates 1–2 cm.

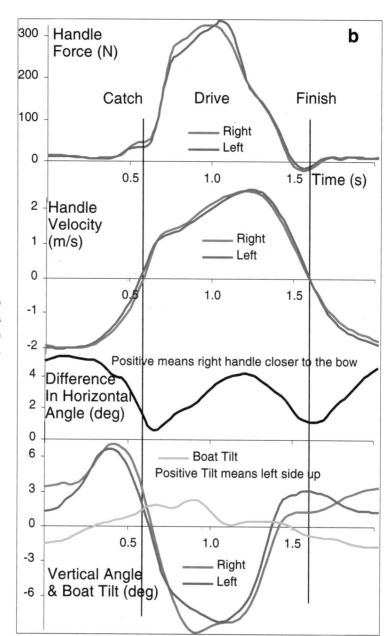

Fig. 4.31 (*Cont.*) Biomechanical data (b) on asymmetry in sculling.

4.4 START

Biomechanical conditions at the racing start are different from steady state rowing, and so also is the rowing technique. The starting velocity of the rower-boat system is zero and rowers have to accelerate it to the cruising speed. The most common starting technique is performing the first strokes at shorter length: ¾ of the full length at the first stroke, then ½, ¾, then longer and longer and achieving the full length at the eighth to tenth stroke.

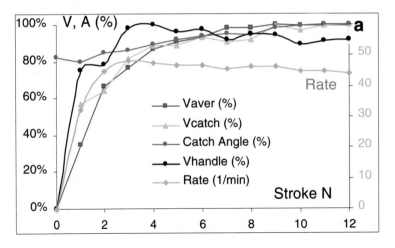

Fig. 4.32
Biomechanical variables: boat and handle velocities, catch angle and stroke rate (a), force curves (b).

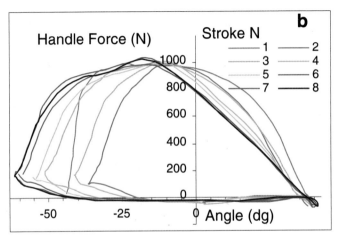

However, there is also an opinion that all strokes at the start must be performed with full length.

There are the following biomechanical reasons for shorter strokes at the start:

- The gearing ratio is lighter at shorter catch angles, because there is no 'dynamic gearing' (see Chapter 6.2.1). This increases propulsive blade force and allows higher acceleration of the system.
- The lighter gearing at shorter strokes also makes rowers' muscles contract faster and more efficiently than slow static efforts.
- The hydro-lift effect doesn't work at low

boat speeds (see Chapter 3.1.1), so pushing the blade outwards at longer catch angles increases its slippage through the water and the amount of energy wasted, which should be avoided.

To analyse the correlation of the catch angle with the boat velocity, the first 10 strokes were measured at the racing start in an international-level crew (Fig. 4.32).

The average boat velocity over the stroke cycle *Vaver* achieved 90 per cent of its maximal value at the fifth stroke, 98 per cent at the seventh and 100 per cent at the ninth stroke. The boat velocity at the catch *Vcatch*

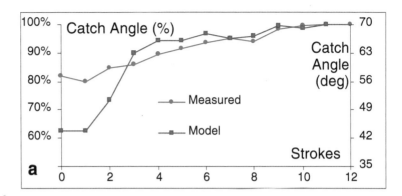

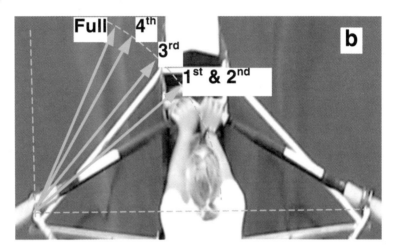

Fig. 4.33 Modelling of the catch angle at the start (a) and its visual presentation (b).

is not the same as *Vaver* because the speed varies during the stroke cycle. The most significant difference was after the first stroke, because there was the highest variation of the boat velocity from the stationary position. *Vcatch* was used for further analysis because it defines the interaction of the blade with the water at the catch.

The catch angles were approximately 80 per cent of the maximal value during the first three strokes. Then the length increased gradually and reached its maximum in the same stroke (the ninth) as the boat speed.

When *Vcatch* was divided by the actual gearing ratio derived using the catch angle (*see* Chapter 6.2.1), the corresponding handle speed was obtained, *Vhandle*, which was signif-

icantly lower during the first two strokes. This means the rower had to work in a slow, heavy, mode that decreased the system acceleration and muscle efficiency.

A hypothesis was made that maintaining a more even actual gearing may increase the efficiency of the start; that is, the catch angle should increase proportionally with the boat speed during the start. The measured angles from Fig. 4.32 were compared on Fig. 4.33 with modelled angles proportional to the boat speed at the catch *Vcatch*.

The optimal sequence of strokes was found to be the following: the first and second strokes: 62 per cent of the full catch angle, the third: 73 per cent, the fourth: 90 per cent and then gradually increasing to 100 per cent at the ninth stroke. The right Y axis on Fig. 4.33a indicates the catch angles in degrees, assuming the full catch angle is 70 degrees. The top view on Fig. 4.33b illustrates modelled catch angles: The first two catches should be made with the handle position above the toes of the stretcher, 'half slide'; the third catch, 'three quarters slide', the fourth, about 10cm shorter than the full length.

4.5 POSTURE AND BACK INJURY PREVENTION

The spine has a very complex design that allows it to offer protection to the spinal cord, transfer weight between the limbs and permit mobility. The last two are of more relevance to the back injury in rowing, which has quite high incidence (between 32 and 75 per cent annually). Structurally, the spine is divided into regions, sacral (the pelvis), lumbar (the lower back), thoracic (the chest) and cervical (the neck), which are connected and all relate to each other. It is important to consider the spine as a whole system and take into account the pelvis, which the spine sits on. The spine and pelvis should move together in synchrony creating 'lumbo-pelvic rhythm'[40]. When the trunk is bent forward, the pelvis usually starts the movement followed shortly afterwards by movement of the lumbar spine; this is simplified in Fig. 4.34.

Fig. 4.34 Visual representation of the lumbo-pelvic rhythm (a) and its analysis in world top scullers (b).

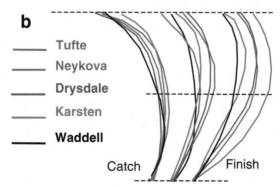

The lumbo-pelvic rhythm could be seen visually and analysed from video using the following method. Fig. 4.34a shows the very different contours of the back in two top world scullers: Olympic champions Rob Waddell in the foreground and Mahe Drysdale in the background. When the contour lines were drawn, scaled and over-lapped, the difference became very clear: Mahe has a straighter lower back and more curvature in the chest, whereas Rob has the opposite.

Then the back curvatures of five of the best world single scullers were compared (Fig. 4.34b) at the catch, the middle of the drive (near perpendicular position of the blade) and the finish. Waddell's back curves were very different compared to the others: more curvature was found in the lumbar area, especially at the catch, and less curvature in the thoracic area in all positions.

To digitize the posture, the back curvature was divided into four zones of the same height relative to the vertical Y axis (Fig. 4.35).

Fig. 4.35
Digital
posture
analysis.

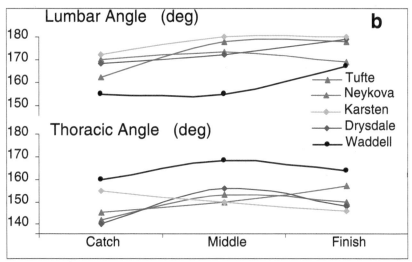

The coordinates of five points A, B, C, D and E were obtained at the locations where the back curvature crosses the border of each zone. Lumbar angle α was determined between lines AB and BC; thoracic angle β was measured between lines CD and DE. The advantage of this method is that it does not require markers on top of the centres of joints as the back curve can be clearly seen from the side. Analysis of the lumbar and thoracic angles confirmed our qualitative observations: the four best scullers have significantly straighter lumbar angles (160–180 degrees) and more curved thoracic angle (140–160 degrees), while Waddell had a more acute-angled lumbar area (150–160 degrees) and a straighter thoracic angle (160–170 degrees).

A straighter lumbar area can help to transfer the force better from hips to shoulders and prevent injuries, but *more curvature in the thoracic area may be more economical because it uses the more elastic properties of the muscles rather than its strength*. The reasons for more thoracic curvature in top world scullers could be related to adaptation to many years of high load as it is more noticeable in experienced scullers. Alternatively, it can be a natural selection of athletes with a specific posture, which allows them to spend less energy in sculling and, therefore, be more successful.

4.6 TECHNICAL EXERCISES OR DRILLS

The simplest way to improve technique is by giving feedback to a rower during normal rowing or after it. However, technical exercises or 'drills' appeared to be the most effective tool for technical coaching. When doing drills, the biomechanics of normal rowing is modified in such a way that allows a focus to

be made on a specific part of the stroke cycle, emphasize it, make it easier or more difficult to do. A big variety of drills can be classified by the following three factors:

- Mechanics: static or dynamic drills;
- Level of details: for elements of sequences;
- Standard or modified mechanical conditions.

Static drills target rowing kinematics: positions, angles and so on. These are the most basic drills and usually beginners start with them: for example, they stop at the catch position, see and feel where their handles, blades and body segments are and hear the coach's comments on them. Then, they stop at the finish, and so on. Sequences can be trained with series of fixed positions and slow transitions between them.

Dynamic drills are more advanced and target rowing kinetics: patterns of force application (force curve), rhythm (patterns of velocity) of the stroke cycle or its elements (drive, recovery), optimal activation of muscle groups, and so on. Examples of effective dynamic drills: 1) catch with short legs drive until the knee angle is 90 degrees, emphasize 'kicking' the stretcher through the toes and knee extension using quads; 2) rowing half-slide, catch at a knee angle of 90 degrees with 'kicking' the stretcher through the heels, emphasize pushing the knees down and hips extension using hamstrings and glutes (*see* Chapter 3.2.2).

Drills for elements are performed focusing on one or a few elements of the stroke, which allows their more intensive improvement: for example, catch only, finish with arms only, oar feathering / squaring, etc.[41,47]

Drills for sequences target better coordination of elements: for example, the sequence of activation of legs, trunk and arms during the drive and recovery, the sequence of the oar squaring and entry at catch, and so on. A good example could be cyclic – performing the dynamics drill 1 above, say, for 3 strokes, then drill 2 for 3 strokes, then 3 strokes using a combination of them whilst focusing on fast switching between quads and hamstrings-glutes.

Drills can be performed at standard or modified *mechanical conditions*: for example, external resistance can be increased with water brake or heavier gearing, or decreased with towing or lighter gearing, which makes rowing conditions heavier-slower or lighter-faster. The first sort of these drills is very often used for training rower's specific strength-power; the second sort is used sometimes for speed training.

For quality coaching it is important to have a sufficient 'toolbox' of drills, to choose a correct drill for a specific technical problem and correct it in the most effective way. This is the 'art' of coaching, which is based on a coach's ability to see–identify–understand the problem and then to choose the most effective 'treatment'. The following general rules and principles may be helpful.

If the target is to win races, not rowing for recreation, rowers should *refer technical drills to the racing speed and stroke rate*. Very often, 'a technical session' means very slow rowing with stops and static drills. It could be good for teaching beginners, but at advanced level it is necessary to also include fast drills. There are a number of reasons for this.

1. Mechanical conditions are very different in slow and fast rowing, at low and high stroke rates: they are as different as walking and running. Inertia forces are negligible in slow rowing, but at a high stroke rate they play a decisive role and change biomechanics dramatically. For example, when the stroke rate is changing from 20 to 40 min^{-1}, the rowing rhythm is changing from 35 per cent to 55 per cent (see Chapter 2.2.2) and inertial losses increasing from 3 per cent up to 7 per cent (see Chapter 3.1.3).

2. Mechanisms of motor control are different at low and high speed movement. At low speed, an athlete has enough time to receive immediate feedback (visual and from proprioceptors) about his body position, so he can control his movements and correct them in real time. At high speed, the quickness of the neuron-muscle loop is not sufficient to control movements at the conscious level, so its pattern should be programmed before the movement starts as it is not possible to control it in real time.

3. It is important to economize correct technique, that is, perform it with the highest efficiency and proper muscle relaxation, which should be practised at a racing stroke rate.

As an example (Fig. 4.36), the catch slip increases from 5 degrees at rate 20 str / min up to 10 degrees at 40 str / min (1) and the

Fig. 4.36 Common profiles of blade work at stroke rates 20, 32 and 40 min^{-1}.

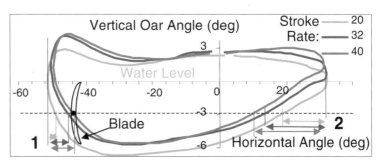

release slip increases from 7 degrees up to 17 degrees (2). This happens because the vertical angular velocity remains the same, but the horizontal velocity increases nearly twice at higher stroke rates.

If a rower targets improvement of blade work at racing speed, he needs either to increase vertical handle velocity proportionally at higher rates, or exaggerate it at lower rates. Both ways make sense and could be practised with 'catch only' and 'finish only' drills, when a quick short vertical movement of the handle is emphasized at various stroke rates.

CHAPTER 5

ERGOMETER ROWING

Ergometer rowing became very popular during the last three decades. The main value of ergometers is very accurate feedback on rowing intensity, which allows precise training of physiology, so rowers spend many hours on erg, especially in the winter period. The influence of erg training on rowing technique is quite a controversial issue. Some coaches reckon that ergs badly affect on-water rowing technique; others believe that erg could be useful for some basic components of rowing technique.

5.1 COMPARISON OF ROWING BIOMECHANICS ON WATER AND ON AN ERG

Biomechanical measurements[34] in rowing on water and on machines of two types (stationary Concept2 – C2 and mobile RowPerfect – RP) revealed that the maximal force applied to the handle on both machines was 34 and 40 per cent higher (C2 and RP respectively) than in a single scull (Fig. 5.1). Average force on machines was 25–26 per cent higher, respectively. Rowers executed 11–12 per cent shorter strokes on the stationary C2, which mainly occurred by means of 30 per cent shorter arms drive. Legs drive was 4–6 per cent longer on C2 than on both RP and on water.

The shape of the force curve was 'wider' in the boat and 'slimmer' on both machines, which was related with a higher ratio of average / maximal forces and earlier peak force in the boat. Maximal handle velocity was 18–20 per cent higher on water than on both ergometers. This difference affects the rower's feeling of the handle acceleration and is related to the difference in gearing ratio. The RP machine accurately simulates negative acceleration of the boat shell at catch. Acceleration of the single scull during the drive was significantly (20–30 per cent) higher than acceleration of the mobile unit of the RP. The latter exceeded the boat acceleration during the recovery phase.

The faster increase in the handle force and legs speed in the boat and on a RP can be explained by the different magnitude of inertial forces caused by interaction of the rower with the stationary or mobile point of support[39]. The differences in magnitude of the handle forces could be explained by dissimilar mechanics, which create different gearing ratios in the boat and on rowing machines (Fig. 5.2).

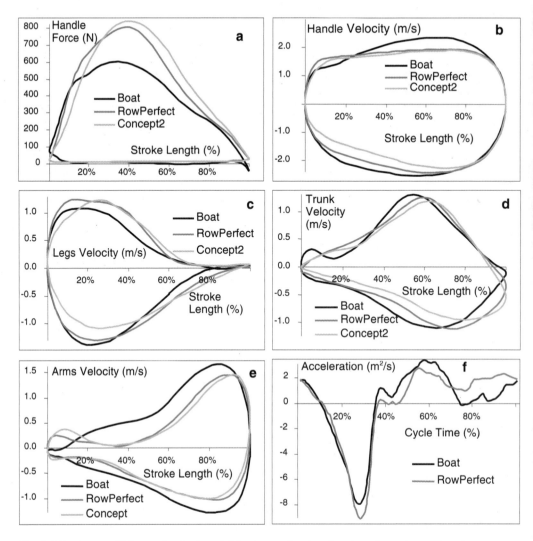

Fig. 5.1 Patterns of biomechanical variables in rowing in a boat and on ergs of two types.

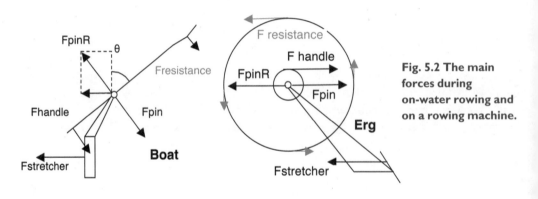

Fig. 5.2 The main forces during on-water rowing and on a rowing machine.

In a boat, the handle force Fh is related to the stretcher force $Fstr$ through gearing ratio of the oar and its angle:

$$Fh = (Fstr - Fin.boat) (Lout / (Lin + Fout)) / \cos\theta \qquad (90)$$

where $Fin.boat$ is the inertia force of the boat shell (relatively small), Lin and $Lout$ are the oar inboard and outboard length, and θ is the oar angle.

On machines, the difference between the handle and stretcher forces is equal to the inertia force Fin of the mobile unit on RP (smaller) of the rower's mass on $C2$ (larger):

$$Fh = Fstr - Fin \qquad (91)$$

In a boat, if a rower applies a certain force to the stretcher, then the corresponding handle force is smaller by the gearing ratio. On machines, the handle and stretcher forces create a couple, so they have similar magnitude. Therefore, at the same stretcher force on water and on ergs, the handle force is about 30 per cent lower in the boat, which is approximately equal to the gearing ratio of the oar (in a single scull it was 2.00m / 2.88m = 0.695).

In the boat the ratio of handle / stretcher forces depends on the oar angle (Equation 90): for example, at a 50 degrees catch angle, it was $0.695 / \cos(50°) = 1.08$, that is the handle and stretcher forces were nearly equal. This explains the smaller difference in the handle force at the catch and finish between on-water and erg rowing. Therefore, the difference in average forces was lower than the difference in the maximal forces. The gearing ratio in the boat varies during the drive, while on both machines it does not depend on the handle position (Equation 91). This explains the difference in the handle velocity profiles (Fig. 5.1b), which significantly affects the rower's perceptions of the drive.

The longer stroke length on water and longer arm travel could be explained by the curvilinear geometry of the arms' movement in the boat and the linear path on machines.

The faster increase of the handle force and leg speed in the boat and on the RP could be explained by the lower inertial forces caused by interaction of the rower with lighter mobile equipment. For the same reason, leg drive was 4–6 per cent longer on the $C2$: higher inertia force helps to achieve a better compression on a stationary erg.

The RP machine quite accurately simulates negative acceleration of the boat shell at the catch. However, during the drive, acceleration of the single scull was significantly (20–30 per cent) higher than acceleration of the mobile RP unit. The latter exceeded the boat acceleration during recovery phase. This difference significantly affects rower's vestibular sensations.

The main value of ergometers is very accurate feedback on rowing intensity, which allows precise training of physiology. Rowing on an erg could be useful for teaching and improvement of basic rowing skills, such as the sequence of body segments, consistency of the force curve, posture, and so on. Ergs with a mobile stretcher allow the practice of more boat-specific skills, such as catch 'through the stretcher' and even synchronization in a crew, when a number of mobile ergs are connected together. However, the biomechanical differences affect rowers' motor control pattern and rowing technique, which cannot be directly transferred from an erg to a boat. Very common technical faults appeared after extensive training using a stationary erg; ergs are 'opening' the trunk too early at catch at slower leg drive and 'soft' catch with late peak force.

As the handle force is relatively higher on an erg, athletes with stronger upper body muscles could have an advantage on machines, while athletes with stronger and faster legs could be better performers on water. The determination factor R^2 between results in a single scull on water and on erg in a homogenous group was found to be 59.2 per cent[44], which means the performance on an erg explains only about 60 per cent of the variation with on-water performance, and the remaining 40 per cent depends on boat-specific factors. Practical observations show that variation between results on water and on an erg could be up to $\pm$ 3–4 per cent, which means two crews with similar on-water results could have 10–15s difference in erg score, and vice versa.

Rowing on water and on erg are two different exercises, so machines should be considered as a cross-training for on-water rowing, though a much more specific exercise than running, cycling or weight-lifting. For the best on-water performance a certain result should be achieved on an erg, which shows rower's sufficient physiological work-capacity. However, the best performers on erg are not always the fastest rowers on water.

5.2 WEIGHT ADJUSTMENT OF ERG RESULTS

Performance on an erg depends on the athlete's body mass: heavier rowers produce higher scores, so it is not always clear which athlete is stronger, better trained, that is, how the level of muscles and energy supply systems is related in two rowers of different body mass. Therefore, weight adjustment factors were introduced to compare erg performance of athletes of different weights.

Though this topic is quite important and popular in the rowing community, there is no common opinion on it. The earliest study[42] was published when ergs were not widely used as a standard testing method of a rower's power production. The author analysed on-water performance and speculated that aerobic power Pae is proportional to $m^{2/3}$, that is to a body surface, which is related to the surface of membranes and oxygen transfer. As the speed is proportional to the cube root of the power $v \approx P^{1/3}$, then $v \approx m^{2/9} \approx m^{0.222}$.

Currently, this proportion is widely used for weight adjustment. In both Concept2 (C2) and RowPerfect (RP) websites it was transformed into a 'weight adjustment factor' k_w, which should be multiplied by the speed V, or a time score T divided by it to obtain an 'adjusted' time Tad and speed Vad:

$$Vad = k_w V, Tad = t / k_w \qquad (92)$$

In a C2, the adjustment k_{C2} was made relative to the 'standard' mass 122.5kg (270lbs) and reversed, because 'the weight-adjusted score becomes a pretty good estimate of a person's potential speed in an eight':

$$k_{C2} = (m / 122.5)^{0.222} \qquad (93)$$

In an RP, the 'standard' mass 75kg was used and 15kg was added to both the rower's and standard masses, probably in an attempt to adjust to inertia losses for the erg with mobile flywheel:

$$k_{RP} = ((75 + 15) / (m + 15))^{0.222} \qquad (94)$$

The adjustment factor on a C2 gives about a 13 per cent faster adjusted speed at 60kg than on a RP; and the difference decreases down to 9 per cent at 120kg.

The next significant step was made by Dudhia[16], who separated aerobic and anaerobic power: the first one remains in agreement with the equations above, but the second one was speculated to be directly proportional to the rower's mass $Pan \approx m$, because 'it

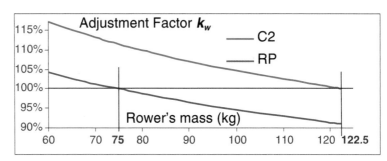

Fig. 5.3 Adjustment factors for C2 (reversed back to use in Equation 92) and RP.

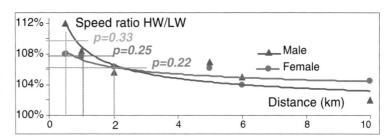

Fig. 5.4 Ratios of speeds in open category vs. lightweights in males and females at various race distances from 500m to 10km.

is defined by the muscles mass'. So, simply relative power in W / kg should be compared $Pr = pan / m$, or the cube root of the speeds: $v \approx m^{1/3} \approx m^{0.333}$

As the race duration of the standard rowing distance of 2km ranges from 5.3 to 7.5 min, the aerobic energy contribution varies from 67 to 84 per cent[49,53,55]. Assuming aerobic power contribution is 75 per cent of the energy during a 2km rowing race at 6.5 min and proportionally summing the above factors 0.222 and 0.333, then $v \approx m^{0.25} \approx m^{1/4}$. Exactly the same function was referred to in the latest study published by Pelz[49]: 'Geometric similarity is a special form of physical similarity based on Bridgman's postulate (Bridgman, 1922) in Pelz and Vergé (2014)[48]. Kleiber's law (Kleiber, 1932, 1975), cited in Pelz and Vergé (2014)[48], that the metabolic rate and hence the mechanical power of an organism is proportional to its body mass raised to the power of ¾th is an allometric scaling. This empirical relationship has been found to hold across the living world from bacteria to blue whales.' If $P \approx m^{3/4}$, then $v \approx m^{1/4} \approx m^{0.25}$.

To compare theory with practice, the data of world records on a Concept2 erg was used (Fig. 5.4).

Assuming the weight of a lightweight and a heavyweight male rower are 75 and 103kg respectively, and in females 60 and 76kg, the average ratio of the speed HW / LW should be 106.3 per cent at factor $p = 0.22$ in the equation $v \approx m^p$, 107.2 per cent at $p = 0.25$ and 109.7 per cent at $p = 0.33$. In a 2km race, the real average ratio was 106.4 per cent, so, it looks like the most traditional and popular factor 0.22 has the best fit to performance data. Higher factors could be suitable at shorter distances: 0.25 could be used in a 1km race, and 0.33 in a 500m race, which reflects a higher contribution of anaerobic energy.

What 'standard' mass M should be used in an adjustment equation? It is important to keep it the same for all rowers to be compared, but selection of the value is a matter of taste: lower values keep lightweights' results the same, but decrease speed of heavyweights, higher values make lighter rowers faster (Table 5.1). 'Added' mass decreases the weight

Standard mass M	Rower's mass m in $k = (M / m)^{0.222}$						
	60	70	80	90	100	110	120
60	100.0	96.6	93.8	91.4	89.3	87.4	85.7
70	103.5	100.0	97.1	94.6	92.4	90.4	88.7
80	106.6	103.0	100.0	97.4	95.2	93.2	91.4
90	109.4	105.7	102.7	100.0	97.7	95.6	93.8
100	112.0	108.2	105.1	102.4	100.0	97.9	96.0
110	114.4	110.6	107.3	104.6	102.1	100.0	98.1
120	116.7	112.7	109.4	106.6	104.1	102.0	100.0

Table 5.1. Weight adjustment factors, per cent, at various 'standard' masses M for erg rowing.

adjustment factor, and doesn't really make sense, especially on a stationary erg.

Conclusion: An erg speed should be multiplied by the following weight adjustment factor k_w or the time score divided by k_w:

$$k_w = (M / m)^p \qquad (95)$$

where m is the athlete mass, M is some 'standard' mass, $p = 0.222$ for 2 and 5km tests. Higher factors $p = 0.25$ and $p = 0.333$ to be used in shorter tests.

5.2.1 Power / Weight Ratio and Boat Speed

How do results on the erg versus rower's weight affect on-water performance? How should ergs be used for ranking and selection of crew boats?

A heavier rower exerts more power, but also displaces more water in the boat, hence creating more drag, which doesn't happen on an erg. Hydrodynamic drag contributes 87 per cent of the total drag[18] and the remaining 13 per cent is aerodynamic drag (with no wind). In the first one, 85 per cent is the skin friction drag D_{fr}, which is directly proportional to the boat skin surface and related to water displacement and mass of the system as $D_{fr} \approx m^{2/3}$. If only the friction drag is considered (the shape and wave drag are omitted), then the inverse proportions of the power and drag should cancel themselves out, $V \approx m^0$, and rowers of any mass should have no advantage. This was stated by Dudhia[16] for aerobic power. McMahon[42] speculated that if boat dimensions were proportional to the rower's weight then it should be $V \approx m^{1/18}$, which gives a 95kg rower 1.7 per cent advantage over a 70kg one. The most recent study of Pelz[48], using a pure allometric scaling approach and non-standard matrix transformations, derived a proportion $V \approx m^{1/36}$, which is 0.7 per cent advantage for heavyweight.

The other factors affecting the drag are:

1. Boat deadweight. FISA rules prescribe the same minimal boat mass for all categories, so the ratio of the equipment per rower

mass is higher for lightweights. This causes three disproportions (*see* Chapter 3.1.5), so lightweights would have:

a) Relatively higher hydrodynamic drag resistance per kg of body mass caused by greater water displacement. This makes speed 0.23 per cent slower at 20kg rower's mass difference;

b) Lower energy losses caused by reduced fluctuations of boat velocity with lighter moving crew mass (advantage + 0.42 per cent for lightweights);

c) Relatively higher inertial losses because the rowers have to move relatively heavier boat mass back and forth (disadvantage − 0.91 per cent for lightweights).

The sum of the above three deadweight factors gives a disadvantage of − 0.73 per cent for lightweights.

2. Only 35 per cent of the aerodynamic resistance depends on the crew size[18], which is also proportional to rowers' body surface $\approx m^{2/3}$ and is cancelled by the reverse power proportion. Rowing equipment contributes the other 65 per cent of aerodynamic drag (oars 50 per cent and boat 15 per cent), and this is very similar for all rower's categories. So, 8.5 per cent (0.13*0.65) of the total resistance does not depend on the crew size and should be overcome by lower power in lightweight rowers, so they would have a 2.68 per cent (0.085³) slower speed. This disadvantage increases in a headwind, because the proportion of the aerodynamic resistance increases, but it decreases at tail wind. The sum of the four factors above tells that lightweights should be 3.4 per cent slower than similar heavyweight events.

To compare the theory with real data, the world best times were compared: the open weight M2x was 1.56 per cent faster than the lightweights, in M4 − this difference was 1.54 per cent; in W2x − 2.77 per cent. Comparison of the average speed of the winners of world regattas over the last 21 years produces very similar numbers: 1.45 per cent for M2x, 1.34 per cent for M4 − and 2.38 per cent for W2x.

An interesting study was published by Nevill[44], where 49 athletes were tested on an erg and on water in single sculls. It was found that the best-fit equation related boat speed Vb, ergometer speed Ve and rowers' mass m as:

$$Vb \approx Ve\, m^{-0.23} \qquad (96)$$

Assuming $Ve \approx m^{0.22}$, agreed above in 5.1.2, this gives us $Vb \approx m^{0.01}$, which means only 0.25 per cent disadvantage for lightweights.

Power trends were used to derive dependence of DF on the mass M of rower plus boat + oars (+ 18kg). For the singles (n = 2296), it was $DF \approx M^{0.50}$ (Fig. 5.5), for 2x / 2 − (n = 1895) and 4 − / 4x (n = 1119) it was

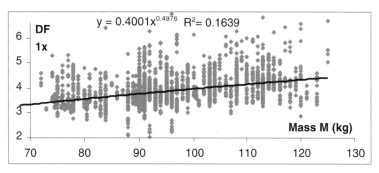

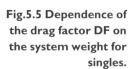

Fig.5.5 Dependence of the drag factor DF on the system weight for singles.

y = 0.4001x^0.4976 R²= 0.1639

DF 1x

Mass M (kg)

	Rower's mass m						
M_{st}	60	70	80	90	100	110	120
60	100.0	99.3	98.7	98.2	97.7	97.3	96.9
70	100.7	100.0	99.4	98.9	98.4	97.9	97.5
80	101.3	100.6	100.0	99.5	99.0	98.5	98.1
90	101.8	101.1	100.5	100.0	99.5	99.1	98.6
100	102.3	101.6	101.0	100.5	100.0	99.5	99.1
110	102.8	102.1	101.5	100.9	100.5	100.0	99.6
120	103.2	102.5	101.9	101.4	100.9	100.4	100.0

Table 5.2 Weight adjustment factors, per cent, at various 'standard' masses, M_{st}, for on-water rowing.

very similar $DF \approx M^{0.63}$ ($R^2 = 0.35$ and 0.26) and for 8 + (n = 728) it was statistically unreliable ($R^2 = 0.006$).

As the speed V, power P and DF are related as $V = (P / DF)^{1/3}$, then for the singles

$$V \approx (M^{0.66} / M^{0.50})^{0.33} \approx M^{0.054} \approx M^{1/18} \quad (97)$$

This means there is a 1.76 per cent difference in speed between 70kg lightweights and 95kg heavyweights in singles. For two and four rowers' boats $V \approx M^{0.011} \approx M^{1/90}$, which means only a 0.28 per cent speed difference. As the first proportion is the closest to observed data of world best rowers and corresponds to McMahon's theory, it should be accepted as the weight correction factor.

Conclusion: To define on-water performance, the erg speed should be multiplied by the following weight adjustment factor k_w:

$$k_w = ((M_{st} + m_b) / (m + m_b))^{0.054} \quad (98)$$

where m is the athlete mass, M_{st} is some 'standard' mass, say, 95kg, m_b is the boat +

oars mass. Table 5.2 applies the above equation for $m_b = 18$kg. Values above 100 per cent mean faster speed and shorter race time whilst those below 100 per cent mean a slower speed and longer time.

Table 5.2 can also be used for direct comparison of rowers of different weights. For instance, if a 90kg rower is 1.8 per cent faster on erg than a 60kg rower then their results on water should be similar.

5.2.2 Mobile Ergs

The main disadvantage of a stationary erg is the high inertia forces which may lead to knee joint injuries. A mobile erg, RowPerfect (RP), was invented by Cas Rekers[50] in 1991 to overcome this problem. After that, other mobile ergs appeared on market: Concept2 introduced slides, which can convert a stationary erg into a mobile one, and, later, the Dynamic Indoor Rower (DIR), Slider (Oartech, Australia) and some other less popular models appeared. All mobile ergs have a floating stretcher, which either connects directly to

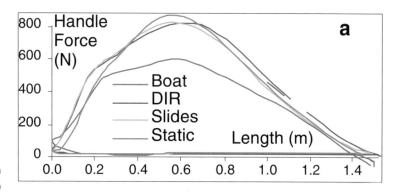

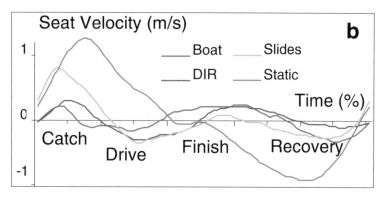

Fig. 5.6 Comparison of force curves (a) and seat velocity (b) in ergs and on-water rowing.

a floating power unit (flywheel) in a RP and Slider, or is connected to a stationary flywheel through a transmission (in a DIR). As the mobile stretcher is associated with a much lower mass than the rower's mass (from 7kg in a DIR to 35kg in Concept2 erg on slides) the inertia forces are significantly lower than on a stationary erg. This enables a higher stroke rate to be maintained and creates biomechanical conditions more similar to on-water rowing.

Comparison of a RP with on water rowing and a static erg was undertaken at 5.1.1 (see above), so here the main characteristics of the DIR, compared to other Concept2 ergs and on-water rowing will be discussed. Rowing on a DIR is quite similar to rowing on an erg on slides: the force increases faster at the catch than on a stationary erg (Fig. 5.6a), which is caused by a smaller moving mass and lower inertia forces. The magnitude of the handle

force is similar on all types of ergs and significantly higher than on water, due to the presence of gearing in a boat (see 5.1.1).

The DIR had the largest inertial efficiency (see Chapter 3.1.3) of 98.1 per cent at 37 str / min, compared to a boat (95.3 per cent), slides (91.6 per cent) and a stationary erg (82.1 per cent). This enables a higher stroke rate on a DIR and, possibly, faster times than on a stationary erg.

It was noticed that the pattern of mobile seat movement could be quite different on a DIR. For some rowers the seat changes direction four times during the stroke cycle, while for others only twice. The explanation of the seat movement on a DIR could be the following.

The seat velocity is closely associated with velocity of the rower's centre of mass (CM). On water, it can be presented as the velocity relative to the frame of reference, which

143

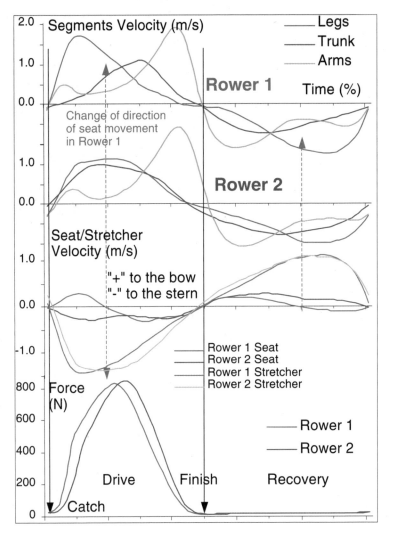

Fig. 5.7 Biomechanical variables in two different rowing styles on a DIR at 37 str / min.

moves with a constant velocity, equal to the average speed of the boat over stroke cycle. In this case, patterns of the seat velocity are similar on water, on a DIR and on slides:

Velocities of the rower's CM and boat (or mobile stretcher on a DIR, or erg on slides) are integrals of their accelerations, which depend on the ratio of handle and stretcher forces. Emphasis on the stretcher force accelerates the rower's CM, but decelerates the boat's CM and vice versa. A rower can control these forces by executing various rowing styles. Using his legs to initiate the drive

increases the stretcher force and acceleration of the rower's CM, but decelerates the boat. Using his trunk early in the drive increases the handle force and accelerates the boat, but decelerates the rower's CM.

Two examples of rowing styles are given in Fig. 5.7. Rower 1 exhibits a consequential rowing style and begins the drive with a leg drive. The seat (and rower's CM) moves to the bow first and then starts moving to the stern, when the rower's legs slow down and the upper body becomes more active. The stretcher decelerates sharply to the stern at the catch, but then its velocity increases faster, which is similar to the boat acceleration on water. During recovery, Rower 1 returns trunk first, his legs follow later but faster. Then he pushes the stretcher earlier and the seat velocity changes direction from bow to stern.

Rower 2 has a simultaneous style with legs and trunk working together after the catch. The seat moves slowly to the stern throughout the drive. Also, the stretcher velocity is much more even: there is no sharp deceleration at the catch, but no fast acceleration during the drive either. During recovery, Rower 2 returns his legs and trunk closer to each other, which causes continuous movement of the seat to the bow. Rower 1 had a faster increase of the handle force than Rower 2, which could be considered an advantage and demonstrates greater effectiveness of the consequential style.

Conclusion: seat movement on a Concept2 Dynamic Erg is a good indicator of rowing style: the consequential style causes a change in direction of the seat movement during the drive and recovery; in the simultaneous style the seat moves continuously towards the stern during the drive and to the bow during recovery. A similar phenomenon can be observed on water or with an erg on slides, but it is more obvious on a DIR because the seat moves relative to the stationary frame.

5.2.3 Handle Drag Factor HDF

Most rowing ergs allow the adjustment of the drag factor, *DF*, while maintaining an accurate indication of rowing speed and power. A lower *DF* makes deceleration of the flywheel lower during recovery, and, hence, the handle velocity is higher during the drive, which a rower will feel as 'lighter' conditions, similar to rowing in faster, bigger boats, with a tail wind or with a lighter gearing ratio of the oar. A higher *DF* makes the handle velocity slower during the drive, which feels 'heavier' and allows higher force production, similar to rowing in slower, smaller boats, in a head-wind or with heavier gearing. There were discussions in the rowing community about an optimal *DF* for testing and training on an erg, but no common opinion was found.

To provide an objective analysis of mechanical conditions and what the rower feels, the concept of 'Handle Drag Factor', *HDF,* was introduced, which can be derived similarly to the boat drag factor:

$$HDF = P / V_{h.av}{}^3 = P / (L / T_d)^3 \qquad (99)$$

where *P* is rowing power and $V_{h.av}$ is average handle velocity during the drive, which is equal to the ratio of the drive length *L* to the time T_d. Simply speaking, *HDF* shows how responsive the handle is: if the power is high, but the handle velocity is low, it feels heavy, and vice versa.

The handle force and velocity were measured at various values of *DF* on Concept2 ergs of two types: the static model D and the DIR. Four samples of 1 minute each at rowing with racing intensity were collected at shutter settings 1, 4, 7 and 10 and *DF* was recorded from the erg monitor (Fig. 5.8). When the drag factor, *DF*, increases, the drive time also increases on both ergs, the applied force grows and the average handle velocity slows. On a DIR, the drive time was shorter and the handle speed was higher than on the static erg at all *DF* settings. On average, *HDF* was 5 per cent lower on a DIR than on a static erg at the same *DF* settings, which could be explained by lower inertia forces. A very high correlation (r = 0.998) was found between the calculated *HDF* and the *DF* recorded from the erg monitor, which confirms validity of the measurements and allows them to be related as:

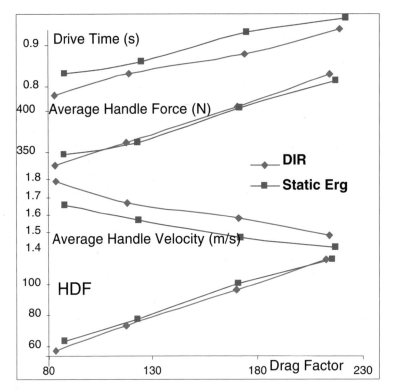

Fig. 5.8 Dependence of handle force, velocity and *HDF* on Drag Factor, *DF*, and on ergs of two types.

$DF = 2.34\ HDF - 51.0$ (for DIR),
$$DF = 2.48\ HDF - 69.1$$
(for static erg)   (100)

To compare the mechanical conditions of rowing on both ergs with on-water rowing, values of *HDF* were derived for various boat types (Table 5.3) using a database of measurements with the BioRowTel system[9] (total n = 5712). Corresponding values of *DF* were derived for the DIR and the static erg using Equation 100. The damper settings *S* were derived through experiment:

$$S = 0.065\ *DF - 4.32$$ (101)

However, the correlation of *DF* and damper settings depends on environmental conditions and the quality of the machine (new or old), so Equation 101 could be used only for an approximate adjustment. The exact

DF value should be obtained from the erg monitor.

In general, rowing in a single could be simulated with the damper setting at 5 on a Concept2 erg, in a double at 3, in a quad and pair at 1, and in a four with a completely closed damper. Rowing in an eight is generally 'lighter' than rowing at the minimal resistance setting on an erg.

Sculling is usually felt to be 'heavier' than rowing, which could be explained by the longer catch angles (heavier dynamic gearing), higher forces at lower stroke rate. Table 5.3 represents *HDF* at some average rowing conditions, while feelings of 'lightness' or 'heaviness' are affected by many other factors:

1. Drag resistance (wind, water temperature, water depth, using water brakes);
2. Oar gearing ratio, including dynamic gearing and blade size / efficiency;

	1 ×	2 ×	4 ×	2 −	4 −	8 +
Table 5.3 Correspondence of HDF in various boat types with DF and damper settings in ergs.						
Sample size n	2214	1235	385	500	657	721
HDF	86.0	71.5	59.0	62.8	50.8	46.8
± sD	12.7	17.6	8.3	14.6	7.9	7.2
DF Static	144	108	77	87	57	47
DF DIR	150	116	87	96	68	58
Damper Static	5.0	2.7	0.7	1.3	− 0.6	− 1.3
Damper DIR	5.4	3.2	1.3	1.9	0.1	− 0.5

3. Specifics of rowing technique and synchronization in a crew (poor synchronization increases inertia forces and makes rowing 'heavier');
4. Stroke rate and rhythm in relation to the stroke length and power.

To achieve the same power at a lower stroke rate a rower has to pull harder and longer, which feels heavier. Also, at a lower rate the recovery time is longer and the rower-boat system or erg flywheel decelerates more, so the rower has to start from a lower velocity at the catch, which adds even more 'heaviness'.

For example, two data samples were taken on a Concept2 static erg at the same $DF = 118$, speed (1:46.6 / 500m) and power (288W), but at very different stroke rates 31.4 and 20.1 str / min. At the lower stroke rate, the stroke length was 11cm (8 per cent) longer and the average forces 110N (26 per cent) higher to produce the same power and speed as at the high rate. HDF values were 71.6 and 79.3 correspondingly, which means 'heaviness' was similar to a double at the high rate, but it was closer to a single at the lower rate. *Conclusion: At the same boat or erg speed rowing at lower stroke rates with longer length and higher force feels 'heavier' and vice versa.*

The HDF factor can be used for a general estimation of rower's feelings of 'heaviness' or lightness' in rowing on water and on an erg.

CHAPTER 6

ROWING EQUIPMENT AND RIGGING

Rowing is a very technical sport, where the equipment can be adjusted through many variables. Specific values of these variables, or a process for their measurement and adjustment, is commonly called 'rigging'.

6.1 RIGGING DEFINITIONS

The most important adjustable rigging variables are defined below: twelve in sculling and eleven in rowing. Typical numbers are given for common equipment, but they could be quite different depending on equipment type (for example, the oar length is much shorter for a Fat2 blade type) and rower's categories.

6.1.1 Oar Settings

Oar length (Fig. 6.1) is measured from the handle top to the outer edge of the blade at the axis of the shaft (1) and inboard from the handle top to the outer face of the button (2).

Actual inboard and outboard are defined from the pin (centre of the oar rotation relative to the boat) to the points where the resultant forces are assumed to be applied: at the centres of the handle and the blade. Actual inboard and outboard lengths are used in the definition of the oar gearing ratio (see Equation 22).

6.1.2 Boat Settings

Span (Fig. 6.2) in sculling (3) is measured between the pin centres at the bottom (because the lateral pitch could affect it at the pin top); and spread (3) in rowing is measured from the centreline of the boat to the pin centre. Overlaps (4) can be measured directly, or calculated:

In *Sculling: Overlap = Inboard * 2 − Span + 4*

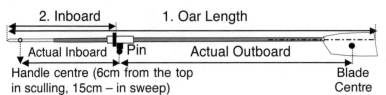

2. Inboard **1. Oar Length**
Actual Inboard Pin Actual Outboard
Handle centre (6cm from the top in sculling, 15cm – in sweep) Blade Centre

Fig. 6.1 Rigging variables of the oar.

Table 6.1 Typical oar rigging lengths (in cm) and their implications.								
Variable	1 ×	2 ×	4 ×	2 −	4 −	8 +	If shorter:	If longer
1. Oar Length	287	288	289	373	374	375	Lighter gearing: higher handle speed at lower force	Heavier gearing: lower handle speed at higher force
2. Inboard	88	88	88	116	115	114	Heavier gearing, longer oar angles	Lighter gearing, shorter oar angles

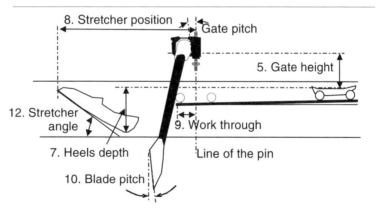

Fig. 6.2 Rigging variables of a boat.

In Rowing: Overlap = Inboard −

Spread + 2   (102)

The gate height (5) is measured from the bottom of its working face to the seat. Usually it is taken to the gunwale first, then the height from the seat to the gunwale is added or subtracted. In sculling, the difference between starboard and port gate heights (6)

is recorded separately. The heels depth (7) is measured from the seat to the bottom corner inside the shoe. The line of the pins inside the boat should be marked and used as a reference to measure the stretcher position (8), to the shoes' toes, and work through (9), to the stern end of the seat.

Blade pitch (10) can be measured either directly with the oar sleeve fixed at the gate

Table 6.2 Typical values of boat settings and their biomechanical implications.			
Variable	Range	At lower values	At higher values
3. Span Sculling	158–160 cm	Longer angles, heavier gearing	Shorter angles, lighter gearing
Spread Sweep	84–86 cm	Same	Same
4. Overlap Sculling	19–21 cm	Longer catch, longer stretcher position	Longer finish, requires shorter stretcher position
-- Sweep	30–32 cm	Same	Same
5. Gate Height	14–18 cm	Shorter length, higher force	Longer length, less force
6. Difference of Gate Heights in sculling	1–2 cm	Even handles heights, more boat roll	Uneven handles height, less boat roll
7. Heels Depth	15–19 cm	Same as 5	Same as 5
8. Stretcher position	55–65 cm	Shorter catch – lighter gearing	Longer catch – heavier gearing
9. Work through	10–20 cm	Same	Same
10. Blade Pitch	4–8°	Deeper blade, requires higher gate height	Shallower blade, lower gate height
11. Lateral Pitch	0–2° out	Less blade pitch at catch, more – at finish	More blade pitch at catch, less – at finish
12. Stretcher Angle	40–44°	Same as 5	Same as 5

and blade shaft in a horizontal position; or the pitch can be measured between the sleeve and the blade, then it is summed with the gate pitch. The pitch is easier to measure with a special electronic pitch-meter applied to the blade or working face of the gate, when the boat is levelled. Lateral pitch (11) outwards is measured at the pin or at the back of the gate, when it is perpendicular to the levelled boat. The stretcher angle (12) is measured from the horizontal axis of the boat.

6.2 The Main Principles of the Rigging Adjustment

6.2.1 GEARING RATIO

The standard definition of gearing is the ratio of the velocities on output to input. Higher, heavier gearing in cycling or cars means higher vehicle velocity at lower engine speed, but lower propulsive force, and vice versa. In rowing, the total gearing can be defined as the ratio of the boat velocity (relative to the water) to the handle velocity (relative to the

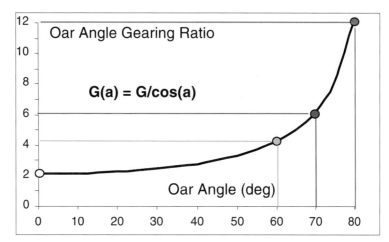

Fig. 6.3 Dynamic gearing at various oar angles.

boat). The total gearing can be defined as a product of the following components:

1. Static oar gearing is the ratio of the actual outboard to inboard (Equation 22). This gearing defines the ratio of the velocities at the blade and at the handle. However, the direction and magnitude of the blade velocity is different from the boat velocity. The static gearing ranges from 2.0 in small boats up to 2.3 in big boats.
2. Blade slip in the water decreases the blade efficiency (see Chapter 3.1.1), but also makes gearing lighter, because it increases blade velocity at the same boat velocity. As the blade efficiency ranges from 70 per cent to 90 per cent[28], the blade slip makes the gearing lighter by 10–30 per cent. A bigger blade area and its deeper placement in the water decreases slip and makes gearing heavier for the rower but it is more efficient for propulsion.
3. Oar angle gearing is defined as the angle of the blade and boat velocities, that is by the oar angle. This makes the gearing heavier by a factor which varies during the drive from 3 times at the catch angle, 70 degrees, down to zero at the perpendicular position of the oar (Fig. 6.3).

4. Span gearing. The rower's biggest segments, legs and trunk, usually move parallel to the boat, but the handle path is circular. Therefore, the handle force vector is not always parallel to the handle velocity (perpendicular to the oar shaft), but the force is transferred from the legs and the trunk to the handle at an angle to the shaft (see Chapter 2.5.5), which varies during the drive. Therefore, the handle velocity is higher than the shoulders' velocity, which means heavier gearing (by 13.3 per cent at A = 60°). The pulling angle is affected by the spread / span (see 6.2.4), so quite often it is used in the definition of gearing.

Only one gearing component is fixed by the oar dimensions. The other three are dynamic and vary through the drive. As the total gearing is a product of all components it also varies from up to 6–7 at catch down to 1.7–2.0 at the middle of the drive.

All above factors have to be taken into account in the search for optimal gearing. Rowing technique here could be more important than equipment adjustment. For example, increasing the stroke length with longer catch angles could make the gearing heavier than a small change of the oar settings.

6.2.2 Case Study on the Oar Length

The purpose of the study was to verify the following hypothesis: *can shorter rowers benefit from using shorter oars?* Four light-weight single scullers (average height 1.76m, weight 65.5kg) performed four trials each with various rigs (Table 6.3) where the actual oar gearing ratio was kept roughly constant at 2.07–2.08. Each trial was 1km long and the stroke rate increased every 250m (20, 24, 28 and 32 str / min). A WinTech Club Racer boat and four sets of Concept2 Smoothie2 Vortex sculls were used together with the BioRowTel system[9] to collect the following data:

- Boat velocity, acceleration, tilt and pitch;
- Horizontal and vertical oar angles;
- Forces at the handle and gate (normal and axial);
- Positions of the seat and trunk;
- Wind speed and direction.

As was expected, using shorter sculls enables bigger angles: shortening the inboard by 10cm increased the total angle by 12 degrees (Table 6.3).

Increasing the angles happened mainly by means of longer catch angles (9 degrees on average), where values of more than 80 degrees were recorded in the tallest sculler. Longer catch angles increased the actual gearing ratio (see 6.2.1), and made the drive time 10 per cent longer, but similarly average handle velocity was slower.

The average forces were quite similar in all rigging settings (3 per cent difference) but a slower handle velocity caused a proportionally 10 per cent lower power production. This resulted in a 3.5 per cent slower boat speed, even though the blade efficiency was 2 per cent higher at the shortest rigging.

To find the optimal rig, the boat speed was corrected using wind speed and direction data, and a prognostic boat speed for absolutely calm conditions was derived. Ratios of prognostic speed in each trial to the average for this sculler in all four trials were derived. A ratio of the oar length to the athlete's height was related to the boat speed and the second order polynomial trend was added (Fig. 6.4, red line). The same analysis was carried out on the corresponding data for the total oar angle (blue line). It was found that the *maximal boat speed could be achieved at 114 degrees total angle*, and at a 157 per cent ratio of the oar length to the rower's height (average oar length 2.76m in this case).

Table 6.3 Rigging and biomechanical data in an experiment with various oar lengths.

N	Oar Length (m)	Inboard (m)	Span (m)	Drive Time (s)	Total Angle (deg)	Aver. Handle Velocity (m / s)	Aver. Force (N)	Power (W)	HDF	Blade Efficiency (per cent)	Boat Speed (m / s)
1	2.89	0.890	1.59	1.093	108.7	1.49	285.2	249.7	74.4	74.3	4.02
2	2.79	0.860	1.53	1.118	111.9	1.44	272.1	233.8	76.3	75.3	3.94
3	2.69	0.825	1.47	1.145	115.6	1.39	278.0	233.1	85.3	75.5	3.93
4	2.59	0.790	1.41	1.198	120.9	1.33	275.6	223.2	95.2	76.3	3.88

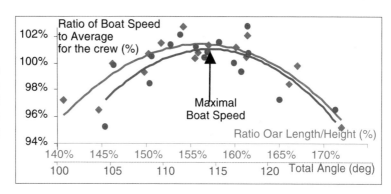

Fig. 6.4 Dependence of the boat speed on the oar length and corresponding stroke length (total angle)

Table 6.4 Optimal rigging based on experiment with the oar length.

Rower's Height (cm)	160	170	180	190	200
Arc Length (cm)	157	160	163	166	169
Oar Length (cm)	272	277	281	286	291
Inboard (cm)	83.0	84.5	86.0	87.5	89.0
Span (cm)	149	152	155	158	161

The results of the study were confirmed through analysis of the database of the BioRow telemetry measurements in singles (n = 4600), where the maximal boat speed was achieved at a total oar angle of 114 degrees. The rower's height H was related to the length of the arc $Larc$ and the linear trend was obtained:

$$Larc = 0.297\,H + 109 \qquad (103)$$

which means that every 1cm of extra rower's height increases the arc by about 0.3cm. The actual inboard $Linb.a$ could be derived using the known arc length $Larc$ and the total oar angle A:

$$Linb.a = (180\,/\,\pi)*(Larc\,/\,A) \qquad (104)$$

Using the optimal total angle $A = 114°$, found above, in Equation 104, obtaining the arc length from the rower's height in Equation 103, and applying the most common oar gearing ratio of 2.11, the optimal rigging shown in Table 6.4 was found for rowers of different height.

6.2.3 Case Study on Oar Gearing and Outboard Length

Another experiment was conducted on two single scullers with three sets of sculls of the same Concept2 vortex-smoothie type, but of different lengths: 271.5 cm, 266.5 cm and 261.5 cm. The inboard was set to 86.5 cm in all sets of sculls. In each session data samples were taken during 20-stroke pieces at stroke rates of 20, 24, 28, 32 str / min and max (Table 6.5).

Table 6.5 Average values of biomechanical variables in the experiment with oar gearing.

	Oar Length (cm)		
	271.5	266.5	261.5
Gearing ratio	1.95	1.88	1.82
Average stroke rate (1 / min)	28.2	30.7	31.5
Drive Time (s)	1.051	0.966	0.930
Angle (deg)	108.5	107.9	111.8
Blade Efficiency (per cent)	78.5	77.2	73.7
Average Handle Velocity (m / s)	1.52	1.64	1.77
Average Force (N)	336.8	368.7	370.5
Rowing Power P (W)	299.0	349.0	375.9
Boat Speed V (m / s)	4.17	4.32	4.38
Handle Drag Factor HDF	81.6	75.8	64.5

The majority of the variables are quite similar in these very different rigging settings (Fig. 6.5). Boat acceleration with the shortest oar length was slightly higher in the middle of the drive, but it was lower during the first half of the drive. The main difference was found in the blade efficiency, which decreased significantly with decreasing the oar length, especially during the first half of the drive.

Shorter oars allowed faster handle velocity, which led to a shorter drive time even at slightly longer rowing angles and, hence, allowed a higher stroke rate and rowing power. However, a shorter outboard at the same inboard makes the gearing lighter by about 12 per cent, which means the blade force became higher at the same handle force. Higher blade force at the same blade area increases water pressure per square cm and, hence, blade slippage through the water.

Therefore, blade efficiency of lighter gearing appeared to be lower and the rower had to expend more energy for moving water at the blade.

However, lighter gearing allows faster rower's movements, so it could increase power production (see Chapter 3.1.2). The HDF factor shows that 'heaviness' of the shortest sculls was similar to rowing in a quad or on a Concept2 erg with the damper setting 1. A medium oar length of 266.5 cm was close to a double or erg damper setting 2 and was the optimal for the given sculler, which corresponded with the results produced by the rigging calculator.

Conclusion:

- *Shorter oars and lighter gearing allow a faster drive and, hence, a higher stroke rate, but decrease blade efficiency.*

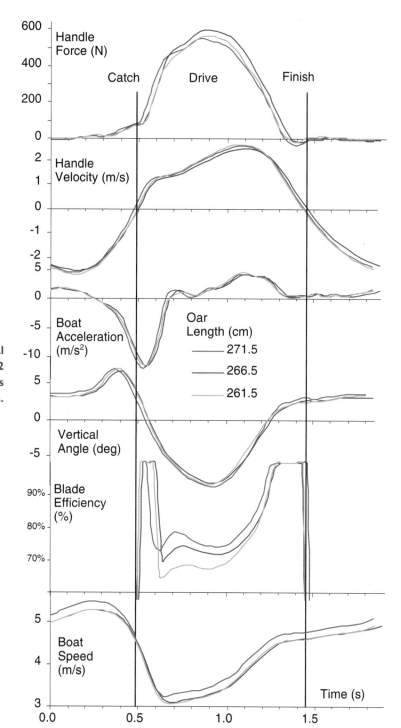

Fig. 6.5 Biomechanical variables in M1x at 32 str / min with various oar lengths.

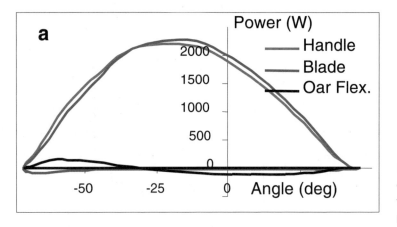

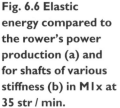

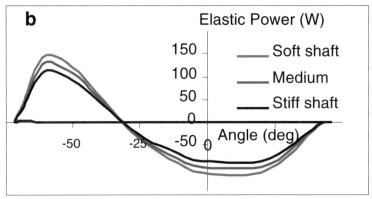

Fig. 6.6 Elastic energy compared to the rower's power production (a) and for shafts of various stiffness (b) in MIx at 35 str / min.

■ *An optimal gearing is a balance between the efficiencies of the rower and the blade and depends on the rower's dimensions and boat speed.*

6.2.4 Oar Stiffness

The stiffness of the shaft is an important variable for oar selection. Manufacturers usually offer three gradations of stiffness: soft, medium, stiff, and provide methods for its measurement (hanging a weight on the oar blade or handle and measuring the deflection). The general opinion is that oar stiffness must match the rower's strength: stronger heavyweight male rowers should use stiffer shafts, while less powerful female lightweights should row with softer oars. However, some coaches believe that the stiffer the oar the better because 'oar bent is the loss of energy'. Others recommend softer oars to prevent injuries.

Bending of the oar shaft could be as much as 10 degrees and could absorb up to 25 per cent of the rower's power over the first 15–20 cm of the drive.

The red line on Fig. 6.6a represents power applied to the handle (product of the handle force and velocity). At the beginning of the drive, the force increases, the shaft bends and part of the handle power is stored in the elastic energy of the shaft (black line). Therefore, the power delivered at the blade (blue line) is less than handle power. When the handle force starts decreasing, the shaft recoils and returns energy to the system. The blade power becomes higher than the handle power. Fig. 6.6b shows the difference in the storage of elastic power between soft, medium and stiff shafts for the same handle force curve. The stiff shaft stores and then returns about 26 Joules of energy, the medium shaft 30 J (15 per cent more) and the soft shaft 34 J (30 per cent more). The total work per stroke of this rower was 1022 J, so the share of elastic energy ranges from 2.5 per cent to 3.3 per cent (stiff and soft shafts). However, at 34 degrees of oar angle, where the peak force is achieved and the stored elastic energy is maximal, it ranges from 6.4 per cent to 8.4 per cent of the rower energy production up to that point in the drive. The maximal flexure of the shaft measured at the middle of the handle ranges from 5.8 cm to 7.6 cm (stiff and soft shafts) at the maximum force of 450 N on each handle.

Most of the elastic energy is stored at oar angles longer than 50 degrees, when the dynamic gearing ratio is about 4. The return of elastic energy happens mainly near the perpendicular position of the oar, when the gearing ratio is about 2. This means more acceleration of the rower-boat system and

higher effectiveness ('whipping effect'). The oar shaft recoils not only at the blade, but also in the middle, where it pushes the pin forward, accelerates the boat and creates a 'trampolining effect' on the stretcher (see Chapter 3.2.5). *Early peak force and optimal timing of the drive are important for effective use of elastic energy of the oar.*

6.2.5 Span and Spread

In the rowing community the span or spread are considered as important rigging variables. The common opinion is that a wider span / spread is 'lighter' and when narrower it is 'heavier'. In some manuals[1,2], even the gearing ratio is defined as a ratio of the span / half-spread to the outboard, though it is incorrect mechanically.

In sweep rowing boats the span works as a lever of the rotational moment of the pin force (see Chapter 4.2.4). In a pair, the rower with the wider span will produce more torque relative to the centre of the boat at the same force (Fig. 6.7a). At the catch it helps to balance the torque of the bow rower and keep the boat straight on course but at

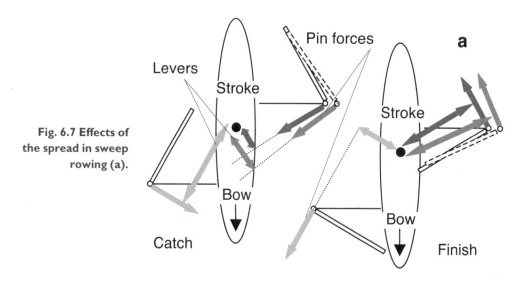

Fig. 6.7 Effects of the spread in sweep rowing (a).

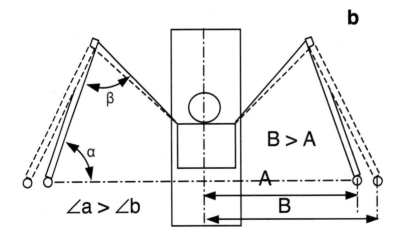

b

Fig. 6.7 (*Cont.*) Effects of the spread in the span in sculling (b).

finish it increases the advantage in leverage of the stroke rower and may turn the boat on the opposite side. Based on the results of rigging surveys at international regattas, in more than half of the measured pairs the stern rower (on whichever side) had a 0.5–1cm wider span.

In sculling (Fig. 6.7b), the span changes the arms-inboard geometry and affects oar and pulling angles. With a narrower span, the oar angle α at catch became larger and pulling angle β became more acute. Both these factors make the gearing heavier, but they work only at the beginning of the drive and practically disappear after the oar angle reaches 20–30 degrees.

Conclusion: the span / spread affects the gearing ratio indirectly through the dynamic oar angle gearing and pulling angle. A wider span / spread makes the dynamic gearing lighter during the first half of the drive, and a narrower span / spread makes it heavier.

6.2.6 Rigging calculator

Equipment dimensions in rowing are much less variable compared to other similar sports, where the dimensions of equipment usually vary in proportion to the athlete's dimensions. For example the ski length in cross-country skiing varies by 17 per cent (from 177 to 207cm), the size of bicycle frames varies more than 30 per cent (from 17 to 23 inches). The rower's height can vary more than 20 per cent (from 1.60m in lightweight females to 2.00m in heavyweight males), but variation of commercially available oars and sculls is less than 3 per cent (from 367 to 378cm for oars and from 282 to 292cm for sculls).

Probably, these specifications are related to the nature of rowing and its history, where equipment was shared in clubs between rowers of various dimensions, while in cycling and in skiing it usually belongs to individuals. However, these days, many elite rowers and single scullers in clubs also use personal equipment, or in National teams it belongs to squads of rowers of similar dimensions. Therefore, it is quite likely that we will see more individualization in rowing equipment in the near future.

Similar conservatism can be found in the gearing ratio relative to the boat's speed. In cycling it is possible to change gearing instantly, proportionally to the cyclist's speed, so the cadence remains at the optimal 90 rev / min $\pm$ 5 per cent all the time. In rowing, the difference between the fastest speeds of a men's eight and a women's single is 25 per cent, and could be up to 40–50 per cent depending on weather conditions. However, the usual difference in the actual gearing ratio (Equation 22, Table 6.1) is only 2–3 per cent. This makes handle velocity much faster, drive time much shorter, and allows higher stroke rates of up to 40–42 str / min in faster big boats, while small boats usually race at 32–34 str / min. The difference in the stroke rate is 20–22 per cent between the slowest and fastest boats and means that the rowers perform at very different biomechanical conditions, which could be outside an optimal range: too fast movements in big boats with a tail wind and / or too slow in small boats with a headwind.

A rowing speed and rigging chart was developed and implemented in an online program[52] in order to model the stroke rate, oar dimensions and gearing ratio in relation to the boat speed and rower's dimensions. The chart consists of two parts: modelling of the boat speed and rigging dimensions.

The boat speed model is based on the boat type, rowing power (taken from the erg score) and rower's weight, and has the following algorithm:

1. The drag factor DF was calculated as a function of the mass (weight) of the rower Wr for each boat type (coefficients a_1 and b_1 were derived from the database of BioRowTel measurements):

$$DF = a_1 Wr + b_1 \qquad (105)$$

2. Rowing power P was derived from the ergometer score Te:

$$P = 2.8 V^3 = 2.8 \ (2000 \ / \ Te)^3 \qquad (106)$$

3. Prognostic speed Vp and time Tp were derived from the rowing power P and DF

$$Vp = (P \ n \ Eb \ / \ DF)^{1/3}$$
$$Tp = 2000 \ / Vp \qquad (107)$$

where n is the number of rowers in the boat, Eb is the blade efficiency (taken to be 81.5 per cent as an average for all boat types). Alternatively, prognostic time Tp could be input straight into the chart and adjusted for the wind speed and direction.

4. A correction for wind applied, based on equations derived from Filter[18].

The second rigging model has two parts: Traditional and Innovative. The traditional section just gives the most typical rigging numbers for a specific boat type, based on the average data of rigging surveys at international regattas[4].

The innovative rigging algorithm is the following:

1. The length of the arc $Larc$ is derived as a linear function of the rower's height Hr, where coefficients a_2 and b_2 were taken from Equation 103.

$$Larc = a_2 \ Hr + b_2 \qquad (108)$$

2. Actual Lin_a and measured inboard Lin were derived from:

$$Lin\_a = (180 \ Larc) \ / \ (\pi \ A)$$
$$Lin = Lin\_a - 2cm + Wh \ / \ 2 \qquad (109)$$

where the handle width $Wh = 12cm$ for sculling and $Wh = 30cm$ for rowing. The rowing angle A is taken as a normative value for each rower's category (see Chapter 2.3.1) and adjusted for U23 as 98 per cent and for juniors as 96 per cent of the value for elite rowers.

3. Drive time Tdr was taken as a function of the stroke rate Rr, where coefficients a_3 and b_3 were taken from 2.2.2.

$$Tdr = a_3 Rr + b_3 \qquad (110)$$

4. Average handle speed Vh was derived from $Larc$ and drive time Tdr

$$Vh = Larc / Tdr \qquad (111)$$

5. Gearing ratio G was derived from Vh and Vp

$$G = (Vp\ Eb^{1/3}\ Ka\ BTF) / vh \qquad (112)$$

where Ka is a correction factor for the circular movement of the blade compared to the linear movement of the boat, which depends on oar angles, BTF, the Blade Type Factor is taken to be 100 per cent for the Big blade and adjusted for the area of various blade types.

6. Actual $Lout\_a$ and measured $Lout$ outboards were derived as:

$$Lout\_a = g * Lin\_a$$
$$Lout = Lout\_a + 2cm + Lbl / 2 \qquad (113)$$

where Lbl is the blade length.

7. Finally, the oar length $Loar$ was derived

$$Loar = Lin + Lout \qquad (114)$$

The innovative rigging model is based on the following three assumptions:

1. The length of the arc should be proportional to the rower's height. The proportion was taken as an average of measurements in all rowers' categories;
2. There is an optimal total oar angle for each rower's category;
3. Average handle velocity over the drive should be proportional to the boat speed.

This proportion was based on average speed in all boat types and average rigging.

These assumptions are not firmly inbuilt in the program, so the user could change them by means of using various rigging constraints and target angles. It is important to emphasize that the Rigging Chart does not give this optimal combination of rower's height, boat speed, stroke rate and rigging (inboard and oar length), simply because it is not known; no research results are available yet to derive it accurately. What it could give is the feeling of how different the rigging variables should be if the target is to maintain similar biomechanical conditions across all rowers' sizes and boat speeds.

6.2.7 Gate Height

The gate height is an important rigging variable, which is related to the drive length and force (see Chapter 2.5.4), blade pitch (see 6.2.8), vertical angles (see Chapter 2.3.2) and its specifics in sculling (see Chapter 4.3). At the catch, a rower has much more freedom to vary the height of the handle pull, because his arm is straight. Therefore, the *height of the handle and related gate height is mainly defined by position at the finish*.

An empirical method is the simplest one to define an optimal gate height. A rower should sit in the boat at the finish position, bury the blades into the water and find the most comfortable height for him. However, an analysis and normative values could be useful to predict the correct height for a rower in various boats, for the understanding of an effective technique and identifying the reasons for errors (Fig. 6.8).

The main requirement for the correct rower's position at the finish is horizontal forearms, that is the elbow and the handle must be at the same level because only this

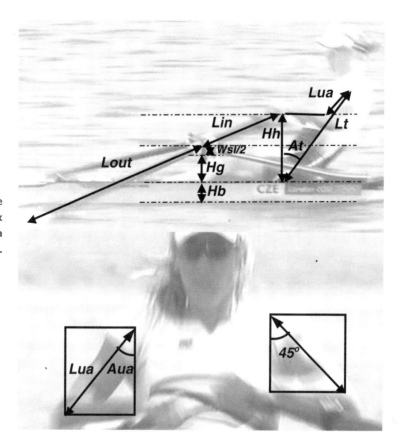

Fig. 6.8 Analysis of the gate height in M1x Olympic champion Mirka Knapkova, CZE.

position allows an effective horizontal pull. The height of the handle *Hh* from the seat can be calculated as:

$$Hh = Lt \cos(At) - Lua \cos(Aua) \cos(At) \quad (115)$$

where *Lt* is the length of the trunk from the seat to the centre of the shoulder joint, *At* the angle of the trunk from vertical, *Lua* the length of the upper arm between the centres of the shoulder and elbow joints, and *Aua* the angle of the upper arm from vertical, for which the optimal value appeared to be 45 degrees to engage the biggest shoulder muscles (*Latissimus dorsi, Trapezius* and posterior part of the *Deltoid* muscles). The optimal height of the gate from the seat *Hg* at the defined handle height *Hh* can be calculated as:

$$Hg = (Hh + Hb + \sin(-V)Lin)*Lout /$$
$$(Lin + Lout) - Wsl / 2 - Hb =$$
$$Hh + \sin(-V)Lin)*Lout / (Lin + Lout) -$$
$$Wsl / 2 - Hb(Lin / (Lin + Lout)) \quad (116)$$

where *Lout* is the length of the actual outboard from the pin to the middle of the blade, *Lin* the actual length of the inboard from the pin to the middle of the handle, *Wsl* the width (thickness) of the sleeve, *V* the vertical angle of the oar relative to the water level, which should be below −3 degrees for a fully covered blade, and *Hb* the height of the seat above water level. Though the model became quite complicated, it produces a quite reasonable gate height of *Hg* = 15.8cm for the following parameters: *Lt* = 50cm, *At* = 30°, *Lua* = 25cm, *Aua* = 45°, *V* = − 3°,

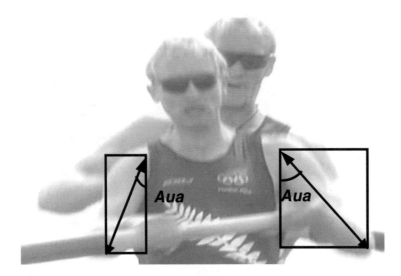

Fig. 6.9 Analysis of the gate height in sweep rowing.

Lin = 84cm, $Lout$ = 175.5cm, Wsl = 5.6cm, and Hb = 10cm.

The large number of variables in the model allows endless combinations of them. For example longer trunk leaning can be compensated for by a more horizontal position of the upper arm. Also, some variables themselves are not fixed for a given rower. For example, the length of the trunk Lt depends on the posture (how straight the torso is) and position of the shoulders (higher or lower *clavicle* and *scapula*).

The model works in sweep rowing as well (Fig. 6.9), but upper arms usually have different angles: the inside arm has a more vertical position (elbow lower), because it produces a higher force at the finish. The derived equations lead to the following conclusions:

- *A higher seat position above water (in a larger boat) requires about a three times smaller decrease in the gate height.*
- *Longer leaning of the trunk at the finish requires a lower height of the handle and gate and vice versa. This is because cos(At) decreases at larger angles. With other inputs remaining as above, a trunk angle of 20 degrees gives a gate height of 17.5cm* whilst for a trunk angle of 10 degrees it is 18.5cm.
- *The lighter the gearing, the lower the gate and vice versa.* However, the effect is quite small. With the other inputs remaining as above, a 10cm shorter outboard, *Lout*, would require only a 0.5cm lower gate.
- *The optimal gate height is important for effective blade work and force application at the finish of the drive.* If the gate is too high it would increase the finish slip of the blade ('washing out').

6.2.8 Blade Pitch

A pitch of the blade (the angle at which the vertical axis of the blade leans, see Fig. 6.10) is required because during the first half of the drive the handle is much lower than the shoulders, making it difficult for rowers to pull the handle horizontally. The force vector at the handle can be resolved into two components: horizontal and vertical. When transferred through the oar as a first-class lever, these components change magnitude (according to the gearing ratio) and direction (to the opposite). The horizontal component

12deg
4deg
Pitch

1

Fig. 6.10 Analysis of the blade pitch at catch (a) and finish (b) in M1x Olympic champion Olaf Tufte, NOR.

creates a propulsive force at the blade and the vertical component makes a downward force, which sinks the blade. A positive pitch angle at the blade is needed to overcome this vertical force and allow the blade to move horizontally.

At the catch (Fig. 6.10a), when pulling through straight arms, an estimated angle of the force vector should be close to 12 degrees. If this pitch angle is set, then 20 per cent of the total force will be directed vertically ($\sin(12°) \approx 0.208$) and the propulsive force will be decreased by 2.2 per cent ($\cos(12°) \approx 0.978$), which is a significant loss.

There is another option: to bend ('grub') the arms and pull more horizontally towards the elbows, which would require less pitch on the blade. Usually, rowers use a combination of these two methods: they 'grub' with the arms, but still pull at a small angle to the horizon, which requires a small pitch. In the case of the most common pitch of 4 degrees, only 0.24 per cent of the propulsive force is lost (9 times less than at a 12 degrees pitch) and the vertical component is only 7 per cent.

Therefore, it does not make sense to set the pitch at zero to pull absolutely horizontally and 'grub' the arms more, as it would require more energy from the muscles for a very small gain in propulsive force. It would eliminate the vertical component completely, which plays a positive role because it pushes

163

Fig. 6.11 Dependence of the blade pitch on the pin's lateral pitch.

the boat upwards, reducing its wetted surface and, therefore, its drag resistance. Also, it is not possible to increase the handle (and the gate) height enough to eliminate 'grubbing' arms, as it should be at an optimal level for other reasons (see 6.2.7).

When altering the gate height, the change of direction of the force vector dP in degrees can be defined as:

$$dP = 180 \, dH_g L_{oar} \, / \, \pi \, L_{arms} \, L_{out} \qquad (117)$$

where dH_g is the change of the gate height, L_{oar} the actual oar length, L_{arms} the length of the arms from shoulders to the handle, and L_{out} the actual outboard length. For common values of the above parameters, *every 1 cm of decrease of the gate height makes the direction of the force vector 0.6 degrees more vertical, and vice versa.* Therefore, a lower gate height requires more pitch and more significant arm 'grubbing' and vice versa.

The pin's lateral pitch (leaning the pin outwards) is useful to overcome the difference in comfortable height of the handle and to maintain a more constant force vector because it increases the blade pitch at the catch and decreases it at the finish (Fig. 6.11).

A 1–2 degrees lateral pitch could be recommended which would increase the blade pitch up to 5–6 degrees at the catch (4

degrees at the middle), and decrease it down to 2.5–3 degrees at the finish.

6.2.9 Stretcher

Similar to the gate height, the exact stretcher settings are not easy to define in an equation as they depend on many variables of the rower, boat and oars, which need to be measured and modelled. The most efficient approach is to use the practical method. The main stretcher measures are defined in 6.1.2, so only the main principles are given below. The stretcher variables affect each other, so their adjustment should be done in the following sequence:

- stretcher angle
- depth
- horizontal position.

1. The stretcher angle was measured to be in the range 37–47 degrees with an average of 42 degrees[4] and the recommended value of 40 degrees[14,45]. The adjustment principles are as follows:
   - A flatter angle allows quicker placement of the heels on the footboard during the drive (so, the glutes and hamstring muscles can be used earlier, see Chapter

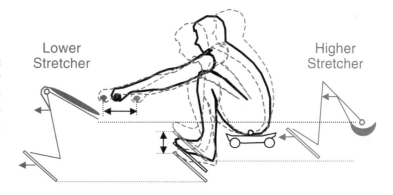

Fig. 6.12 The effect of the stretcher height on the drive length and muscles engagement.

Lower Stretcher

Higher Stretcher

3.2.4), but it is limited by ankle flexibility at extension: too flat an angle doesn't allow full knee extension at the finish.

- A steeper angle allows more horizontal force to be applied at the start of the drive[12], but it is limited by ankle flexibility at flexion: too steep an angle makes it more difficult for leg compression at the catch and could make the drive length shorter.

A very simple solution to combine the above advantages is to make the stretcher plate angled with a steeper toes part and a flatter heels part, which could be found in some manufacturers of rowing equipment. The advice could be to set the stretcher angle as flat, as it doesn't make any ankle tension at the extension at the finish.

2. The stretcher depth is traditionally measured as a vertical distance between the bottom corner inside the shoes and the top of the seat. Its recommended range is 15–19 cm, but the measured settings could be found from 12 to 22cm with an average of 17cm[4]. The following rules affect individual adjustments (Fig. 6.12):

- A lower stretcher allows a longer handle position at the catch, but limits the applied force because a rower could be lifted from the seat and lose it (see Chapter 2.5.4). Also, a lower stretcher

allows easier compression at the catch, increases quads utilization, but prevents early usage of hamstrings and glutes.

- A higher (and steeper) stretcher allows more horizontal drive and greater force production[12,58], but makes compression at the catch more difficult. It allows early usage of hamstrings and glutes (and trunk opening), but it is not easy for quads usage.

Conclusion: Set the stretcher depth to provide an optimal compression at the catch: the shins should be vertical, the knees at armpit level and the contact with the seat should be maintained at the rower's strongest efforts.

1. The horizontal position of the stretcher should be set up after all other settings as it can be adjusted quickly and does not affect other settings. It can be measured (from the line of the pins) at the toes Lt[10] or heels Lh[14]. Both of these measures can be used as they are simply interrelated:

$$Lt = Lh + Ls * cos(\alpha) \qquad (118)$$

where Ls is the length of the shoes and α is the stretcher angle. Measured at the toes, Lt is in the range 50–70 cm and it depends on many factors: the rower's height / legs length, shoulder width and trunk breadth, inboard / span / overlap, trunk angle at the finish. The position of the stretcher affects the catch and finish angles:

■ Moving the stretcher towards the stern increases the catch angle and, possibly, the total angle if the finish angle is maintained. However, setting the stretcher too far aft may limit the finish angle, if the handle hits the rower's chest.

■ Moving the stretcher towards the bow increases the finish angle and could be used to reduce trunk activity at the finish, providing there is good compression at the catch. An excessive finish angle could cause pulling the oars inwards, especially at narrow sculler's shoulders, wide span and low handles.

The traditional advice could be suggested: *At the correct stretcher position, the top of the handles must just touch the ribs when the legs are straight and the trunk is vertical.* A good indication of correct stretcher position is a perpendicular angle between a forearm and an oar at the finish.

Another stretcher variable is splay, an opening angle between the shoes, but it is usually fixed and can't be changed without redesigning the shoes' mounting plate. Only the 'New Wave rowing shoe fixing system' allows easy splay adjustment. Though manuals suggest a splay of 25 degrees[45], measurements give it in a range of 0–12 degrees with an average of 6 degrees[4]. The splay affects pressure distribution on the feet; a wider angle shifts it to the inside of the feet and vice versa.

CHAPTER 7

PERFORMANCE ANALYSIS IN ROWING

7.1 TRENDS OF PERFORMANCE

7.1.1 Long-Term Trends in Endurance Sports

Rowing results vary significantly from year to year because the boat speed at world regattas is randomly affected by weather conditions. To make performance analysis more objective, long-term trends of world records over 1900–2005 were analysed in similar endurance events, such as 1500m running[43] and 400m freestyle swimming[60] and compared with the results of world champions in rowing (Fig. 7.1a).

The trend lines in all analysed sports have quite similar patterns. Five periods common for all analysed sports could be defined during the twentieth century:

T1. *Before 1920: Fast growth* of performance 1–1.5 per cent per year, which can be explained by initial development of sporting technique and training methods. It is interesting that the trend in M8 + is already quite flat during this period and initial development occurred before 1900, which can be seen from the records of the Royal Henley Regatta (Fig. 7.1b).

T2. *1920–1950. Slow growth* (0.5 per cent per year) caused by two World Wars, amateur status of the athletes and less competition due to separation of the East and West sport systems.

T3. *1950–1980. Very fast growth* of performance 1–2 per cent a year. The Eastern bloc joined in Olympic sports in 1952. Sport became a political factor and professional activity, which caused a boom in the volume of the development of training, methods and the use of drugs in sport. This performance growth was even faster in women, because it coincided with initial development in some women's events.

T4. *1980–1996. Slower growth* of 0.5–0.8 per cent a year. The influence of training approached its biological limit; effective training methods became widely known, there were improvements in the drug control. Rowing performance continued to grow relatively quickly (1.5 per cent a year) than in athletics and swimming. It could be assumed that the reasons were equipment development (plastic boats and oars replaced wooden ones, big blades, and so on) and an active position of FISA in the wider promotion of rowing and the popularization of modern training technologies.

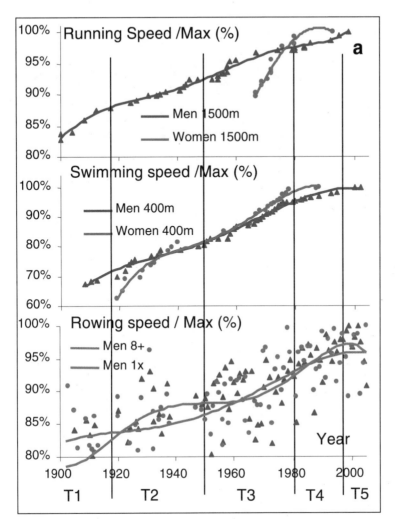

Fig. 7.1 Performance analysis in running, swimming and rowing over the twentieth century (a) and results of Royal Henley Regatta over 165 years (b).

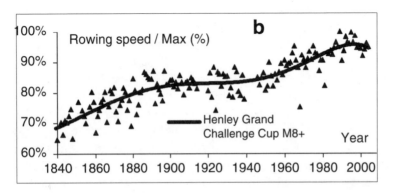

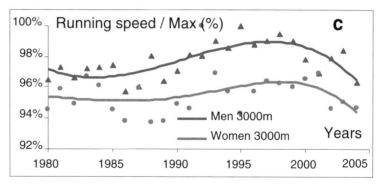

Fig. 7.1 (Cont.) World best times in running (c).

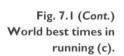

T5. *1996 to now. A stable period* and even a decreasing of performance, which can be seen in the latest trends of the yearly world best times in athletics (Fig. 7.1c). It could be speculated that the reasons were further development of doping control methods (such as blood doping tests) and sociological factors. Nevill and Whyte[43] reckoned that 'many of the established ...endurance running world records are nearing their limits. ...the athletic and scientific community may continue to explore greater performance

gains through use of pharmacology and the evolving science of gene doping'.

7.1.2 The Latest Trends in Rowing Results

In rowing, the idea of nearing the limits of human performance could be confirmed by significantly slower growth in small boats (Fig. 7.2). However, in big boats the results are still significantly increasing, which could be explained by continuous developments

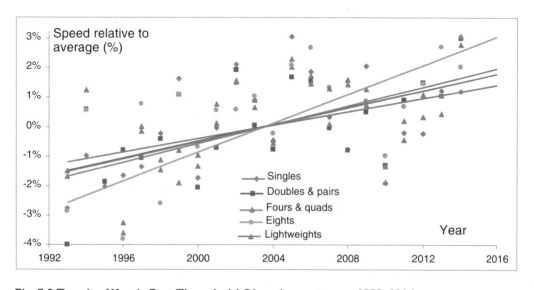

Fig. 7.2 Trends of Yearly Best Times in 14 Olympic events over 1993–2014.

Table 7.1 World best times at 2014, performance growth, the year of the expected new WBT and prognostic Gold Time in 2016.

Event	WBT at 2014	Growth (per cent per year)	Expected new WBT	Gold Time 2016
W8 +	05:54.2	1.54	2016	05:53.9
M8 +	05:19.3	1.28	2015	05:20.4
LM4 −	05:45.6	1.27	2019	05:45.3
M4 ×	05:33.2	1.21	2019	05:34.2
LW2 ×	06:49.4	0.95	2016	06:48.3
M2 −	06:08.5	0.94	2022	06:12.4
LM2 ×	06:10.0	0.89	2022	06:08.9
M4 −	05:37.9	0.82	2024	05:44.1
W2 −	06:53.8	0.71	2023	06:55.1
W4 ×	06:09.4	0.65	2028	06:12.4
M1 ×	06:33.3	0.65	2028	06:35.6
W2 ×	06:38.8	0.64	2025	06:41.6
M2 ×	06:03.3	0.61	2032	06:06.0
W1 ×	07:07.7	0.42	2035	07:14.9
Average		0.85		

of training methodology; more and more countries create high-performance training systems, where larger numbers of talented rowers could be assembled and trained together using the most modern methods.

To define general boat speed trends the speed of the winners and finalists of the world championships and Olympics could be analysed. However, the World Best Times (WBT) were not always shown in the finals, but in the races with the fastest weather conditions, sometimes in heats and semi-finals. Therefore, the following approach was used: the Best

Times of the Year (BTY) were derived for the latest 21 years from 1993 until 2014, and linear trends were assembled based on these data series. It was found that the average boat speed in 14 Olympic events grew by 0.85 per cent per year (Table 7.1). The time factor explains 27 per cent of the performance variability and the rest is explained by other factors, mainly by weather conditions.

The biggest growth of 1.3–1.5 per cent per year was found in both men's and women's eights, where a new WBT is expected within the next two years. Small sculling boats had the slowest growth

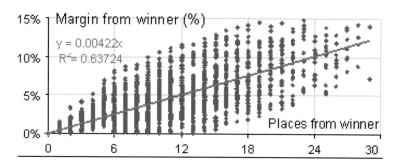

Fig. 7.3 Dependence of the boat speed on ranking in fourteen Olympic events in the adult category and its trend.

of 0.4–0.6 per cent, which would forecast a new WBT in 15–20 years from now.

A different method was used to calculate a prognostic 'Gold Medal Time' for the next Olympic Games: 2016. The linear trends were calculated based on results of the winners of world championships and Olympics, which were not necessarily the fastest in the respective year. Therefore, these trends reflect the speed in some average weather conditions. Each Gold Time GT was calculated using the linear equation:

$$GT = aY + b \qquad (119)$$

where a and b are the slope and intercept of the linear trend specific for each event and Y is the prognostic year (2016 in this case).

7.2 MARGINS BETWEEN FINALISTS

Analysis of the margins between finalists could be useful for race planning and selection of crews for regattas. It can help to find a percentage of prognostic times, if the target is a specific rank in the finals. The analysis was done on a database of results of World Championships and Olympic Games from 1993 until 2009 (n = 3760). The problem was that often finals A, B, C and others were held on different days, which meant the weather conditions were different and it is not pos-

sible to compare the boat speeds reliably. The margins of all place-takers (ratio of their time to the winner's time) were plotted relative to their ranking, the linear trend was calculated and outliers were filtered within the limit of ± 3SD of the trend line (Fig. 7.3).

Based on the slope of the trend line, every one place lower in ranking means a 0.42 per cent slower boat speed. For example, eleven places difference between the first and twelfth places should have a 4.64 per cent difference in the boat speed. This value varies across different events, which reflects homogeneity of competitors (Table 7.2): M2x with the most uniformity, without strong leaders, W2– with the biggest margins from the leaders.

The winners of finals B were usually faster than the slowest crews in finals A (Table 7.3), which reflects tougher competition for the first place in a final. Similar regularity could be found when comparing finals C to B, D to C and others. The margins in men's events were a little tighter than in women's. No significant time-trend of this data was found over the whole analysis period.

In juniors, the data was available only for the first two finals for most years, so the trend is less reliable. The slope was slightly steeper than in adults with an average of 0.443 per cent difference between places (Fig. 7.4).

Interestingly, the smallest margins (the highest homogeneity of results) in juniors were found in M2x and M4x, the same as in the adults (Table 7.4).

Table 7.2 Slopes of speed / place trend line, per cent, in fourteen Olympic boat classes.

M2 ×	M4 ×	M4 −	LM2 ×	M8 +	LW2 ×	LM4 −
0.30	0.36	0.39	0.40	0.42	0.42	0.43
W8 +	M1 ×	M2 −	W2 ×	W4 ×	W1 ×	W2 −
0.44	0.44	0.45	0.48	0.49	0.50	0.53

Table 7.3 Average margins from winners in World Championships and Olympics during 1993–2009, per cent.

Average	1st	2nd	3rd	4th	5th	6th
Final A	0.0	0.5	0.8	1.4	2.1	3.0
Final B	2.8	3.1	3.4	3.8	4.3	5.1
Final C	4.8	5.2	5.8	6.9	7.7	8.1
Final D	7.6	8.2	8.9	9.4	10.6	12.6
Men	1st	2nd	3rd	4th	5th	6th
FA	0.0	0.4	0.8	1.3	2.0	2.9
FB	2.5	2.9	3.2	3.5	4.0	4.7
FC	4.5	4.9	5.5	6.5	7.1	7.3
FD	6.8	7.7	8.2	9.2	9.7	10.4
Women	1st	2nd	3rd	4th	5th	6th
FA	0.0	0.5	0.9	1.5	2.3	3.2
FB	3.1	3.5	3.8	4.1	4.8	5.5
FC	5.0	5.5	6.2	7.3	8.4	9.0
FD	8.3	8.8	9.7	9.6	11.4	14.9

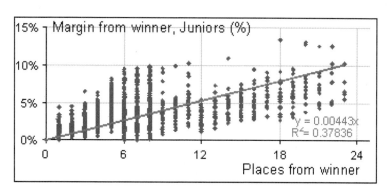

Fig. 7.4 Dependence of the boat speed on ranking in juniors.

Table 7.4 Slopes of speed / place trend line in Juniors' events, per cent.

JM2x	JM4x	JM2 −	JW1x	JM4 −	JM1x	JM4 +
0.29	0.33	0.34	0.38	0.38	0.39	0.42
JW4x	JW2x	JM8 +	JW2 −	JW8 +	JM2 +	JW4 −
0.43	0.51	0.52	0.53	0.67	0.74	0.82

Table 7.5 Average margins from winners in Junior World Championships during 1993–2009.

Finals	1	2	3	4	5	6
FA	0.0	0.8	1.3	2.0	3.0	4.1
FB	3.2	3.9	4.4	4.3	4.2	5.1
FA boys	0.0	0.6	1.2	1.8	2.7	3.8
FB boys	2.7	3.4	4.0	3.4	3.9	4.8
FA girls	0.0	0.9	1.6	2.4	3.4	4.5
FB girls	3.8	4.6	4.9	5.5	4.8	5.6

An analysis in the U23 category gave similar results to adults and juniors, but statistics was less reliable, because less data was available (only from 2001).

Concluding, on average, a crew has chances to get into final A if its speed is no more than 2.5 per cent slower than the winners' speed in men's events and 3.0 per cent in women's, in both adults and junior categories. For final B these margins were 4.5 per cent and 5 per cent; for final C, 6.5 per cent and 8 per cent, correspondingly. The margins vary between events with the smallest values in M2x and M4x, and the largest in W2.

Event	Gold	Silver	Bronze	4th place	5th place	6th place	Average
LM2x	38.8	38.1	37.1	39.6	39.2	37.3	38.4
LM4 −	40.7	39.9	39.7	39.7	39.8	40.3	40.0
LW2x	36.1	34.4	38.0	36.0	36.9	38.2	36.6
M1x	36.0	33.5	35.7	34.0	34.2	35.8	34.9
M2 −	40.2	39.4	38.6	38.9	38.0	37.6	38.8
M2x	37.9	40.4	38.6	38.4	38.1	38.0	38.6
M4 −	39.7	39.2	39.8	39.9	38.5	39.7	39.4
M4x	36.7	38.9	37.8	39.8	36.9	37.4	37.9
M8 +	39.2	40.0	40.1	40.4	39.8	40.1	39.9
W1x	33.9	34.2	31.3	33.3	33.8	32.9	33.2
W2 −	37.1	36.3	38.9	36.2	37.6	36.5	37.1
W2x	37.0	36.2	39.9	37.7	35.8	37.7	37.4
W4x	36.6	39.1	37.2	37.7	37.1	35.8	37.2
W8 +	36.5	38.4	39.4	38.3	36.0	39.0	37.9
Average	37.6	37.7	38.0	37.8	37.3	37.6	37.7

Table 7.6 Average racing stroke rate in finalists of the World Championship 2014.

7.3 RACING STROKE RATE

During races, the stroke rate is the only variable that can be seen and measured with the naked eye. Analysis of the racing stroke rate during rowing regattas was usually performed manually in real time or using video footage[31]. During the last few years, the stroke rate data acquired with a GPS timing system became available and its accuracy significantly improved. Compatibility of these two methods was verified and the data was combined to analyse the stroke rate in various boat types over the last decade.

During the World Championship in 2014 the average stroke rate in medallists in fourteen Olympic events was 37.7 min^{-1}, which is slightly higher than in 2010 (37.1) and 2004 (37.3), but lower than in 2002 (38.1) and 2000 (38.3). This means there is no clear trend, so *the stroke rate does not vary significantly over the years.*

No statistically significant difference was found in the average stroke rate between finalists (Table 7.6). The Relative Effective Work per Stroke (EWpS) was calculated based on the speed and stroke rate data (see Chapter 2.2.1) for the finalists of the World Championship, 2014 (Table 7.7).

Boat	Gold	Silver	Bronze	4th	5th	6th
			Table 7.7 Relative Effective Work per Stroke in finalists of the World Championship, 2014, per cent.			
LM2x	3.2	3.9	7.2	− 2.5	− 6.0	− 5.0
LM4 −	2.7	2.6	2.2	2.5	− 2.7	− 7.0
LW2x	5.2	8.3	− 3.5	1.7	− 2.7	− 7.8
M1x	2.5	11.3	− 1.4	1.3	− 1.7	− 10.8
M2 −	5.3	3.0	2.1	-2.9	− 2.1	− 5.2
M2x	5.6	− 3.7	0.7	1.0	0.9	− 4.2
M4 −	5.7	4.5	2.7	0.3	− 2.6	− 10.0
M4x	8.2	1.9	1.5	− 4.9	0.4	− 6.2
M8 +	6.2	3.6	1.4	− 1.8	− 3.2	− 5.7
W1x	4.4	1.8	7.8	0.6	− 7.1	− 6.5
W2 −	6.8	5.7	− 2.8	1.5	− 5.8	− 4.7
W2x	5.3	5.7	− 4.8	− 2.1	1.2	− 4.5
W4x	7.1	− 3.1	1.0	− 3.0	− 2.3	0.7
W8 +	9.1	2.1	− 2.4	− 1.9	1.8	− 7.7
Aver.	5.5	3.4	0.8	− 0.7	− 2.3	− 6.0

On average, the winners had significantly higher EWpS, which means *the races were won by higher effective work per stroke: every one higher place 'cost' about 2 per cent of higher EWpS.* However, there were some exceptions: in LM2x, LW2x, M1x and W1x the winners had higher stroke rate, but lower EWpS than some medallists.

7.4 RACE STRATEGY

The race strategy is defined as the total distribution of crew effort during a race. It could be expressed as a sequence of four numbers rep-resenting the ratio (per cent) of boat speed during each 500m section to the average boat speed over 2km for the crew[30].

The most typical race strategy of the winners in world regattas (speed in each 500m section relative to the average speed over a 2km race) was as follows: the first 500m were rowed about 3.1 per cent faster, the second and third 500m 1.0 per cent slower and 1.8 per cent slower respectively and the last 500m close to the level of the average speed over the race. No significant difference was found in the pattern of race strategy between the finalists, except the sixth place takers, who were relatively faster

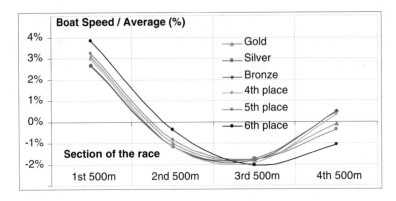

Fig. 7.5 Average race strategy in the finals of World Championships and Olympic Games during 1993–2014.

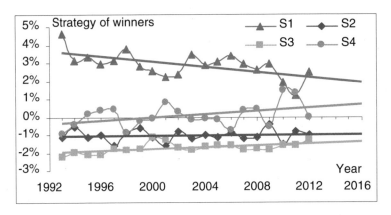

Fig. 7.6 Trends of the strategy of the winners of World Championships and Olympic Games.

at the start and slower at the finish (Fig. 7.5). Silver and bronze medalists and those in fourth place were slightly faster in the final section than the winners and fifth place takers. This suggests that *the races were won because of proportionally faster boat speeds in all sections of the race* and most of the competitors' strategies are close to the general pattern.

Trends of the race strategy were analysed over the last few years (Fig. 7.6) and it was found that the race strategy of the winners is getting more and more even over the race: if during the early 1990s the common pattern was + 3.5 per cent, − 1 per cent, − 2 per cent, − 0.5 per cent, then these days it became + 2 per cent, − 1 per cent, − 1.5 per cent, + 0.5 per cent. From the current trends

we can forecast the following typical strategy of the winners for 2016: + 1.9 per cent, − 1.0 per cent, − 1.4 per cent, + 0.7 per cent. This means *the boat speed during the race is becoming more and more even.*

7.5 SEAT RACING AND CREW SELECTION

Seat racing is quite a popular method of crew selection for big boats. It is very important to run the procedure in the most objective way, because the results may define an athlete's career and affect the team's performance and morale.

| Race N | Race Time | Rowing Power (W) | | | | |
		Rowers A–F	Rower G (W)	Rower H (W)	Rower I (W)	Rower J (W)
1	6:33.0	267.4	267.3	272.5		
2	6:33.7	253.1		259.1	284.8	
3	6:43.0	247.3			277.1	271.2
4	6:39.8	244.5	259.2			279.5
Average Time		6:36.4	6:36.4	6:33.3	6:38.3	6:41.4
Average Power		253.1	263.3	265.8	280.9	275.4

Table 7.8 Results of the seat racing in a crew.

7.5.1 Case Study: Seat Racing

A coach has firmly selected six rowers for an eight, and four other rowers bidding for two seats. Four 2km races were performed, where four rowers were rotated on two seats and the ranking was made by the average time for a rower in all races. The boat was equipped with the BioRowTel system, which measured the handle force, oar angles and other variables, and the rowing power was derived (Table 7.8).

It was found that in the course of racing the average power of the six constant crew members (rowers A–F) gradually decreased by 22.9 W or 8.6 per cent, which should decrease the boat speed by 2.7 per cent or ~ 10s for above race times. The reason was quite obvious: the athletes got tired, so at the end of racing they were not able to apply the same power as in the first race. Therefore, rower H seeded for the first two races had the best average time 6:33.3 and rower J seeded for the last two races had the slowest average time 6:41.4, though his rowing power was higher (275.4W) than in rower H (265.8W). Without biomechanics, rower H would be selected

unfairly. *Fair seat racing is not possible in one boat only. It should be done between two or more boats racing one against another:* the eight and pair or two fours in this example, so fatigue would affect all rowers similarly.

An important factor to be considered in seat racing is weather conditions: wind speed and direction. It is very likely they could change in a few minutes between the races and severely affect the results. This strengthens the above conclusion: *it is very important to measure performance in relative margins between two or more boats racing together, but not in the absolute times of a boat racing repetitively.* Also, it is always better to race with a tail wind, variation of which has a much lower effect on the boat speed than variation of a headwind. The races in the example above were done in a headwind, which increases the uncertainty of the results.

Though biomechanical measurements provide very useful information, there are limiting factors in using them as a selection tool:

1. Even with the current selection of the most informative measured characteristics it is not possible to measure everything in a

boat. There are other known and unknown variables affecting performance and measurements; for example, the effect of power transfer through the hull from one rower to another (see Chapter 3.1.3). Also, there is a risk of occasional error.

2. It is possible to measure the biomechanics and physiology of rowers. However, there are psychological factors that may play a decisive role in competitions. Some athletes are good performers in training and testing, but fade under the pressure. Others perform better and better, when psychological pressure is increased by the importance of a competition.

The psychological factor may affect seat racing: rowers already selected for a crew, consciously or subconsciously, may perform better or worse on the basis of preference to a rower still bidding for a seat. This makes seat racing a sort of indirect voting for new team members. If it is undesirable, the selection should be announced for all rowers at the same time, so all of them must race to their full effort.

The objective selection for big boats must be performance-based on standard races over 2km in small boats (singles and pairs). Power on an ergometer could be taken into account, then seat racing could be used if performance of two or more rowers is close or a rower doesn't fit well in the crew. After the selection is made, the coach should adjust the individual rower's technique for the best performance in a crew. The purpose of biomechanics is to help in this process, but not replace selection races. The factors affecting performance in a crew versus small boats are: synchronization of movements of crew members and stroke timing (see Chapter 4.2), coordination of force application to the handle and stretcher (see Chapter 4.2.2), and boat balance and asymmetry in sculling (see Chapter 4.3).

7.6 EFFECT OF THE WEATHER ON PERFORMANCE

It's an obvious fact that the boat speed depends on the wind speed and direction and water temperature. Thanks to Klaus Filter[18], it is possible to analyse experimental data, which was obtained in the 1970s in the DDR. Filter wrote: 'The physical property of water changes depending on the temperature...The mobility of water molecules decreases at lower temperatures', which increases the frictional resistance. *The boat speeds decrease by 1.3 per cent (~ 4s over 2km), when the water temperature drops from 20°C down to 5°C (Fig. 7.7). If the water gets warmer, up to 30°C, then the boat goes 0.6 per cent faster (~ 1.8s over 2km).* The power trend fits very well to the experimental data ($R^2 = 0.99$).

The wind resistance data was obtained using a wind tunnel. Filter wrote: 'The system crew-boat above the waterline causes a resistance of approximately 13 per cent of hydrodynamic resistance.' This means that the wind resistance comprises 11.5 per cent of the total resistance. Boat and riggers contribute 15 per cent to the wind resistance (1.7 per cent of the total resistance), rowers' bodies contribute 35 per cent (4.0 per cent) and oars 50 per cent (5.7 per cent). 'These shares can increase by up to 4 times under headwind conditions and decrease to zero with a sufficient tailwind.'

The straight winds and winds at an angle of 30 degrees to the boat have a higher effect on smaller boats (Fig. 7.8): 5 m / s headwind makes singles 17.4 per cent slower and eights 12.2 per cent slower, a tailwind of the same speed makes singles 7.5 per cent faster and eights 5.1 per cent faster. According to Klaus's data, a cross-headwind at 60 degrees has a similar effect on all boat types (about 10 per cent slower at 5 m / s) and a cross-tailwind

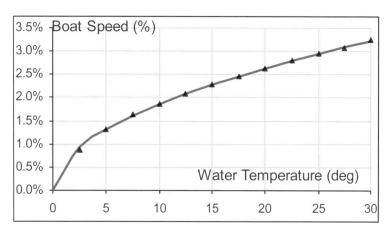

Fig. 7.7 Dependence of the boat speed on water temperature. Points: experimental data, line: fitted power trend.

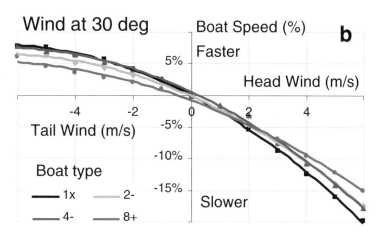

Fig. 7.8 Dependence of the speed of various boat types on wind direction and speed. Points: experimental data, lines: fitted second order polynomial trends.

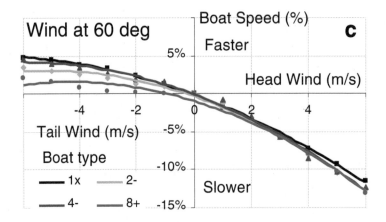

Fig. 7.8 (Cont.)

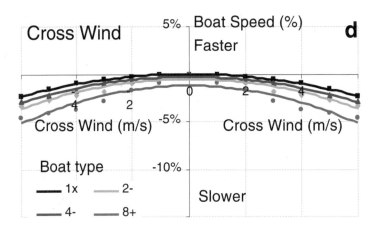

of the same speed is more favourable to smaller boats. Crosswinds have a higher effect on bigger boats: a 5 m / s crosswind makes singles 1.6 per cent slower and eights 4.1 per cent slower. The second order polynomial trends fit quite well to all experimental data ($R^2 > 0.99$) except 60 degrees and crosswinds in eights ($R^2 = 0.93$ and 0.53 respectively).

Is it possible to verify the above data with results of world regattas? The winner's speed normally lies within a range of ± 5 per cent from the average speed in the event. The slowest speeds (typically 8 per cent slower than average) and the fastest speeds (3.9 per cent faster) correspond to a head / tail wind of 3–4 m / s according to the above data. It

could be estimated that the strongest winds had higher speeds (for example a 5m / s wind is classified only as 'a gentle breeze' n = 3 on the Beaufort scale). Therefore, it is possible that the charts slightly overestimate the influence of the wind. It is noticeable that a headwind has the highest effect on lightweight events, which is understandable due to their lower mass and power. Also, it seems doubles are less affected by wind than pairs.

The above data allows us to build a model that can predict the boat speed at various wind and water temperature conditions. The model was implemented as a Web application in combination with a rigging chart (see Chapter 6.2.6).

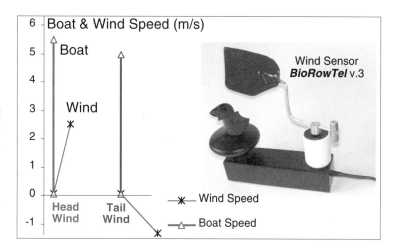

Fig. 7.9 Measurement and evaluation of the wind effect.

What could be done to decrease wind resistance? Filter recommends the following: 'In crews where the height of the sitting athletes is noticeably different, the tallest should be in the bow to give the best coverage … Crews should wear caps where they can cover their hair under stronger headwind conditions. The clothing has no influence as long as it does not flutter.'

With a sensor placed directly on the boat canvas, the BioRowTel system[9] allows very accurate measurements of wind speed and direction (Fig. 7.9). It makes it possible to derive an absolute speed, which could be shown by the crew at zero wind. Comparison of the absolute boat speeds in various pieces helps to evaluate rowing technique and to precisely determine the effect of variations in a crew combination, rigging or rowing style.

CHAPTER 8

VARIOUS CROSS-DISCIPLINARY TOPICS

8.1 EFFECT OF THE EXERCISE DURATION

$$rV = rD^p \quad (1)$$
$$rV = rT^q \quad (2) \tag{120}$$

The most common practical question was the following: 'If we have some known normative speed / rate data for one distance, how can it be extrapolated for another workout of a different duration?' To answer this question, an equation was derived describing dependence of speed and power (y) on the distance and time of the workout (x). Previously, the power or logarithmic functions were used for this purpose[22,56]. The power function $y = x^a$ was used here for simplicity. Instead of absolute values of speed V and distance / time D / T, their ratios (per cent) to corresponding values obtained in a 2km race were used:

Two sources of data were used, both obtained on Concept2 ergometers: the world best times at various distances, and the average data for a group of 20 elite rowers (unpublished data). The last sample fits very well with the power regression line ($R^2 = 0.99$), but world record data has lesser fit ($R^2 = 0.96$) because of some outliers (for example, world men's record on 500m 1:10.5 = 119.4 per cent to 2km record 5:36.6):

Fig. 8.1 shows that men have a higher factor in the equation 120(1) (p $= - 0.08385$) than women (p $= - 0.07104$). This means *men are better sprinters, while women are relatively*

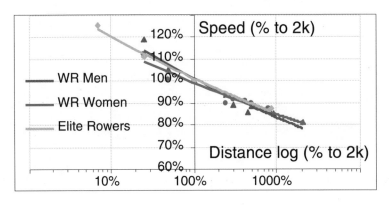

Fig. 8.1 Ratios of the speed to distance of the workout.

Table 8.1 Rowing speed, power and stroke rates at various workout durations.						
			Effect of the stroke rate (1 / min)			
Distance (m)	Speed (per cent)	Power (per cent)	25 per cent	50 per cent	75 per cent	100 per cent
250	117.5	162.2	39	45	50	55
500	111.3	138.0	37	40	44	47
1000	105.5	117.5	35	37	38	40
2000	100.0	100.0	34	34	34	34
5000	93.1	80.8	32	31	29	27
6000	91.8	77.5	32	30	28	26
20000	83.7	58.6	30	27	23	20

better at long distances. The general factors in all studied groups were found to be: p = − 0.07748 and q = − 0.07228.

The sources of metabolic energy at various distances are physiology issues, so only the mechanical aspects are discussed here. The second and third columns of Table 8.1 show normative percentages of speed and power at various distances based on general trends.

To achieve the variation of power P at various distances, a rower has two options: to vary stroke rate R or the work per stroke WPS:

$$P = WPS / T = 60 \, WPS*R \qquad (121)$$

where T is duration of the stroke cycle. Practically, WPS means the applied force because the stroke length does not usually change much and can even show the opposite trend of getting shorter at higher rates. Usually, both options are used together. Rowers use a higher stroke rate and apply more force at shorter distances, and vice versa, so the

'constant WPS' method doesn't make sense here.

Various strategies can be used to vary power and speed. Some rowers and crews prefer to vary stroke rate and maintain forces more or less constant. Others vary the applied force quite significantly. Also, various strategies could be used at shorter and longer distances:

■ At short distances a rower may not have enough capacity / skills to increase speed and stroke rate, and will have to use a higher force and WPS.
■ At long distances, force and WPS may drop due to muscle fatigue, which must be compensated for by a higher stroke rate.

Stroke rate and force application must be optimized individually to achieve the best performance. The last four columns of Table 8.1 show how stroke rate and applied force may vary when using different strategies. Percentages of 'Effect of the stroke rate' show its share in the variation of power / speed:

- 100 per cent means all variation of power is achieved by the variation of stroke rate while WPS remains constant.
- 50 per cent means variation of the power is produced by equal variations of both stroke rate and WPS.

A racing stroke rate of 34 str / min was used as the most common for 2km races.

In training, athletes usually perform exercises with efforts lower than in racing (100 per cent of their speed / power at the given distance), so the percentage of intensity shows speeds at corresponding relative efforts. Table 8.1 would work perfectly on an erg, because the indicated speed is affected only by power. In a boat speed is also affected by weather conditions (see Chapter 7.6).

8.2 ROWING BIOMECHANICS AND PSYCHOLOGY

Coaches quite often mentioned the psychological effect of biomechanical information and methods. They say that objective measurements help the coach to communicate with rowers in a positive way. Their feedback shows how biomechanical assessment creates confidence and sets clear targets for improvement. Here the psychological effects of biomechanical measurement and evaluation procedure are summarised. As no psychological research methods were used, these are only subjective observations, though they were quite consistent. Biomechanics could assist psychology in three main areas: to increase motivation, to decrease anxiety and to improve collaboration in teams.

1. *Motivation.* An understanding of biomechanical laws and principles, and experimenting with technique based on objective data, sets the creative climate in a rowing team and motivates coaches and rowers to find new ways to improve performance. Comparison of personal data with gold standards could create a challenge for rowers and improve their motivation.

2. *Anxiety.* When evaluating biomechanical data, we initially always try to find and emphasize something positive in the technique. Combined with objective identification of 'points to improve', it sets clear targets and helps rowers and coaches to adopt positive thinking. Firstly, the length of the stroke at the catch was increased during the February–April period (Fig. 8.2, point 1), although force application became slightly lower. Then, during the April–June period the force was significantly increased, the force curve became more 'front-loaded' (point 2) whilst length was maintained. This objective evidence confirms that rowers and coaches are on the right path and helps to increase awareness and decrease anxiety.

3. *Collaboration.* The current generation of young rowers has been raised in a highly technological age, so belief in charts and numbers presides over verbal explanations. Sometimes coaches ask me to tell rowers something specific and to confirm it with the data. They say: 'I repeat it to them every day but they would understand and accept it better in your scientific terms.' Thus, objective data helps coaches to prove their technical ideas and to improve communication and collaboration in teams.

In addition there are the following factors:

4. *Perception of technical changes.* During repeated measurements, after the first testing, analysis and feedback session, rowers were given a chance to improve their technique and see the changes. It was found that if a rower needs, say, to increase stroke length by 10 per cent and he tried to

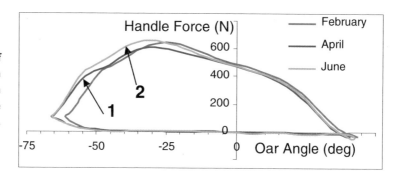

Fig. 8.2 Example of progression of an Olympic champion throughout the season.

do exactly this, the measurements usually show only 1 per cent improvement. It was called the 'ten-fold ratio of perceived changes'. This means that *if you want to change a variable of rower's technique by 10 per cent, you have to try to change it by 100 per cent.* Of course, this ratio significantly varies in different athletes.

5. *Long-term changes in technique.* Having worked with many experienced rowers, it was found that quite often they try to reproduce previous practice, which they feel has brought them success in the past. However, their technique gets worse and worse: fast leg drive becomes 'bum shooting', a once long and powerful body swing

becomes so-called 'gymnastics' at the finish, when the trunk still moves to the bow but in vain as the blades are already out of the water, and so on. It appears that the human body and mentality are so smart that they will always try to find the easiest way to do everything. If a rower relies on feelings only and tries to do 'as before', then, stroke after stroke, day after day, year after year, his stroke becomes shorter and shorter, less and less powerful and effective. Our objective measurements show it very clearly. Always try to find something new; extend the limits of your technique. Try to make every next stroke better than the previous one.

REFERENCES

1. Adam, K., Lenk, H., Nowacki, P., Rulffs, M., Schroder, W. 1977. *Rudertraining.* Limpert Verlag GmbH., Germany, pp. 98–99, 170.
2. Adam, K., Lenk, H., Schroder, W. 1982. *Kleine Schriften zum Rudertraining.* Bartels & Wernitz Druckerei und Verlag KG, Germany, pp. 268–272.
3. Affeld, K., Schichl, K., Ziemann, A. 1993. 'Assessment of rowing efficiency.' *International journal of sports medicine,* 14, S39 S41.
4. Aitken S., et al. 2011. Rigging survey at World Rowing Junior Championships 2011. British Rowing RowHow Rigging Forum. http://www.britishrowing.org / education-training / rowhow
5. Atkinson, E. 1896. 'A rowing indicator.' *Natural Science,* 8, 178.
6. Atkinson, B. 2001. Effect of Deadweight. http://www.atkinsopht.com / row / deadwght.htm
7. Barrow, J.D. 2009. Rowing and the Same-Sum Problem Have Their Moments. DAMTP, Centre for Mathematical Sciences, Cambridge University. http://arxiv.org / abs / 0911.3551
8. Bartlett, R. 1999. *Sport Biomechanics: Preventing Injury and Improving Performance.* New York: Routledge. pp. 11–21.
9. BioRowTel Rowing telemetry system. http://www.biorow.com / PS_tel.htm
10. Burnell, R. 1973. *The Complete Sculler.* Simpson of Marlow.
11. Cabrera, D., Ruina, A., Kleshnev, V. 'Simple 1 + dimensional Model of Rowing Mimics Observed Forces and Motions.' *Human Movement Science,* 2(25), 192–220.
12. Caplan, N., Gardner, T.N., 2005. 'The Influence of Stretcher Height on the Mechanical Effectiveness of Rowing.' *Journal of Applied Biomechanics,* 21, 286–296.
13. Caplan, N., Gardner, T. 2006. 'A fluid dynamic investigation of the Big Blade and Macon oar blade designs in rowing propulsion.' *Journal of Sports Sciences,* 1–8.
14. Daigneault, T., Smith, M., & Nilsen, T. S. 2002. FISA Intermediate Rigging Level 2.
15. Dal Monte, A., Komor, A. 1989. 'Rowing and sculling mechanics.' *Biomechanics of Sport.* p. 54–11.
16. Dudhia, A. 2008. Effect of Weight in Rowing. http://www-atm.atm.ox.ac.uk/rowing/physics/weight.html#section7
17. Fairbairn, S. 1934. *Chats on Rowing.* Hefner & Sons, Cambridge, p 69.
18. Filter, K. 2004. The system crew – boat. Lecture.
19. Fukunaga, T., Matsuo, A., Yamamoto, K., Asami, T. 1986. 'Mechanical efficiency in rowing.' *European Journal of Applied Physiology.* 55 / 5, 471–475.
20. Garland, S., Hibbs, A., Kleshnev, V. 2007. 'Analysis of speed, stroke rate and stroke distance for a world class breaststroke swimmer.' *Proceedings of BASES Annual Conference,* Bath, UK. p.125.
21. Gjessing, E. 1979 Kraft, Arbeids og Bevegelsesfordeling I Roing en Analysemodell. Presented during FISA seminar in Tata, Hungary.
22. Gordon, S.M. 2008. *Sport training.* Moscow, FK, 256
23. Holt, P.J.E., Bull, A.M.J., Cashman, P.M.M., McGregor, A.H. 2003. 'Rowing technique: The influence of fatigue on anteroposterior movements and force production.' *International Journal of Sports Medicine,* 24, 597–602.
24. James, S.L. & Brubaker, C.E. 'Biomechanical and neuromuscular aspects of running.' *Exercise and Sport Science Reviews,* 1973(1), 189–216.
25. Klavora, P. 1977. *Three predominant styles: the Adam style; the DDR style; the Rosenberg style.* Catch (Ottawa), 9, 13.

26. Kleshnev, V. Device for power measurement in rowing. SU Patent 1650171.

27. Kleshnev, V. 1991, 'Improvement of dynamical structure of the drive in rowing.' PdD thesis, St Petersburg Institute of Sport, p. 49.

28. Kleshnev, V. 1999. 'Propulsive efficiency of rowing.' In Sanders, R.H. and Gibson, B.J. (eds.). *Scientific proceedings: ISBS '99 : XVII International Symposium on Biomechanics in Sports*, pp. 224–228.

29. Kleshnev, V. 2000. 'Power in Rowing.' *XVIII Symposium of ISBS, Proceedings, Hong-Kong*, pp. 96–99.

30. Kleshnev, V. 2001. 'Racing strategy in Rowing during the Sydney Olympics.' *Australian Rowing*. 24(1), 20–23.

31. Kleshnev, V. 2001. 'Stroke Rate vs. Distance in Rowing during the Sydney Olympics.' *Australian Rowing*. 25(2), 18–21.

32. Kleshnev, V. 2002. 'Moving the rowers: biomechanical background.' *Australian Rowing*. 25(1), 16–19

33. Kleshnev, V. 2004. Technology for technique improvement. in: Nolte V. (ed.) *Rowing Faster*. Human Kinetics. pp. 209–228.

34. Kleshnev, V. 2005. 'Comparison of on-water rowing with its simulation on Concept2 and Rowperfect machines.' *Scientific proceedings: XXII International Symposium on Biomechanics in Sports*, Beijing. pp 130–133.

35. Kleshnev, V. 2006. 'Method of analysis of speed, stroke rate and stroke distance in aquatic locomotions.' *Scientific proceedings: XXII International Symposium on Biomechanics in Sports*, Salzburg. pp 104–107.

36. Kleshnev, V. 2010. 'Boat acceleration, temporal structure of the stroke cycle, and effectiveness in rowing.' *Journal of Sports Engineering and Technology*, 233, 63–73.

37. Kunz, C.O., Kunz, N.M. 2005. Stroke cycle phase shift rowing. US Patent No. 6 881 112.

38. Lazutkin, V.M. 1980. 'Coordination of oarsman movement at catch.' *Annual Grebnoi sport (Rowing sport)*, Moscow. pp. 23–26.

39. Martindale W., Robertson D. 1984. 'Mechanical energy in sculling and in rowing an ergometer.' *Can J Appl Sport Sci*, 9, 153–63.

40. McGregor, A.H., Patankar, Z, Bull, A.M.J. 'Spinal kinematics in elite oarswomen during a routine physiological "step test".' *Medicine & Science in Sport and Exercise 2005*, 37(6), 1–14–1020.

41. McLaughlin, S. (2004), A Comparison of two Methods for Teaching Beginners the Sport of Rowing. Masters Thesis, University of Western Ontario.

42. McMahon, T.A., 1971. 'Rowing: a similarity analysis.' *Science*, 173, 349.

43. Nevill, A., Whyte, G. 2005. 'Are there limits to running world records?' *Med. Sci. Sports Exerc*. 37, No.10, pp.1785–1788.

44. Nevill, A. et. al. 2010. 'Scaling concept II rowing ergometer performance for differences in body mass to better reflect rowing in water.' *Scand J Med Sci Sports 2010*, 20, 122–127.

45. Nilsen, T., Nolte, V. 2002. Basic Rigging. 'Be a Coach' FISA handbook, Level 1.

46. Nolte, V. 1991. Introduction to the biomechanics of rowing. FISA Coach 2 (1), 1–5.

47. Nolte, V., McLaughlin, S. 2005. 'The balance of crew rowing boats.' *Malaysian Journal of Sport Science and Recreation*, Vol. 1 (1), 51–64.

48. O'Neill, T. 2014. *Coaching Manual: Oarsport*, Nottingham, UK. www.oarsport.co.uk/coaching.

49. Pelz, P., Vergé, A. 2014. 'Validated biomechanical model for efficiency and speed of rowing.' *J. of Biomechanics*, 47(2014), 3415–3422.

50. Rekers, C. 1993. 'Verification of the RowPerfect rowing ergometer.' *Proceedings of the Senior Coaches Conference*. British Amateur Rowing Association, London.

51. Rodriguez, R.J., Rogriguez, R.P., Cook, S.D. & Sandborn, P.M. 'Electromyographic analysis of rowing stroke biomechanics.' *Journal of Sports Medicine and Physical Fitness*, 1990(30), 103–108.

52. Rowing Speed & Rigging Chart. 2010. http://www.biorow.com/RigChart.aspx

53. Russell, A.P., Le Rossignol, P.F., Sparrow, W.A. 1998. 'Prediction of elite schoolboy 2000–m rowing ergometer performance from metabolic, anthropometric and strength variables.' *Journal of Sports Sciences*, 1998, 16, 749–754

54. Sanderson, B., Martindale, W. 1986. 'Towards optimizing rowing technique.' *Med. Sci. Sports Exerc.*, Vol. 18, No. 4, pp. 454–468.

55. Schwanitz, P., 1991. Applying Biomechanics to Improve Rowing Performance. FISA Coach 2(3), pp.2–7.

56. Secher, N.H. 1993. 'Physiological and biomechanical aspects of rowing.' *Sports Med.*, 15, 24–42.

57. Shimoda, M., Kawakami, Y. & Fukunaga, T. 'An application of acceleration analysis to evaluation of a rowing technique.' *Proceedings of the XIII International Symposium for Biomechanics in Sport* (edited by T. Bauer), 1995, 95–100.

58. Soper, C., Hume, P. 2004. 'Towards an Ideal Rowing Technique for Performance.' *Sports Med*. 34 (12), 825–848.

59. Toussaint, H.M. & Beek, P.J. 'Biomechanics of competitive front crawl swimming.' *Sports Medicine*, 1992(13), 8–24.

60. Volkov, N., Popov, O. 1999. *Current development of sport records*. RGUFK, Moscow, p.82.

61. Williams, R. 2011. All together now. *Rowing & regatta*, #50, March 2011, 34–35

INDEX

RELATED TITLES FROM CROWOOD

High Performance Rowing
978 1 86126 039 0

Sculling
978 1 86126 758 0

Indoor Rowing
978 1 84797 191 3

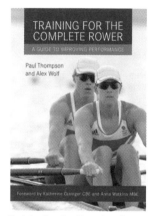

Training for the Complete Rower
978 1 78500 086 7

Rowing and Sculling
978 1 84797 746 5

In case of difficulty ordering, please contact the Sales Office:
The Crowood Press
Ramsbury
Wiltshire
SN8 2HR
UK

Tel: 44 (0) 1672 520320

enquiries@crowood.com

www.crowood.com